The Family Sto

WOMEN AND MEN IN HISTORY

This series, published for students, scholars and interested general readers, will tackle themes in gender history from the early medieval period through to the present day. Gender issues are now an integral part of all history courses and yet many traditional text books do not reflect this change. Much exciting work is now being done to redress the gender imbalances of the past, and we hope that these books will make their own substantial contribution to that process. This is an open-ended series, which means that many new titles can be included. We hope that these will both synthesise and shape future developments in gender studies.

The General Editors of the series are *Patricia Skinner* (University of Southampton) for the medieval period; *Pamela Sharpe* (University of Bristol) for the early modern period; and *Penny Summerfield* (University of Lancaster) for the modern period. *Margaret Walsh* (University of Nottingham) was the Founding Editor of the series.

Published books:

Gender, Church, and State in Early Modern Germany:
  Essays by Merry E. Wiesner
Merry E. Wiesner

Gender and Society in Renaissance Italy
Judith C. Brown and Robert C. Davis (eds)

Women and Work in Russia, 1880–1930:
  A Study in Continuity through Change
Jane McDermid and Anna Hillyar

The Family Story: Blood, Contract and Intimacy, 1830–1960
Leonore Davidoff, Megan Doolittle, Janet Fink and Katherine Holden

The Family Story

Blood, Contract and Intimacy
1830–1960

LEONORE DAVIDOFF

MEGAN DOOLITTLE

JANET FINK

&

KATHERINE HOLDEN

Longman
London and New York

Addison Wesley Longman Limited
Edinburgh Gate
Harlow
Essex CM20 2JE
England
and Associated Companies throughout the world

*Published in the United States of America
by Addison Wesley Longman Inc., New York.*

© Megan Doolittle, Leonore Davidoff,
Janet Fink and Katherine Holden 1999

The right of Megan Doolittle, Leonore Davidoff, Janet Fink
and Katherine Holden to be identified
as the authors of this work has been asserted by them
in accordance with the Copyright, Designs and
Patents Act 1988.

First published 1999

ISBN 0 582 303508 PPR
ISBN 0 582 303516 CSD

Visit Addison Wesley Longman on the world wide web at http://www.awl-he.com

British Library Cataloguing-in-Publication Data

A catalogue record for this book is available from the British Library

Library of Congress Cataloging-in-Publication Data

A catalogue record for this book is available from the Library of Congress

Set by 35 in 10/12pt Baskerville

Printed and bound by Antony Rowe Ltd,

Contents

v

Acknowledgements

Since this book has four authors and draws heavily upon individual research projects, which in some cases go back many years, it would be impossible to mention everyone who has contributed to our thinking or helped us along the way.

However, we would like to thank in particular Mary Blake, Jo Campling, Julie Charlesworth, Catherine Crawford, Lesley Davis, Tom Davis, Anna Davin, Ida Davidoff, Joyce Doolittle, Quenten Doolittle, Lisa Doolittle, Amy Erikson, Ron Fink, Tony Foley, John Gillis, Diana Gittins, Miriam Glucksmann, Anita Goransson, Fred Greene, Gro Hagemann, Edward Higgs, Hyla Holden, Joan Holden, Ursula Holden, Pat Holland, Elaine Jordan, Ludmilla Jordanova, Helen Kendall, Joan Landis, Hakon Leiulfsrud, Asa Lindqvist, Trevor Lummis, Moira Martin, David Morgan, György Péteri, Roderick Phillips, Michael Roper, Alison Rowland, Sonya Rose, Michael Sinfield, Paul Thompson, John Tosh, Karen Wallis, Christine Walters, Virginia Whitehead.

Brenda Corti and Mary Girling have, as always, cheered us on and smoothed the way. Many thanks to them and the secretarial staff in the Sociology Department at the University of Essex, Sue Aylott and Diane Streeting.

We gratefully acknowledge support from the following institutions and funding bodies: the Faculty of Humanities at the University of the West of England; the Open University; the Research Promotion Fund and the Fuller Fund (Sociology Department) at the University of Essex; and the Economic and Social Research Council. We also received support and useful critical feedback from the Social History Society Conference, York in 1995, and the Third Carleton Conference on the History of the Family, Ottawa in 1997. Leonore Davidoff had the benefit of discussing issues raised in the book at the Swedish Collegium for Advanced Study in the Social Sciences when she was a fellow in 1996 and Katherine Holden received support from the Harold Hyam Wingate Foundation in 1996–97.

Finally, special thanks to our editors Penny Summerfield and Hilary Shaw for their helpful comments and general encouragement.

The publishers would like to thank the following for permission to reproduce copyright material:
The Society of Authors, on behalf of the Laurence Binyon Estate, for the poem 'For the Fallen (September 1914)' by Laurence Binyon, and to Jeanette Winterson, the author, for extracts from *Oranges are Not the Only Fruit* (Pandora, 1985).

Preface

History books tend to favour individual narratives and it is comparatively rare to find one written jointly by four people. But it is also perhaps fitting that a book which insists that a family should not be treated as an undifferentiated unit, acting or speaking with a single voice, should be produced by a 'family' of authors.

This was not a pre-planned team project, nor did we conform to any traditional academic hierarchy. Rather this work grew organically as we realized that in our individual researches on fatherhood, singleness, illegitimacy, and domestic services we had common concerns and interests which could be linked in order to tell a wider family story. Despite our geographical separation, rather than submitting an edited collection of chapters we decided to work together, sharing the writing and editing of each chapter and generating ideas during our frequent meetings.

It was a genuinely collaborative project. Detailed plans, particularly of the first three chapters, were created, re-created and sometimes discarded at early meetings. As subsequently we worked through chapter drafts together, they were amended and sometimes reincarnated in completely new forms. Although individuals took initial responsibility for particular chapters, we all commented in detail on each other's texts. Most of the chapters were passed around, changed and expanded by at least one and sometimes several of us. While many favourite ideas and examples ultimately got left on the cutting-room floor, they served an important purpose in helping to focus and refine our thinking. In addition to our formal meetings, we often met separately, in pairs or threes, face to face or by phone, while e-mails and letters flew around the country fast and furiously throughout the research and writing period, which lasted nearly two years. We all gained immeasurably from participating in this creative process and most importantly are still good friends.

Aspects of our personal family histories are implicit within this book. We are all mature women but come from diverse backgrounds with different sets of familial relationships and living arrangements, although sons and/or brothers feature strongly in all our families. Some of us were born in England, for others it is our country of adoption. Between us we have a rich and varied experience of paid and unpaid work outside the academy. The variety in our own life experiences and approaches to research has added depth to our analysis and helped to bring different perspectives to bear on the subject matter. This explains the range of voices and evidence to be found in the book.

As we worked together on this project and attempted to meet sometimes unrealistic deadlines, our own families often demanded prior attention: whether through illness or the need for childcare, starting or leaving school, needing living space in our houses or fleeing the nest, going to live abroad or giving birth to a new generation. Yet they also contributed richly to our family story and without them we could not have written this book.

'To the Spirit of Creative Friendship'

PART ONE

Family Paradoxes

CHAPTER ONE

Introduction

Of course that is not the whole story, but that is the way with stories; we make them what we will . . . The only thing for certain is how complicated it all is, like string full of knots. It's all there but hard to find the beginning and impossible to fathom the end.

Jeanette Winterson, *Oranges are Not the Only Fruit*[1]

Knots within the story of the family are difficult to unravel not only because of the many forms of its telling. There is a deep yearning in late twentieth-century debates about the family to find a beginning that, it is hoped, will both explain the present and take us confidently into the future. This yearning has produced an ongoing search for a golden age of stable, loving and supportive families upon which to model hopes and dreams for ourselves and future generations. But our understanding of where such a golden age might be located is interwoven with personal memories of family life and society's collective stories about families in the past.

At the personal level we frequently look to our own childhoods as a measure by which comparisons of past and present might be made. Yet all too often memories of this period in our lives can become imbued with nostalgia or, where too painful to recall or acknowledge, are publicly shaped to conform to acceptable norms of childhood and childhood experiences.[2] What may result is a conflict between a general understanding of childhood, as an idealized time of innocence and protection, and individual memories of personal unhappiness. Experience and the norm are thus able to

1. Pandora Press, 1985, p. 93.
2. See Alistair Thomson, 'Anzac memories: putting popular memory theory into practice in Australia', in Rob Perks and Alistair Thomson (eds), *The Oral History Reader* (Routledge, 1998), p. 301.

simultaneously subvert and uphold the idea of a golden age located in childhood.

Our collective story about the family has, however, a different emphasis. Because of current economic, political and cultural preconceptions about the nature of family relationships, we are led to understand that a golden age can be traced to a time when the marital couple and their children lived independently of other kin but in close proximity to them; when men were the principal breadwinners and their wives and children were economically dependent upon them; and when wives and mothers took almost sole responsibility for domestic chores and childrearing; in short, the period when the nuclear family form was the preferred choice for couples and when, thereby, society and families operated within a mutually supportive framework. This public story is, however, equally unhelpful, for, in consistently foregrounding the nuclear family, it denies the complexities of familial relationships in the recent past while holding out the nuclear unit as the means by which a golden age might be restored in the future. The first purpose in our narration of the family story is, therefore, to challenge myths and assumptions about this golden age and to shift the nuclear family from its central, idealized position.

Building on such an approach, our second purpose is to explore and, where possible, define the form and nature of familial and quasi-familial relationships which have existed outside the nuclear unit. To do this we have chosen to highlight the ways in which the concepts of *blood*, of *contract* and of *intimacy* can illuminate the meaning and significance of such relationships while demonstrating how these concepts also interact and conflict with our understanding of the meaning of family. Through the idea of *blood*, we argue that although families are usually understood to be related by blood, this view of family ties is by no means an uncomplicated one. The marital relationship, for example, is not one of blood, although this is hardly ever acknowledged. On the other hand, with current advances in medical science, children and siblings have brought to the foreground the significance of blood relationship. We use the notion of *contract* to illustrate that, although it is less often associated with family life, relationships are often predicated upon implicitly contractual arrangements of caring and financial reciprocity – as in the marriage contract. And finally we consider the tensions within the concept of *intimacy*, which is understood to lie at the very core of family life. For although intimacy encompasses the most private physical, sexual and emotional aspects of relationships, based on trust and loyalty, it also incorporates the seemingly oppositional characteristics of power and control.

By emphasizing the assumptions and contradictions contained within these three particular concepts, we are able to illustrate the multi-layered nature of ties which exist not only between individuals but also inside, outside and across families, households, institutions and the workplace. In addition, such an approach demonstrates that the core nuclear group is, and was, surrounded by other figures whose friendship, employment, duty or loyalty were integral to its maintenance. And, similarly, that since the beginning of this century the state itself has provided, out of our insurance contributions, statutory provisions for particular patterns of family life. Our family story, therefore, incorporates these additional but often disregarded elements of support, interaction and obligation.

From this, the collective and personal stories of the family through our period are shown to be complex, interwoven narratives. These have been constructed through and by not only representation, myth, memory and anecdote, but also by local and national shifts in the law, social policy, economic and political institutions, culture and demography as well as global events such as the rise and decline of Empire. These are also stories which, despite our present assumptions, incorporate a much wider range of familial and quasi-familial relationships than those of the nuclear unit of husband, wife and dependent children.

Although in many ways familiar, their telling has not been an easy task. Unlike the events and ideas of political, military, religious or even social and cultural history, we (almost) all live or have lived in some sort of family arrangement. Personal experience and desires intrude, consciously and unconsciously; every pundit can be an expert on the family. Then, too, the family has been and continues to be a problem area and is often regarded as in crisis. Therefore, a considerable body of family studies centres on policy-based issues. These have been related to the therapeutic, particularly psychoanalytic, models of the family. As we shall explore further, unlike many other historical fields, the family is almost always seen as the site of morality, even if it is not explicitly identified as such. Moral issues around the family are freighted with contemporary anxieties and colour historical investigations.

Finally, 'the family' is still often implicitly taken to be an essential and natural entity. And behind this exclusion is the unspoken assumption that the family is about women and children, about femininity and infancy. But this tipping of the family into a naturalistic,

taken-for-granted sphere carries many dangers. It results in faulty
generalization: the family is this, the family is that. Such generalization is then compounded by privileging that central singular term,
the family. This abstract notion – often actually an ideal – makes real
consideration of plurality, let alone diversity, or the admission of
fundamentally different ways of operating, difficult. As a result, a
form of circular thinking develops in which studies of the family
are framed by our understanding about what *the family* means and
ought to mean and, from this understanding, what issues are considered significant to its research and investigation.[3]

Yet undoubtedly the family *is* an unusual social entity for it covers
issues around physical as well as social reproduction, nurturance
and transmission of custom, sexuality and desire, illness and health
– the messy small change of the quotidian. It also addresses mys-
teries which all societies must confront around birth and death.
Unlike many other cultures, Western culture is deeply coloured by
a linear, rather than cyclical, understanding of time. Claims to common ancestors, kindred, lineage, a House, or group fix our sense
of life's progressive journey within onward flowing time.

Several consequences stem from these deep-seated assumptions.
The first is one of intellectual status. The investigation of such
matters, especially those intimately related to the body, to matters
of possible pollution, both material and symbolic, has been trivialized
and held in low esteem. In social science it is theory, particularly
high, abstract theories, 'that are most divorced from blood, sweat
and tears, that have the highest prestige'.[1] In history it has been the
public world of diplomacy, politics, war and economics which has
dominated the profession. Not coincidentally, groups defined as
less powerful, those associated themselves with low status and polluting activities – women, children, paupers, slaves – have until
recently been low on, or even missing from, the academic hierarchy
of attention.

In intellectual terms, the family has become a dumping ground
for the brute materiality of our embodied human condition.
Although recently there have been efforts to bring the body back
into social and historical analysis, these have tended to emphasize
the social construction and representation of bodies through medical sociology and history, in feminist theory and the theorizing of

3. Elizabeth Minnich, *Transforming Knowledge* (Temple University Press, 1990),
p. 177.
4. Arthur Stinchcombe, 'The origins of sociology as a discipline', *Acta Sociologica*,
Vol. 27, No. 1 (1984), p. 52.

homosexuality. While each of these is important in itself, they have not sufficiently recognized the physicality of bodies which makes up much of what actually has gone on in families and households. For example, the feeding of babies and children and the tending of the bodies of the infirm and the elderly are central to the organization of families charged with their care.

While all academic disciplines have their own vocabularies and come from different perspectives, all operate from a similar premise when it comes to the family. As we will attempt to show, almost every event, institution, belief system, cultural artefact has a familial dimension, but in so many cases this is hidden. At whatever level the discipline operates, the family is everywhere and the family is nowhere to be seen. Why has this been so? It can be argued that it has been impossible to 'see' the place of the family within social thought because of the perspective of most major thinkers. As Daniel Bertaux has noted:

> between the level of classes and that of isolated individuals lies . . . the level of *families*. That this has not been perceived so far is entirely consistent with the blindness of the founders of sociology to the female half of the population.[5]

It is heartening that recently the problem has begun to be recognized. As the sociologist Jon Bernandes argues, the standard nuclear family type provides little insight into 'family lives' which both historically and today are so varied and diverse as to defy attempts to fit them within any model.[6] David Morgan has stated that 'the family' in his view is 'not a thing but a way of looking at and describing, practices which might also be described in a variety of other ways'.[7] But recognition is not enough. The roots and extent of the problem have to be addressed.

How is it possible to unravel the dense tangle of love, hate, pity, care, duty, loyalty, calculation, self-interest, patronage, power, dependency and, at the same time, continue to make sense of the family?[8] Yanking the strands into some sort of order only pulls the knots tighter. Rather a tug here, a tweak there and the threads will

5. Quoted in John Golby (ed.), *Studying Family and Community History: 19th and 20th Centuries* (Cambridge University Press, 1994), Vol. 3, p. 108.
6. Jon Bernardes, *Family Studies* (Routledge, 1997), pp. 1–25.
7. David Morgan, *Family Connections: An Introduction to Family Studies* (Polity Press, 1996), p. 199.
8. Myra Marx Feree writes of the family as a 'tangle of love and domination' which we have here extended: 'Beyond separate spheres', *Journal of Marriage and Family*, Vol. 52, No. 4 (1990), p. 879.

slowly come undone. Sometimes it might be necessary to cut through the knots of rhetoric, but eventually we should be able to weave the many-coloured, multi-layered picture which is the nearest to understanding we can hope for.

In this task, we should be warned by the derivation of the word 'family'. In its Latin root, *famulus* meant servant, which became *familia*, a household. For many centuries, the adult male head of that household was not considered part of it. It seems that the heart of the family was the relationships between the dependants it embraced. This reminds us that familial relationships have always been implicitly structured around issues of power, dependency, service and protection. And so, in some family relationships, we find contractual elements, long recognized by sociologists who have tried to analyse the family in terms of self-interest and exchange.[9] Although many are uneasy about such calculation besmirching our ideal of the family, there is no reason why self-interest should not co-exist with love and affection. Nineteenth-century commercial, manufacturing, farming and professional families, who raised capital mainly through kinship and friendship networks, routinely expected their nearest and dearest to pay market rates of interest; even sons, brothers or nephews inheriting a family business were expected to pay the market price for their share.[10]

Moreover, familial relationships were found *and still are found* in a range of other institutions and places where we no longer expect them. All-male organizations such as the guilds and confraternities of early modern Europe operated along familial lines with senior men as fathers, juniors as sons. Inheritance of skill, even property might pass within the guild from the elder generation to the younger, bypassing genetic offspring.[11] Other all-male institutions have demanded from their members particular forms of loyalty and duty to the organization and its practices which are familial in their language and nature. The Freemasons and the Mafia not only have hierarchies of Fathers (Godfathers), Sons and Brothers, but in many ways turn the organization itself into 'The Family', a term openly used by the Mafiosa. Even while men within these organizations care for each other with the most intense loyalties, feminine elements

9. The best-known historical example remains Michael Anderson, *Family Structure in 19th Century Lancashire* (Cambridge University Press, 1971).

10. Leonore Davidoff and Catherine Hall, *Family Fortunes: Men and Women of the English Middle Class 1780–1850* (Routledge, 1994), Part II.

11. Mary Anne Clawson, 'Early modern fraternalism and the patriarchal family', *Feminist Studies*, Vol. 6, No. 2 (Summer 1980).

are expunged from within their own psyches through ritual humiliation. Despite the declared aims of taking care of their own families, in extreme cases loyalties to 'The Family' override those afforded to individual families, whose material and emotional needs, even lives, will be sacrificed in the name of the blood Brotherhood.[12] Even within highly structured bureaucracies, familial relationships may hold the key to recruitment and operation, despite modern explicit revulsion against nepotism. In the nineteenth century the armed services assumed that senior officers would act as Fathers of the Regiment, counselling, protecting but also disciplining the junior ranks regardless of age.[13] Military nursing, which evolved from the Crimean War, followed with an expectation that while all nurses were Sisters, ladies gave orders and expected service as they would from daughters or servants. Civilian nursing, with its ambiguously familial titles of Matron and Sister, continued this tradition.[14] While it might be expected that small businesses, farms and professional practices would continue to use family members, it has been found that even in large, formal organizations such as public companies recruitment to managerial positions often embraces family ties; there seems to be a reassertion of personal forms of ownership and control.[15] Senior managers as mentors develop fatherly relationships with their protégés and putative sons.[16]

But popular familial imagery, together with all the emotional and psychic meanings with which it is imbued, is also deployed in other contexts and for different purposes. For example, Laurence Binyon's poem 'For the Fallen' is best known for its powerful call to remember the dead of the First World War:

> They shall grow not old, as we that are left grow old:
> Age shall not weary them, nor the years condemn.
> At the going down of the sun and in the morning
> We will remember them.

12. Renate Siebert, *Secrets of Life and Death: Women and the Mafia* (Verso, 1996); Marie M. Roberts, 'Who wears the apron? Masonic misogyny and female Masonry', *Transactions of the 8th International Congress on the Enlightenment*, Voltaire Foundation, 1991.
13. Myna Trustram, *Women of the Regiment: Marriage and the Victorian Army* (Cambridge University Press, 1984).
14. Anne Summers, *Angels and Citizens: British Women as Military Nurses 1854–1914* (Routledge & Kegan Paul, 1988).
15. R. Scase and R. Goffee, *The Real World of the Small Business Owner* (Croom Helm, 1980); W. Carroll and S. Lewis, 'Restructuring finance capital: changes in the Canadian corporate network 1976–1986', *Sociology*, Vol. 25, No. 3 (1991).
16. Michael Roper, *Masculinity and the British Organisation Man* (Oxford University Press, 1994).

At the same time the poet also reveals that the moral and mythical meaning of family can be heavily drawn upon to exemplify the respective duties and responsibilities of state and citizen. Thus his poem opens:

> With proud thanksgiving, a mother for her children,
> England mourns for her dead across the sea.
> Flesh of her flesh, spirit of her spirit,
> Fallen in the cause of the free.[17]

Binyon thereby uses the idea of the Mother Country, who was owed the personal and intimate loyalties of her 'sons and daughters', together with the more diffuse attachment of patriotism, to explain and excuse why men and women fought and died for a cause which was not their own. In such ways and at such moments of national crisis, the contradictory elements of family, represented by women, order, love and birth, and of war, symbolized by men, chaos, hate and death, can be successfully interwoven so that, at the experiential level, individual families are disrupted and their members offered up to protect a 'Mother' who demands sacrifices not asked for by individual mothers.

But in peacetime there was also Queen Victoria as Mother of her people, including the vast empire she came to rule. Anti-slavery campaigners clinched their arguments with the phrase: 'Am I not a man and a brother, am I not a woman and a sister?' if only in Christ and at a suitable distance.[18] The Coronation in 1953 was celebrated as an event in which British society 'is felt to be one large family' and the Commonwealth countries 'are conceived of as a "family of nations"'.[19] In the late twentieth century the Royal Family is also known colloquially as The Firm, thus illustrating the ways in which the monarchy, as institution, has sought to balance its quasi-familial relationships with the people and contractual ties to the state. And finally Christian imagery never forgets the Holy Mother, the Father in Heaven and his sacrificed Son.

Why, then, is there not a vocabulary which embraces all these elements? We seem always forced to describe every relationship 'within the language of family relationships',[20] which in English is,

17. Laurence Binyon, 'For the fallen', in *The New Oxford Book of English Verse* (Oxford University Press, 1972).

18. Claire Midgley, *Women Against Slavery: The British Campaigns 1780–1870* (Routledge, 1992), p. 99.

19. Edward Shils and Michael Young, 'The meaning of the coronation', *Sociological Review*, Vol. 1, No. 2 (December 1953), pp. 78–9.

20. Jeffrey Weeks, 'Pretended family relationships', in D. Clark (ed.), *Marriage, Domestic Life and Social Change: Writings for Jacqueline Burgoyne* (Routledge, 1991), p. 228.

ironically, comparatively poor in terms for relatives. For example, we do not have words to distinguish between mother's parents and father's parents or to separate aunts and uncles from the mother's or father's side, despite the different significance which they might have within a family's inner circle. Somehow, therefore, we have to push back the limitations of this language.

This does not mean we seek 'the true' or even 'truer' meaning of the family, but rather to think with the terms given by historical actors while at the same time being as careful as possible about our own vision, so clouded with personal and social perceptions of present as well as past. In this we search for change and variation in both concept and context, and for similar relationships which bear other, or even no, names at all. The purpose of such work is not to deny the centrality of family in our understanding of past and present, but rather to acknowledge the significance of that centrality and its resultant impact on the vocabulary and ideas available to us to describe practices and relationships peripheral to the familial context.

The first section of the book, therefore, highlights the ways in which the nuclear family, or its supposed opposite, the extended family network, has been afforded so much research and prescriptive literature. Through a detailed discussion in Chapter 2, we focus upon the history of the family and how it has been shaped by these existing preconceptions and models. This is followed in Chapter 3 by an examination of the concepts of *self*, of *kinship*, of *home* and *household*, and of *identity*, which are shown to constitute parts of the meaning and of our understanding of the family and ourselves. The tensions and contradictions inherent within these concepts and their relationship to the family are considered and alternative means for their re-use or re-interpretation are offered. Throughout we demonstrate that family and gender are inseparable. At the core of family life is shown to be the mother, who has also been the central focus of the caring professions, law, and psychology, despite the fact that, as Chapter 5 highlights, it was fathers who 'made' families. Our position thus mirrors that of John Gillis, who has eloquently argued that 'In a world largely emptied of a sense of place, mothers have become fixed points in our mental landscapes'.[21]

That fixed point, however, also reinforces the gendered divide of the world in which men are not confined within the boundaries of home and family, which women are expected to create and be. As

21. John Gillis, *A World of Their Own Making: Myth, Ritual and the Quest for Family Values* (Basic Books, 1996), p. 176.

so many of our myths and fairy tales confirm, young men go out into the world to seek their fortune while young women, like Sleeping Beauty and Rapunzel, remain locked in their towers awaiting rescue by their prince and only then marry and live happily ever after as his wife in his house. This unspoken blueprint has deeply coloured the practice of family history, as demonstrated by John Demos, one of the founders of the field, in the 1970s:

> The family, in particular, stands quite apart from most aspects of life. We have come to assume that whenever a man leaves his home 'to go out into the world' he crosses a very critical boundary.[22]

These icons, boundaries and images are a constant of our period.

But the narrative of the family has also been moulded by larger historical changes. The specific contexts for our discussion of the family story are, therefore, laid out in the opening chapters of Parts Two and Three (Chapters 4 and 7). Here we concentrate upon the significant changes to English society during the years 1830 to 1960. We trace the major demographic shifts of the period, and their effects upon the size of families and households and upon relationships between their members. We look at how scientific, medical and technological advances impinged upon and, in some cases, shaped the experience of family life. We highlight how social reforms and economic growth generally brought material benefits to families across all strata, while acknowledging that class and status continued as major divides within the population. We point to the importance of gender in understanding how the worlds of work and of home were increasingly separated and how, as a result, the nuclear family – with the breadwinner husband and dependent wife and children – came to be understood as the normative experience.

Although these chapters are broadly linked by theme, we also demonstrate the unique features of each period. For example, Chapter 4 illustrates the significance of religion, the impact of industrialization and the importance of institutional life in the nineteenth century, while Chapter 7 highlights the impact made by legislative and welfare reforms on the shape and quality of family life in the twentieth century and how, in turn, state, social and medical policies were framed by existing familial ideals and practices. At the same time our discussion emphasizes the ways in which rapid change was accepted, resisted or adapted to by familial groups and how they themselves influenced elements of social change.

22. John Demos, *A Little Commonwealth: Family Life in a Plymouth Colony* (Oxford University Press, 1974), p. 186.

To these changes, and their role in shaping the history of the family, we also add intellectual shifts. These are taken up in Chapter 3 and in the case studies of Chapters 5, 6, 8 and 9, where the issue of identity, a central preoccupation of our time, is incorporated into the history of the family. We argue that basic identities are formed in childhood, a fact all too frequently overlooked. Minds as well as bodies are usually born into, are cared for and grow within familial contexts of some sort. And, as our case studies demonstrate, the time and nature of that context is crucial to the development of an idea of self and of identity. Work in this area is only just beginning, and there is still much to be learnt about how the population in the more distant past *experienced* a sense of self, how their identities were formed, and the ways in which kin relationships were invoked and utilized in day-to-day life.

Within modern Western perception, there are still gaps in understanding how identity is formed. We question the mechanisms by which individuals as subjects identify, or do not identify, with the positions within groups, communities and nations to which they are summoned and aligned.[23] In raising these questions we return to our original point about mortality and reproduction. While group identity is social, it is carried by individuals who have a limited lifespan, and thus new members must be initiated into the group. Cultural as well as material inheritance has created the family just as the family moulds our inheritance.

The in-depth case studies also try to link our ideas about familial relationships with historical evidence.[24] Here the attempt has not been to take the statistical norm but to look at relationships which have generally been neglected for a variety of reasons. Chapter 5 focuses on nineteenth-century fatherhood, on men as fathers, on fathers as the absent presence as head of the family/household. Chapter 6 turns to the subterranean, taken-for-granted world of nineteenth-century domestic service and lodging, which provided the basis for so much family life. Chapter 8 highlights the state of singleness and the lives of single women in the twentieth century, shadowy but necessary, feared but used, family members who have escaped most family stories. Finally, Chapter 9 turns to the silences and secrets with which family members have protected themselves

23. Stuart Hall 'Introduction: who needs "identity"', in S. Hall and P. DuGay, *Questions of Cultural Identity* (Sage Publications, 1996), pp. 13–14.

24. '. . . a case study is most often an intermediate production in the effort to link ideas and evidence', Charles Ragin and Howard Becker, *What is a Case: Exploring the Foundations of Social Inquiry* (Cambridge University Press, 1992), p. 225.

against outsiders as well as from each other and, in so doing, have
helped to define who and what is 'family'.

All the studies have in common, therefore, a certain perspective.
None of them privileges marriage or motherhood, the two major
icons of the family. All involve power relations of a complex nature.
All, at least potentially, point to an element of illicit or illegitimate
sexuality. And finally all, in various ways, have served to define the
norm of the family and its practices while, at the same time, actually providing a range of relationships alternative to the core.

Our emphasis throughout is upon language and how the family
and its history have been both constructed and 'read' through the
written and spoken word, although valuable discussions could equally
be drawn from, for example, the visual worlds of art, photography
and material artefacts or the spatial work of town planners, archi-
tects and interior designers. Within the limits of written texts we
have sought, therefore, in Parts Two and Three of the book, to use
as wide a range of material as possible and have cited court cases,
novels, reports by state and voluntary organizations and prescriptive literature.

Oral histories and autobiographies are also particularly drawn
upon, to listen for the voices of previously silenced family and
household members. The interwoven stories contained within the
case studies are told by different voices using a range of approaches
and methods. The ways in which we interpret these sources illustrate our determination not simply to recount life stories but rather
to consider how family forms and familial identities are implicated
in the formation of an individual's sense of self and identity. We
question how narrators shaped their worlds to fit the picture they
wished to present within the structures and meanings available to
them, and seek to identify the myths and silences which were built
into every account. In short, how do people tell their family stories?
Which key relationships and aspects of their past lives do they
emphasize? What range of narrative forms and vocabulary is available to them to make sense of their earlier selves? Where are the
conflicts, tensions and silences in accounts of their past?

This careful unpicking of the history, concepts and instances of
the historical family acknowledges its multi-layered complexities. At
the same time it should allow the reader to grasp the warp and weft
which runs through our discussion of familial and quasi-familial
relationships in whatever context they emerge in these pages. Family history is one means by which the complex interaction between
self, identity and society can be approached and understood.

The relationships of blood, contract and intimacy, which frame so much of our discussion, support and entangle all of us but in different ways and for different reasons. The book's content and our methodology reflect the material shifts in family life and the changing significance of the concept of the family over the 130-year period covered. At the same time they bring out the separate interests of the authors and acknowledge the diversity of our audience. The first section, where we lay out our position in relation to the current state of family history and make explicit the concepts employed, is central to the overall argument but it may be of less interest to some readers than the contextual chapters and in-depth studies that follow. These too differ in their source materials and the extent to which they adopt a broad sweep or a case study approach. The variations in style, content and approach point also to one of the central themes. Though we may look for common cultural and social patterns of family life, in the past and the present, no two family stories are ever the same.

CHAPTER TWO

The family and the historian

Darling, look, the history of us!
Review by E.P. Thompson of Lawrence Stone's *The Family, Sex and Marriage in England, 1500–1800*, 1977[1]

There is enormous interest and concern about 'the family' in our society. It is seen as a vital social institution which is in great danger of disintegration, a prospect loaded with dire social consequences. Politicians and polemicists of all kinds draw upon this concern to demand support for a wide range of ideological platforms, from anti-abortion crusades to environmental struggles. The vast scope of such concerns reflects the diversity of ideas, models and experiences of family life which co-exist in England today. But the emotional impact of drawing upon the notion of 'family values' to discuss social issues relies on a small number of key common-sense understandings of how modern families have developed historically.

It is in popular history and in ordinary understandings about the past that many of the most common preconceptions and assumptions about the history of the family have arisen. Those visions of families in the past which have had most grip on the popular imagination are both reflected and sometimes created by academic historians. Theorists and researchers from other disciplines, especially sociology, economics and demography, have also been the source of these understandings, but all have brought popular ideas to their research as basic assumptions, either implicitly or as questions to be tested. Although some researchers have been critical of and even discarded elements of the popular story of the family as too simplistic or relevant only to a very small proportion of families,

1. *New Society*, 8 September 1977.

many fundamental premises are still taken for granted. In order to develop a wider and deeper understanding of families and historical change, it is necessary to trace the origins of these popular ideas, and to examine existing challenges to their validity.

In this chapter we particularly seek to question the conceptual distinctions between the ways families interact with society in general, and the relationships which are internal to family life. By focusing on relationships understood as working within families, wider connections have been lost; but by assuming the family is a single social unit relating to the rest of society, these 'internal' relationships have in their turn become hidden. It is only by combining both into an analysis that histories of the family can be understood. Our second purpose is to explore ways in which these interrelated sets of connections and relationships are loaded with differences of power. These disparities are most familiar to us in terms of gender, age and class, but most social inequalities can be identified as operating within and through families.

The most pervasive underlying assumptions about families in the past are that they underwent a dramatic and decisive change when industrialization occurred, and that this change was part of the 'progress' of Western societies from traditional to modern, with an accompanying sense of regret for a lost rural and organic family life. It is supposed that before this great divide, families were extended, containing several generations of kin, especially grandparents. These family groups worked and played together in unpolluted rural surroundings, and relied on each other for support in organic, if hierarchical, communities without the interference of governments, bureaucracies, or outside cultural or social influences. It was ties of blood which knit people together and gave them social support and status, and timeless rituals associated with birth, death and marriage cemented these ties. On the other hand, relationships in such families were less emotionally intense. Parents did not have the same bonds with their offspring as we expect today, because so many children died; and because marriages were usually based on property and land, affection between spouses was not seen as important.

According to this model, after industrialization families became smaller, limited to the parent/child nuclear form, and, when contraception became available, to fewer children. Within these families, stronger emotional ties could develop, not least because the struggle for survival had eased. Separate roles for husbands, wives and children emerged, with men operating in the public sphere of work, and women confined to the home. Children became precious and valuable, embodying freedom and joy, protected from the harsh world of labour and allowed to remain innocent of adult knowledge in order to develop as individuals through play and education. The family became a private place, a haven from the evils of modernity, a defence against the encroachments of urban life and disciplines of the factory and office. But to ensure that traditional values were not completely lost in this transition, supposedly timeless rituals have been cherished and revived.

Paradoxically, according to these stereotypes, as the family became more private, the state in various forms began to extend into family concerns, through civil registration of birth, death and marriage, through an increasing range of health professionals, through financial support such as child allowances and old age pensions, through compulsory education and the truant officer. The involvement of the state is seen as a sign of a progressive and humane society which cares for the weak and dependent, but also as interference with individual independence – the nanny state.

The ideas of feminists have had some impact on these commonsense stories, to the extent that women are widely perceived as losers in the process of modernization, by being isolated in the home and economically and socially dependent on men. Recent moves towards gender equality are seen as beginning to rectify this as women enter the public world as workers, although the double burden of housework and paid work continues. On the other hand, the anti-feminist backlash labels women with jobs as selfishly escaping their familial duties.

There is also an important class dimension in this story of historical change. The popular perception is that the first to embrace the ideals of companionate marriage, separate spheres, innocent childhood and small families were the middle classes as they emerged from industrialization. These values and practices were supposed to have gradually trickled down to almost all levels of society, as knowledge and prosperity spread downwards through the classes, leaving only a small residuum of the profligate defying domesticity, with too many children and disordered family lives spilling awkwardly into public view. There is also an assumption of a trickle-up effect, as the aristocracy eventually took on the bourgeois family form, perhaps most clear in the ways the Royal Family has gradually de-emphasized its aristocratic trappings to present itself as a normal family, the care of its children no longer left entirely to servants and schools.

Assumptions about ethnicity and cultural differences have also been made. These are not easy to locate, partly because they have been so pervasive. But the family of the past has been seen as a white English family, loaded with traditional English values which elevate the privacy of the home, romantic love as the basis of marriage, and strict but kindly childrearing. Other ethnicities and cultures, by contrast, are seen as having family histories which are less well developed. The denigration of Asian arranged marriages or the supposed profligacy of the Irish as backward are just two examples of this kind of stereotyping.

These assumptions about families in the past must be taken apart and questioned. We turn first to the issue of when the modern family emerged, and go on to look at the processes which separated home and work, the changing forms of families, the emotional contexts of family life and the involvement of the state in families. We will examine how these stereotypes have arisen, and the many other ways we might locate historical change and interpret existing histories of the family.

Modernization and the family

According to the popular story, the emergence of the modern family is usually placed rather vaguely in the past, some time before living memory. However, it is usually seen as a historical turning point, a fixed time when industrialization took place, rather than a process over a long period. It is sociologists in particular who have sometimes conflated the complexities of industrialization to a brief, transitional episode with a distinct before and after. On the other hand, historians of industrialization have grappled with this issue of periodization for many decades. Modern history is generally defined and located as history after the first impact of industrialization, and yet many historians have come to question the concept of a turning point as a radical change in economy and society. Instead, a picture composed of gradual and uneven changes co-existing with continuities in long-established social and political concerns has emerged as an alternative view.[2] Similarly, historians of gender have questioned the idea that there was a pre-industrial golden age for women, when they occupied a more equal place,

2. For a broad survey of these debates, see D. Cannadine, 'The present and the past in the English Industrial Revolution, 1880–1980', *Past and Present*, No. 103 (1984), pp. 149–72.

living and working alongside men, which collapsed under economic and social changes which established separate, and more unequal, spheres.[3] As we shall see, many historians of the family also see continuities over many centuries, some of which persist today. The search for a precise turning point is necessarily an elusive one, whether for the end of an idyllic past and the start of the modern nightmare, or for the beginning of progress from backward poverty to modern affluence. The standard periodization for the modern era focuses on the decades between the 1780s and 1840s as the crucial era of change.[4] Discontinuities in society and economy between pre- and early industrialization before this time and the emergence of a recognizably modern industrial society by the mid nineteenth century are not difficult to find, even if they occurred in gradual and uneven ways. People living and writing during this period certainly felt that they were living through such times. Patrick Colquhoun wrote in 1814:

> It is impossible to contemplate the progress of manufactures in Great Britain within the last thirty years without wonder and astonishment. Its rapidity, particularly since the commencement of the French revolutionary war, exceeds all credibility.[5]

We have chosen the 1830s as a starting point for this reason, although we recognize the necessarily arbitrary nature of any date as a marker for modernity.

It would be surprising indeed if this transition, however uneven, did not also mark significant changes to families, changes which have had long-lasting effects. One example is the very influential idea of the breadwinner husband and dependent wife. This emerged as a model from liberal economic theory, at the same time as wages were more frequently being paid to the individual worker, with men commanding higher earnings than women and children. While gendered divisions of labour were undoubtedly very marked before the 1780s at every level, from the household to the community and the nation, the distinctive roles of wage-earner husband/father and domestic housewife/mother began to appear by the 1850s among a wide range of social groups, giving us one important indication of the connections between industrial and economic change and

3. Judith Bennett, '"History that stands still": women's work in the European past', *Feminist Studies*, Vol. 14, No. 2 (Summer 1988).
4. Maxine Berg, 'Rehabilitating the Industrial Revolution', *Economic History Review*, Vol. 45, No. 1 (1992), pp. 24–50.
5. P. Colquhoun, 'Treatise on the wealth, power and resources of the British empire' (1814), quoted ibid., p. 26.

family life. This family pattern may have been out of reach for many, and rejected by others, but it became a key model for family relationships and structures, one which influenced not only families and domestic life but a wide range of public policies, from trade union negotiations, to state support for maternity care, to the design of houses. On the other hand, this model concealed other practices and ideas, both survivals and adaptations from earlier periods, and new ways of living which grew up and existed alongside the more dominant breadwinner/housewife form. Thus the issue of periodization of family history is an important one which demands approaches which question the idea of a turning point when modernity became established, but which also seeks to locate social and economic changes associated with the role of families in the growth of industrial capitalism.

The idea that the family holds a distinct and important position in industrial society was one of the cornerstones of functionalist sociology, and it was in the work of Talcott Parsons in the United States in the 1940s and 1950s that the most influential sociological paradigm for the family of advanced industrial capitalism was developed. Parsons's vision of society placed the family as a key element of the social order.[6] In his view, modern nuclear families were necessary to meet four basic needs in industrial society: the regulation of sexual behaviour, the reproduction of the next generation, childcare and the socialization of children into the values of the society, and the provision of psychological support for adults.

He argued that this modern family emerged in urban-industrial societies from wider kin groupings which were multi-functional, performing social, political, religious and educational roles, as well as being central to production and the economy. Obligations to this wider kin group were more significant than any affection within a smaller, nuclear group in order to ensure that the wider group remained cohesive. In contrast, the modern family has few structural obligations to wider kin groups, which means that the economic system is unhampered by such obligations, while a stable, if limited, range of affective relationships is available, contained within the family. Within the functional family, only the male breadwinner moves between work and home, so there is little likelihood that the needs of the nuclear family will clash with those of society. The breadwinner is also freed to respond to the demands of the labour

6. For a detailed analysis of Parsons's ideas about the family, see David H.J. Morgan, *Social Theory and the Family* (Routledge & Kegan Paul, 1975).

market as a highly mobile worker, a crucial attribute in the post-war American social context.

Parsons was not the only social theorist to tell the story of the history of the family in this way. But at the time that the history of the family began to develop as a field of research, his mapping of social systems, within which the family fitted so cosily with capitalist production, was undoubtedly the most influential theoretical framework. In the post-war United States and Britain, the concern to rebuild family life after the disruptions of war, the developments in the study of demography and populations which were focusing on the population crisis of underdeveloped (i.e. traditional) societies, and the growing interest in psychoanalytic versions of intimate family interactions – phenomena we explore further in Chapters 3 and 7 – combined to reinforce the move towards structural explanations for historical changes to the family.

Thus it was another functionalist who first took up this story and placed it in a specific historical context. Neil Smelser looked at the industrial revolution in England, and examined the early cotton textile industry to locate the ways that industry and family were reshaped, performing distinct social and economic functions in the transition from traditional to modern family.[7] He examined the shift in cotton production from the domestic putting-out system, where raw materials were provided by entrepreneurs to families who processed them at home, to the factory, and how the existing family-community structure changed when 'the worker and his [sic] family' could no longer work together. He concluded that a key effect was that the control of fathers over childrearing was threatened, causing social unrest. The end result was the segregation of the labour of adults (i.e. men) from children and the emergence of a school system, a clear indication that economic functions were being separated from the family in the process of modernization.

Smelser was unique in trying to link explicitly historical research to functionalist theory, but many historians of the family have used its underlying framework, often without acknowledging or questioning its values. Thus, while there has been a sustained critique of the functionalist approach within sociology, the particular problems associated with this vision of historical change are rarely identified by historians.

7. Neil Smelser, *Social Change in the Industrial Revolution: An Application of Theory to the Lancashire Cotton Industry 1770–1840* (Routledge & Kegan Paul, 1959).

However, there are several key aspects which present problems for historians. This framework encourages a vision of the family as a single social body which moved and adapted to wider changes. Families have been counted and classified, their economic functions described, and their responses to historical change traced, as if 'the family' was a historical actor. Treating the family as a single, closed entity has made it difficult to look at internal relationships in terms of gender, generation or other inequalities. Feminists have been particularly critical of the general lack of acknowledgement of power relations within families. For example, historians have almost invariably examined intergenerational relationships in terms of *parents* and children, often without questioning the different positions, roles and experiences of mothers and fathers. Children have also often been viewed as a single group, whatever their ages, whether teenagers or toddlers, and differences between sons and daughters are often ignored, the experiences of boys generally receiving much more attention.

The rigid framework which set out four specific functions of modern families has left little room for the wide variations in culture, class and ethnicity as well as historical constructions of family life, which lie outside the functionalist model. Thus the literature has focused on those kinds of families which best fit the model, such as the emerging middle-class nuclear family, usually in an American context, or working-class families responding to industrial change.[8] There is even less room for dysfunction or contradiction, and in the context of the family and industrialization, this has meant that the multiplicity of ways in which families and their members survived difficult times have been reduced to those solutions which were 'successful' in adjusting them to industrial capitalism. Alternative visions and strategies of kinship, of co-operation or community which developed outside the functional family are thus doubly excluded as valid subjects.

Marxists have been important in developing this critique of functionalism, although to a large extent they have accepted the direct linkage between family forms and historical change. Because Marx himself had very little to say about the family, the key text has been Frederick Engels's work *The Origin of the Family, Private Property and the State*, published in English in 1891. Engels brought Marxist ideas about the connections between historical changes in production

8. e.g. James Casey's *The History of the Family* (Blackwell, 1989).

and social change to bear on the family, showing how families changed from a primitive to a civilized pattern as the means of production in societies changed. He argued that when legal equality between the sexes was fully established, and all women entered 'public industry', the family would no longer be needed as the basic unit of society. Until that process was completed, he placed the hierarchical relationships of gender within families on a par with class relationships, the husband as the bourgeoisie and the wife as the exploited proletariat. Thus, although Engels saw economic change as the trigger for changes in the family, he did not see the family as functional to industrial capitalism. The inner contradictions of the family under capitalism would, he suggested, lead to its demise, rather than to its adaptation to become a cornerstone of modern society.

Marxist feminists began to build on these basic premises to examine women and work during the transition to industrial capitalism, particularly the reversing of women's initial entry into waged industrial employment, the role of ideology in stabilizing the family under capitalism, and, as we shall see below, the role of domestic labour. But this has placed the family as an adjunct to production, as the site where the system of production is reproduced through the renewal and sustenance of its workers, which has marginalized the actual work of reproduction, of giving birth and bringing up each new generation.

A key problem with both functionalist and Marxist approaches is the assumption that it was the family which changed in response to wider economic and political developments, i.e. the family was the dependent variable in the processes of modernization. This has had the effect of concealing the ways that families have shaped and formed economic and social life, and of ignoring the important effects that families have had on historical processes. For example, the middle classes drew upon their family connections to raise capital and credit, particularly the property of wives and female relatives held in trusts, to build their entrepreneurial projects, relying heavily on close kin ties between sons, brothers, brothers-in-law and nephews to form business partnerships.[9] Thus familial relationships and connections deeply coloured and shaped nineteenth-century enterprise culture.

9. Leonore Davidoff and Catherine Hall, *Family Fortunes: Men and Women of the English Middle Class 1780–1850* (Hutchinson, 1987), ch. 4.

While many historians do not explicitly bring the theoretical frameworks of functionalism or Marxism to bear upon their research, these have become part of commonly held understandings around the idea of the role of families in the processes of modernization. When they are made explicit, it becomes possible to challenge a number of key perceptions. It is clear, first, that industrial capitalism and the modern nuclear family did not emerge together at a specific historical point, nor did modern families emerge in a single form, ideally equipped to function in modern industrial society. Neither can the family be understood as a single social and economic entity which was influenced and changed by economic and social forces, without actively shaping the processes of modernization.

Separation of home and work?

The story of the abandonment of the traditional family for the sleek and functional nuclear form can be seen in the assumptions about the changes in family relationships as production gradually moved away from the household and into the factory. While not denying the overall shift in work practices which has meant that most paid work in industrial societies is done outside the household, there are substantial debates about the historical processes in which this shift took place, and it is in feminist history that these have emerged most clearly. The historical specificities of these changes (and other continuities) pointed to a much more complex picture, and even to the need to redefine the notion of work itself.

Some kinds of work have never been done within households. Mining, the merchant navy and the armed services are prime examples of this. Commercial enterprises based on workshop rather than household also existed long before the nineteenth century: for example, as early as the 1520s, journeyman ribbon weavers in Coventry worked away from their homes for entrepreneurial masters.[10] Individual waged labour was known from at least the sixteenth century, although it was usually combined with working on the land for subsistence.

On the other hand, it seems that the early phases of industrialization brought about an intensification of household production

10. Peter Laslett, *The World We Have Lost*, 3rd edn (Methuen, 1983), p. 13.

in the expansion of the putting-out system, especially but not exclusively in textiles. As the pace of industrial development and growth quickened, workshops and households only very gradually became separate spaces, while factories usually remained both small-scale and restricted to specific industries, or even specific processes within industries. By 1850, only 5 per cent of the workforce had jobs in factories, and less than 25 per cent were employed in mechanized workplaces of any kind (excepting agriculture).[11] It was not until the late nineteenth century that industrial production had become firmly located away from the small household-based workshop.

In exploring the changing nature of women's work in this transition, feminist historians have found a very wide range of experiences. In some trades, at some times and in some regions, paid work for women became more widely available, partly because their wages, and those of children, who were also widely employed, were lower than men's. This could even delay technological progress which involved heavy investment, for example in hosiery in Leicester.[12] But in many other sectors, opportunities for women and children narrowed, as in some rural areas, where work once done at home in addition to agricultural labour disappeared (for example, straw plaiting), or as agricultural practices changed, demanding different kinds of labour (for example in dairying, which was once a woman's concern). Pressure for women to withdraw from waged work could also influence the ways work practices were reshaped. Thus, although a key feature of industrial change is widely seen as the exclusion of married women and children from production, it is clear that this process was uneven, and in some ways never completed, as for example in small shopkeeping, doctors in general practice, and the clergy, all of whom have relied on wives and family to provide important services.

Debates about domesticity and women thus fit rather uncomfortably within this complex range of experiences of work. Nineteenth-century feminists were sure that the prime cause of their oppression was their confinement to the private, domestic sphere, and traced this confinement to a number of social, legal and political sources. The earliest campaigns to give women rights over property, to education and to professional recognition emphasized women's

---

11. Wally Seccombe, *Weathering the Storm: Working-Class Families from the Industrial Revolution to the Fertility Decline* (Verso, 1993), p. 24.
12. Nancy Grey Osterud, 'Gender divisions and the organisation of work in the Leicester hosiery industry', in Angela John (ed.), *Unequal Opportunities: Women's Employment in England 1800–1918* (Basil Blackwell, 1986).

exclusion from the public world, and feminist historians have often
accepted this explanation at face value without examining the important class (and other) differences between women's experiences
of work.

On the other hand, feminist historians have challenged the idea
that domesticity was necessarily confining for women, arguing instead that this role emphasized companionship, common interests,
and 'love and friendship' both within and across families. Women's
shared culture could lead to collective action, often informal, within
an oppositional female culture.[13] However, while this approach
shifted attention to the history of women, it tended to bypass
women's place in networks of family and kinship, downplaying the
important role these played in women's cultures, and neglecting
the experiences of women who did remain within their allotted
domestic sphere, whether by choice or necessity.

Even if the experience of domesticity was far from universal, the
ideology of separate spheres was certainly influential. Catherine
Hall pointed to the importance of the evangelical movement, coinciding with the emergence of a new entrepreneurial and professional middle class, which placed an emphasis on the special and
separate role of women as the carriers of social and religious virtue,
only possible if women were shielded from the vicious and competitive public world of men and the market.[14] One of the indications
of the effectiveness of this ideology was the way places and activities
seen as tainted by this public world were increasingly barred to
women, while the sacred duties of maintaining the virtuous home
and raising children to embrace middle-class values and practices
were elevated. For example, by the mid nineteenth century, middle-
class women faced increasing social criticism if they openly walked
or rode horseback, except for health or recreational reasons, which
restricted their ability to engage directly with the public world.[15]
Within this framework, a woman's direct involvement in paid work
was seen as inappropriate, casting doubt on her femininity as well
as undermining the status of her family, especially of her male relatives. This pattern reinforced her economic and social dependence
on such relatives. Of course, for many, even of the middle class, this

13. Carol Smith-Rosenberg, 'The female world of love and ritual: relations between women in nineteenth-century America', in *Disorderly Conduct: Visions of Gender
in Victorian America* (Oxford University Press, 1985).
14. Catherine Hall, 'The early formation of Victorian domestic ideology', in *White,
Male and Middle Class: Explorations in Feminism and History* (Polity Press, 1992).
15. Davidoff and Hall, *Family Fortunes*, p. 286.

goal was always unattainable. Many women earned a living for themselves and their families, even when their options for employment
became increasingly limited.

The notion of separate spheres has hidden the ways that families
have always crossed the boundaries between work and home in
their daily lives. Explorations of these boundaries have led to a
questioning of standard definitions of work. The meaning of work
as paid employment, rather than its more general sense as labour,
emerged in the early modern period. Raymond Williams argued
that this change reflected the emergence of capitalist productive
relations in general.[16] In economics, work was firmly placed within
the market, with exchange marking the boundary between public
and private domains, between paid work and unpaid domestic
labour. However important unpaid labour might be in society,
according to this economic model it had no value. This theoretical
framework, common to both Marxist and neo-classical economics,
contained crucial gender implications, as women's work became
less and less identified with exchange and the market, and increasingly tied to unpaid domestic labour.

This model was built into government statistics from the 1881
census, when women working at home were explicitly classified as
'unoccupied' and were removed from occupational tables. This
practice was eventually consolidated under the influence of Charles
Booth and the economist Alfred Marshall, so that when Booth
constructed a time series of occupations for the nineteenth century, he simply moved all working wives and female relatives in the
previous census statistics of occupations to the unoccupied category
to present a consistent series, a practice continued ever since by
most historical statisticians.[17]

Feminist debates about the economic value and meaning of
housework which arose in the 1970s centred on attempts to put
domestic work back into economic thinking. Thus the economic
value to society of housework was highlighted to help to explain
the relationship between productive and reproductive work.[18]
Attempts to include domestic labour in existing economic models,
both Marxist and neo-classical, were never successful because the

16. Raymond Williams, *Keywords: A Vocabulary of Culture and Society* (Fontana, 1988),
p. 335.
17. Edward Higgs, 'Women, occupations and work in the nineteenth-century
censuses', *History Workshop*, No. 23 (Spring 1987), pp. 70–3.
18. Maxine Molyneux, 'Beyond the domestic labour debate', *New Left Review*,
No. 116 (1979).

public/private dichotomy was one of the fundamental premises of both. The logical outcome of these arguments was the 'Wages for Housework' campaign, which demanded that women's domestic work be recognized through the form of a wage, and which has closely allied itself to demands for workers' rights for women in the sex industry.

A very different approach to this impasse has been to undermine the notion that domestic and other work should be so neatly separated.[19] A key historical example is women's involvement in philanthropy, which could extend far beyond the limits of domestic duty into highly public political campaigning while remaining within a rhetorical framework of care and nurture, rather than the market. Josephine Butler's work against the Contagious Diseases Acts, and the lobbying of the Co-operative Women's Guild for better conditions for wives and mothers, are two examples of this.[20]

Finally, the theoretical separation of work and home is most clearly undermined when we look at the place of domestic service. We investigate the place of servants in families in Chapter 6, pointing to the growing contradictions between the ancient master/ servant relationship and the nineteenth-century construction of domestic employment. Domestic service became that work which was done mainly by women living in their employer's household to maintain the new consumer goods produced by industry, and to delineate the social status of their employers. By the First World War domestic workers increasingly rejected the service relationship by 'living out', establishing clearer boundaries in their lives between work and private life, although the idea that servants were 'one of the family' persisted. Because domestic service defies the split between work and home, its history has become neither part of family history nor part of the history of work, remaining in an upstairs/downstairs limbo of period drama.

It was not just wives, mothers and servants who were in theory at least located in the domestic sphere. Another crucial element in the debates about the separation of home and work is child labour. The removal of children from paid work into an unproductive domestic world is seen as one of the most 'civilized' elements of modernization, and this assumption underlies many standard

19. From the large literature on women and work, one example of an approach which looks at the interconnections between work and home is Judy Lown's *Women and Industrialization: Gender at Work in Nineteenth-Century England* (Polity Press, 1990).
20. Frank Prochaska, *Women and Philanthropy in Nineteenth-Century England* (Clarendon Press, 1980), pp. 224–7.

accounts of children during the transition to modern society, not least in the stories told by those who laboured as children themselves. As Charles Shaw wrote:

> Imagine a mere boy, running in and out of this stove-room, winter and summer, with its blazing iron stove, his speed determined by his master's speed at his work. Coarse oaths, and threats, and brutal blows in many cases followed any failure to be at the bench at the required moment. Thank God there is no mould-running or wedging now. Mechanical contrivances have done away with these cruel forms of child-labour. But such was the condition of life of thousands of youths 'when I was a child' and the great humane Parliament of England, composed of lords and gentlemen of kind and beneficent hearts, never once thought of the little Pottery slaves.[21]

However, this transition shows more than a shift towards humanitarian concerns for children in the industrial workplace. It also marks an important change in the way children's labour was seen. Ludmilla Jordanova pointed out that, in the eighteenth century, the perception of the problem of child labour was that idle (i.e. unemployed) children were a social danger, because it was through labour that children learned social values as well as work skills necessary for adult life.[22] The very gradual decline of child labour since then has pointed to some important issues for the history of the family. Most significant are the disruption of authority within families when children became earners in their own right when working for employers outside the immediate family network; the importance of their work, both paid and unpaid, to family survival; and the changing representations of children as their places in economic and social life were reshaped.[23] And because of these important gaps, in many ways histories of the family and of childhood have remained separate fields, as explorations of child labour have tended to remove children's working lives from wider contexts. There are exceptions, such as Anna Davin's work, which show

21. Charles Shaw, *When I Was a Child, by an Old Potter*, extract in John Burnett, *Useful Toil: Autobiographies of Working People from the 1820s to the 1920s* (Penguin, 1984), p. 299.

22. Ludmilla Jordanova, 'Conceptualising childhood in the eighteenth century: the problem of child labour', *British Journal for Eighteenth Century Studies*, Vol. 10 (1987).

23. Michael Anderson, 'Sociological history and the working-class family: Smelser revisited', *Social History*, Vol. 1, No. 3 (1976); David Vincent, *Bread, Knowledge and Freedom: A Study of Nineteenth-Century Working Class Autobiography* (Methuen, 1981), chs 4–5; Hugh Cunningham, *The Children of the Poor: Representations of Childhood since the Seventeenth Century* (Basil Blackwell, 1991).

how children lived within interlocking networks of family, school, work and neighbourhood, a mixture of domestic and public spaces and relationships.[24]

The model which most clearly placed women, servants and children as dependants within the home also placed men as the breadwinners, the earners of wages or profits in the public world, returning to a domestic haven for emotional and material repair and replenishment. However, there has been much less critical attention to this side of the home/work dichotomy. It is clear from some accounts that many men were unable to fulfil this role, and that some were also unwilling, an apparent 'flight from commitment' beginning to emerge by the late nineteenth century.[25] However, the importance of the breadwinner model has been emphasized by its links to political movements such as the Chartists and the trade unions, forming a key element in the demand for the extension of citizenship by working-class men.[26] The material power and authority within families which came with achieving the position of sole breadwinner have only just begun to be explored in historical terms.[27]

Thus issues of the boundaries between work and home can be seen as crucial in reconceptualizing the story of families in the past. The gradual and uneven shifts between large-scale and domestic production make the tracing of these boundaries difficult, but more importantly the ideological construction of women's work around the private sphere, untouched by market forces, and the representations of the childhood ideal as free from labour, concealed the crucial economic contributions of supposedly dependent women and children working at home.

The emergence of the nuclear family?

The comfortable fit between the modern family and modern industrial society is further disturbed when we turn to look at family

24. Anna Davin, *Growing Up Poor: Home, School and Street in London 1870–1914* (Rivers Oram Press, 1995).

25. John Tosh, 'Domesticity and manliness in the Victorian middle class: the family of Edward White Benson', in Michael Roper and John Tosh (eds), *Manful Assertions: Masculinities in Britain since 1800* (Routledge, 1991).

26. Anna Clark, *The Struggle for the Breeches: Gender and the Making of the British Working Class* (Rivers Oram Press, 1995); Keith McClelland, 'Masculinity and the "representative artisan" in Britain 1850–80', in Roper and Tosh (eds), *Manful Assertions*.

27. Colin Creighton, 'The rise of the male breadwinner family: a reappraisal', *Comparative Studies in Society and History*, Vol. 38, No. 2 (April 1996).

structures. The popular perception of the transformation of families from traditional, multi-generational groups of kin to the nuclear form was questioned for the first time by historical demographers associated with the Cambridge Group for the History of Population and Social Structure. They concluded from their research that family structures underwent surprisingly little change between the sixteenth and nineteenth centuries, and that the extended family was never a common phenomenon in England after the Reformation – perhaps not even before. The proportion of households containing more than two generations between 1622 and 1854 was estimated at 5.7 per cent.[28] This startling conclusion was reached through the methodology of family reconstruction, first developed in the 1960s, where family sizes and structures could be estimated for a community, with parish registers used as a source of information about births, marriages and deaths. The Cambridge Group thus turned modernization theory on its head, pointing to long-standing continuities in family forms throughout the extended processes of industrial development and population change. But while the various technical difficulties of constructing these data sets were gradually overcome, some of the wider questions about what these figures meant became more pressing.

The central concern with these findings has focused on the conflation between family and household. The Cambridge Group methodology assumed that persons living in households who were not closely related were only peripheral additions to a family core, and on the whole it has been this 'family' core which has interested them. Thus households have been seen as families plus less important, unfamilial relationships. Even when the distinction between household and family has been acknowledged, researchers have tended to look at either one or the other, losing the richness of the networks of relationships between them.

As we will see in Chapter 3, a more fruitful way of viewing the relationship between household and family is to recognize households as social entities in their own right, entities which may have connections with families both within and external to themselves. Similarly, families can be understood as being sited both within and between households.

Today, a household is generally understood as a group of people living together, not necessarily related, sharing domestic space and at least some economic and domestic arrangements concerning

28. Laslett, *The World We Have Lost*, p. 98.

food, cleanliness and possibly the care of dependants. The current census definition of this 'common housekeeping' is the sharing of a daily meal, or sharing a living or sitting room. Households can also consist of a single individual. Thus not all households are set up around the desire for family life in its narrower senses. But because there have been few ways of describing or naming household groups which are not obviously familial, the imagery and language of family are often used to fill this gap.

Households in the past also might consist of people whose connections with each other were not familial in the ways we would define them, including servants, apprentices, lodgers, visitors, pupils, and other kinds of workers. But such households often considered themselves as a kind of family, and the hierarchies working within them contained ambiguous connections of both kinship and contract. The head of the household, also head of the family, united these interwoven relationships in a social and economic unit, within which his (or less often her) children and other blood relations could usually claim a privileged position. To see these households as nuclear families with other people added on, as in the Cambridge Group statistics, is plainly inadequate; on the other hand, to define them as simply another type of family ignores the complexity of the possible relationships of contract and service within and between nuclear family, wider kin and unrelated household members.[29]

Another problem with conflating family and household is that it has masked those family relationships which extend outside the boundaries of shared living space. For example, several generations of a family may live in the same community, and sustain relationships very like those of a household, with daily exchanges of both material and emotional support. And yet a definition based on household membership would identify each part of such a network as an independent family unit. The importance of such networks in the past has been explored by Miranda Chaytor, in an early seventeenth-century town, and by Michael Anderson, in a North-West textile town rapidly expanding as people came looking for work in mid nineteenth-century factories.[30]

If some family research has tended to conflate household and family, others have turned their attention to the household as a

29. Olivia Harris, 'Households and their boundaries', *History Workshop*, No. 13 (1982), pp. 143–52.
30. Miranda Chaytor, 'Household and kinship: Ryton in the late sixteenth and early seventeenth centuries', *History Workshop*, No. 10 (Autumn 1980); Michael Anderson, *Family Structure in 19th Century Lancashire* (Cambridge University Press, 1971).

social entity which is detachable from familial experiences and practices. Sociological analyses based on the household as a social and economic unit have made it possible to look at the connections between home and work, between activities and relationships normally seen as divided along a public and private fault line. Thus, for example, Pahl's research on work and the family relied on the notion that households were units for getting various kinds of work done. These units were tied to each other in many complex ways and had fluid boundaries as members moved back and forth at different stages of the life course, but were fundamental in understanding how work was defined and allocated in society.[31] This kind of analysis was very important in questioning the boundaries of public and private, and revealing the ways households engaged with economic life rather than simply reacting to the outside world. But it avoided questions about familial relationships and practices contained within or lying outside households.

In general, economic models have been less open to an examination of the fluidity of households, nor have divisions within households been seen as important to their analyses, with the important exception of the work of feminist economists. Nancy Folbre has pointed out that the neo-classical model, which underpins most economic thinking, cannot include any analysis of the inner workings of the household, particularly the relative bargaining powers between the generations and the sexes.[32] These powers are not simply determined by market position, but by largely patriarchal legal and cultural frameworks. This treatment of the household as a single social and economic actor has contributed to the marginalizing of the complexities of the relationships which not only exist within it, but which spill out of its boundaries.

A tendency to see the household as a discrete social unit has the same pitfalls as treating the family in this way, in that it hides the differences of gender and generation which operate within it. Differences of class and ethnicity can also disappear. In particular, the concept of household strategies, very widely used by economists and sociologists as well as social historians, has been questioned because it makes assumptions about the household as a unified social actor. It was feminist sociologists who pointed out that households were key sites for the sexual division of labour and unequal distribution of resources, rather than social units pursuing joint

31. R.E. Pahl, *Divisions of Labour* (Basil Blackwell, 1984).
32. Nancy Folbre, 'Of patriarchy born: the political economy of fertility decisions', *Feminist Studies*, Vol. 9, No. 2 (1983), p. 267.

strategies and managing available resources to produce agreed outcomes.[33]

Research based on household strategies has also tended to perpetuate the public/private split by separating those strategies applied to the world of work, which are seen as rational, and those applied to the world of the family, which are relegated to the realm of altruistic affection. Researchers who attempt to ignore the non-material, and therefore less quantifiable, factors which might dominate a household's decisions will have difficulties explaining their strategies. An example might be the tensions around family rituals, like holidays or Christmas, where a household's strategy emerges from a tangle of emotional obligations as well as material considerations, and where power to determine the eventual outcome is often unequal.[34]

Closely related to the strategies approach has been the investigation of the ways families changed internally over time. Initially this was described as the life cycle, but the term 'life course' has come to be more widely used, because it avoids the implication that individuals pass through set stages in a fixed cyclical series, which are unrelated to other groups or processes. 'Life course' allows connections to be made between households, individuals and wider historical change as family structures experience shifts and transitions. Tamara Hareven's analogy of the family as a moving shoal of fish whose members move in and out of the group, establishing or re-forming similar groups over time, has provided a highly flexible image for these processes.[35]

Paradoxically, this approach, while stimulating much empirical work on the histories of various stages of the life course such as childhood, youth, marriage, old age, and widowhood, results in analyses which are less connected to the wider society than the more static strategy model. Sources are used to create snapshots of different populations who happen to be in that particular stage at particular periods of time, rather than investigations of families going through historically mediated transitions.[36]

33. J. Brannen and G. Wilson (eds), *Give and Take in Families* (Allen & Unwin, 1987); Janet Finch, *Family Obligations and Social Change* (Polity Press, 1989).

34. Christine Delphy and Diana Leonard, *Familiar Exploitation: A New Analysis of Marriage in Contemporary Western-Type Societies* (Cambridge Centre, 1992).

35. Tamara Hareven, 'Family time and industrial time: family and work in a planned corporation town 1900–1924', in *Family and Kin in Urban Communities 1700–1930* (New Viewpoints, 1977), p. 5.

36. For the debates on using a family strategies approach, see Leslie Page Moch *et al.*, 'Family strategy: a dialogue', *Historical Methods*, No. 20 (1987).

Part of the problem for historians, even of the nineteenth and early twentieth centuries, has been the need to rely on a predominant single historical source, the national census, which has also assumed a paradigm of families as social units which can be clearly distinguished. The census was designed around the presumption that family and household were the same social entity which could be captured and counted at a single point in time to provide a general picture of the population. The historical construction of the census has been the subject of analysis, most notably by Edward Higgs,[37] who has pointed out that those who designed and supervised the censuses were profoundly influenced by the ideas of political economy and utilitarianism, which sharply separated the family from the public world. They struggled to fit the population of Britain into this framework, with only limited degrees of success.

Defining the family and household was central to these attempts, and a solution was developed which relied on counting the heads of households, always an adult male unless the only adults in the household were female. Everyone else present, whether wives, children or others outside this 'natural' circle, were all attached like a body to this head. Thus lodgers were found to be a particularly difficult group to categorize. This is shown in the increasingly complex tests used to judge whether they formed a discrete unit or were part of another's household, eventually focusing on who prepared meals. Physical boundaries between households were also subject to some debate, particularly in periods of overcrowding where a single 'house' might contain many households. Furthermore, the data collected for the census could only give a snapshot of household forms at a single point in time, and thus the fluidity of families and households has tended to disappear. The census as a major analytic tool for historians, particularly historical demographers who have counted and averaged household sizes and structures based on this data, has severe limitations in developing an understanding of families which did not fit its rigid model.

Demographic analyses have been used more flexibly as a base for exploring specific or local family experiences. This approach was led by Michael Anderson's study of Preston in the mid nineteenth century,[38] where he found significant variations in family forms, structures and networks, and used these to explore the

---

37. Higgs, 'Women, occupations and work'.
38. Anderson, *Family Structure in 19th Century Lancashire*. It also enabled him to develop a critique of Smelser's thesis about the ways family engaged with factory production.

effects of industrialization on families in the North-West. Data from census collectors has continued to be widely, if sometimes uncritically, used by historians doing other local studies, as information about relationships within households or about the occupations of household members can rarely be established in any other way.

While local and specific studies have proliferated, the wider assumptions about household and family structures, outlined by Peter Laslett and the Cambridge Group, have until recently remained largely unchallenged. However, Wally Seccombe has argued that, although the average numbers in households may have been the same for many centuries, the composition of families did change in significant ways, as waves of industrial development shifted the material means of survival available to families and households. Thus, while early modern households often included farm servants, by the late nineteenth century this relationship was a much less common phenomenon, while, on the other hand, purely domestic servants were rare until the nineteenth century, reaching a peak just before 1914.

The fertility decline, that' phase of demographic change beginning in the 1870s which brought into being the mid-twentieth-century norm of the two-parent/two-child family, has been easier to trace empirically than earlier changes, and the 1940s marks a clear watershed in terms of declining family size. However, explanations for the fall in birth-rates remain contested, and it is historical demographers who have dominated these arguments.

Historical demography as a separate discipline developed relatively late, not becoming fully recognized until the 1920s, and for many years remained a narrow field, closely tied to governmental agencies, especially the Registrar General's Office. Demographers saw themselves as hard scientists and, because of the scientific paradigm and the form in which their data was collected, they limited themselves in the questions they could ask. Such concepts as the social construction of reproduction, or gender as a political relationship, both central to the understanding of fertility historically, simply do not lend themselves well to being treated only through quantitative methods and abstract modelling.[39]

In the 1960s and 1970s, some researchers investigating the fertility decline began to include family relationships, the status of women and the value of children in their analysis, but they still

---

39. Susan Greenlagh, 'The social construction of population science: an intellectual, institutional, and political history of twentieth century demography', *Comparative Studies in Society and History*, Vol. 38, No. 1 (January 1996), p. 49.

tended to exclude crucial historical and political forces for change. Even the definition of culture that most were using was narrow and mechanistic, based on ideas like the extent of communication about contraception. In 1979, the feminist historical demographer Sheila Ryan Johannson pointed out that most demographic histories focused on families and that most also assumed that the interests of husbands and wives were identical in respect to family size.[40] She went on to point out the predominance of negative stereotypes of women, who in taking decisions about childbearing were dubbed selfish, either refusing to have children in times of perceived population dearth, or spawning too numerously when overpopulation was feared.[11] The failure to consider changing power relations between men and women in discussions of fertility can be seen as a critical omission, with the exception of the few feminist demographers, historical or otherwise – for example, Johannson herself, Diana Gittins and, more recently, Alison MacKinnon.[12]

However, there is now an increasing questioning of these notions in the context of the fertility decline in England. The idea that changes in the reproductive behaviour of couples can be understood at the national level within a hierarchical model of social class, with working-class couples gradually accepting the model set by a more progressive middle class, has been challenged by Simon Szreter, who places much more emphasis on local changes, especially the variability of local labour markets in terms of age and gender. However, even this more nuanced framework assumes the family structure we are so familiar with, because the main body of his data, the 1911 fertility census, was based on a nuclear family model.[13]

Seccombe has argued that fertility decisions became a site for gender struggles, as relationships between husbands and wives necessarily affected and were changed by new perceptions about fertility choices.[11] Susan Greenlagh also focuses on the lack of attention to real power differences within families who were making

40. Sheila Ryan Johansson, 'Demographic contributions to the history of Victorian women', in Barbara Kanner (ed.), *The Women of England from Anglo-Saxon Times to the Present: Interpretative Bibliographic Essays* (Archon Books, 1979).
41. Alison MacKinnon, 'Were women present at the demographic transition? Questions from a feminist historian to historical demographers', *Gender and History*, Vol. 7, No. 2 (August 1995).
42. Johansson, 'Demographic contributions'; Diana Gittins, *Fair Sex: Family Size and Structure, 1900–39* (Hutchinson, 1982); MacKinnon, 'Were women present'.
43. Simon Szreter, *Fertility, Class and Gender in Britain, 1860–1940* (Cambridge University Press, 1996), pp. 74–5.
44. Seccombe, *Weathering the Storm*, ch. 5.

fertility decisions.[45] By implication all these arguments should also include the fertility 'decisions' of those not in couples, including pre-nuptial pregnancy, stepchildren, or adulterous pregnancies, although these groups have yet to be seriously investigated. The question of changes in household size beyond the declining numbers of children in families, due to the decline in live-in domestic service, to changes in lodging practices and availability and structures of household spaces, and to informal fostering and adoption of other people's children, also remains marginal.

From this survey it is apparent that family forms did change during our historical period, but it is also apparent that we really know very little overall about how and why groups defined themselves as families and/or households in the past. Clearly early modern households did not contain the same kinds of family forms as those of the late nineteenth century, even if they added up to the same number of people. In the twentieth century, the complex processes which eventually led the majority of people to live in households of small nuclear families or single people are still being unravelled.

The family becomes an emotional haven?

Interest in the history of the family was sparked off for many by the work of Philippe Aries on the history of childhood. In this pathbreaking study Aries identified a fundamental change in the ways society understood children. In the past, he argued, they were not seen as intrinsically different from adults. Thus images of children showed only small people and there were no specific toys, books or pastimes allocated to childhood. He saw the change to modern constructions of childhood, especially its association with innocence, nature and a need for parental love, nurture and protection, as part of the Enlightenment with its changing ideas about the place of 'man' in nature and society generally.[46] Aries was the first historian of the 'sentiments' approach to the history of the family, an approach which has been most concerned with the question of whether modern families have developed a unique and important world of affection and emotion which was not available in the past.

---

45. Susan Greenlagh, 'Anthropology theorises reproduction: integrating practice, political economic and feminist perspectives', in *Situating Fertility: Anthropology and Demographic Inquiry* (Cambridge University Press, 1995).

46. Philippe Aries, *Centuries of Childhood: A Social History of Family Life* (Jonathan Cape, 1962, first published 1960).

This debate has had two opposing positions, the first being that because relationships associated with families belong to the 'natural', they have remained fundamentally the same throughout history. Thus, for example, Linda Pollock has identified many first-hand accounts of parenting to build an argument that the concerns of parents for their children have not changed over the centuries. On the other hand, it is argued that social barriers and cultural limitations prevented such 'natural' feelings from being expressed in pre-modern families, feelings which modernization and individualism have liberated. For this view, the most influential example is Lawrence Stone's *The Family, Sex and Marriage in England*, a broad sweep from the fifteenth to the nineteenth centuries, which traces the growth of affective individualism through the rise of companionate marriage and child-oriented parenting.

An important critique of both sides of this debate has focused on the problems of sources. Because there is very little evidence about how people felt about their families, especially for groups such as the poor, women and children with little access to literacy, historians have relied heavily on a few sources, many of them prescriptive, which give a very limited picture. Both Aries and Stone have been particularly criticized for generalizing from sources relating to social elites, such as diaries and records of property. Questions of how to interpret this evidence have also highlighted the problems faced in trying to understand feelings like affection or duty in earlier historical periods. For example, in Pollock's work, there is a lack of social context for much of her evidence, and a deeper analysis of these sources in terms of class, gender, economic and legal positions, and an examination of these texts as social constructs themselves, would seriously undermine her conclusions.[17]

Work on the twentieth century has increasingly drawn upon oral history as a source, which has given historians the opportunity to ask their interviewees about their family lives. Historians of women – for example, Elizabeth Roberts and Joanna Bourke – have been particularly interested in the domestic relationships of women.[48] Oral history was derived from sociological methodologies, and particularly influential in explorations of the family was the work of

47. Linda Pollock, *Forgotten Children: Parent–Child Relations from 1500 to 1900* (Cambridge University Press, 1983) and *A Lasting Relationship: Parents and Children over Three Centuries* (Fourth Estate, 1987).

48. Joanna Bourke, *Working Class Cultures in Britain 1890–1960* (Routledge, 1994); Elizabeth Roberts, *A Woman's Place: An Oral History of Working Class Women, 1890–1940* (Blackwell, 1984).

the Institute of Community Studies in Bethnal Green during the 1950s and 1960s, which used the interview as a way of exploring such things as care of children and kin relationships.[49] While these approaches can never give an insight into the past before living memory (or at least recorded memory), and require careful interpretation and contextualization, they have provided a rich source for investigations into relationships in families.

But there are far more serious problems with this debate than the availability and interpretation of sources, and it was feminist historians who in the 1970s began to unpack and investigate its underlying premises. Rayna Rapp, Ellen Ross and Renate Bridenthal, in an early Marxist feminist critique, pointed to a whole range of inadequacies, identifying a lack of attention to the crucial links between the inner worlds of family relationships and those of material survival, and the subordinate positions of women in families, challenging the assumption that the family is a natural, biological unit, and acknowledging the many emotional ties which develop between and outside families. From this emerged the counter-factual assertion that there was no such thing as family, only relationships.[50] While this was a salutary shock to the dominant preconceptions of the time, forcing an examination beyond, behind and around the family, it also obscured those times and places where family and kinship were organizing principles of great cultural and material power. Thus, for example, in the nineteenth century, despite the formalization of entry into the professions through impersonal qualifications and examinations, it was still primarily family connections which opened doors and oiled the wheels of the law, the Church, and the military.

Unfortunately, these early feminist critiques did not launch a large body of feminist work on the history of the family, as feminist history pursued parallel lines of enquiry, dominated by the American model of women's culture and the British emphasis on women and work. Both these interests sought to give women historical agency, some empowerment, and to continue the feminist project of reclaiming a place for women in the past, but, in both, women

49. e.g. Brian Jackson and Dennis Marsden, *Education and the Working Class* (Routledge & Kegan Paul, 1962); Peter Mariss, *Widows and their Families* (Routledge & Kegan Paul, 1958); Peter Townsend, *The Family Life of Old People* (Routledge & Kegan Paul, 1957); Peter Wilmott and Michael Young, *Family and Kinship in East London* (Routledge & Kegan Paul, 1957).

50. Rayna Rapp, Ellen Ross and Renate Bridenthal, 'Examining family history', in Judith Newton, Mary Ryan and Judith Walkowitz (eds), *Sex and Class in Women's History* (Routledge & Kegan Paul, 1983).

in families tended to disappear. However, more recent feminist work has begun to look again at the shaping of gender in contexts of family relationships, a leading example being Ellen Ross's examination of motherhood in London's poorest communities.[51]

It was Black feminists who reminded feminist sociologists of the importance of developing concepts of family which were inclusive of a range of family practices and processes, particularly with the work of Carol Stack on women in Black American families.[52] While American debates about the Black family engaged feminists, in Britain questions of ethnicity and family were rarely tackled, despite criticisms of ethnocentrism in feminist stances which placed families as necessarily oppressive to all women in the same ways. This was set out by Hazel Carby:

> Three concepts which are central to feminist theory become problematic in their application to black women's lives: 'the family', 'patriarchy' and 'reproduction'. When used they are placed in a context of the herstory of white (frequently middle class) women and become contradictory when applied to the lives and experiences of black women. . . . We would not wish to deny that the family can be a source of oppression for us but we also wish to examine how the black family has functioned as a prime source of resistance to oppression.[53]

Historical work on slavery and the family in the United States has developed around the issues of how race, gender and class worked together,[54] but in Britain work on feminist histories of race, ethnicity and families has remained very limited, with work on women's engagement with imperialism dominating recent research.[55]

Thus feminists have, on the whole, had little to say about what family life might have been like for women in the past, tending

51. Ellen Ross, *Love and Toil: Motherhood in Outcast London 1870–1918* (Oxford University Press, 1993).

52. Carol B. Stack, *All Our Kin* (Harper Row, 1974).

53. Hazel V. Carby, 'White women listen! Black feminism and the boundaries of sisterhood', in Heidi Safia Miraz (ed.), *Black British Feminism: A Reader* (Routledge, 1997), p. 46.

54. e.g. Elizabeth Fox Genovese, *Within the Plantation Household: Black and White Women of the Old South* (University of North Carolina Press, 1988) and Brenda Stevenson, *Life in Black and White: Family and Community in the Slave South* (Oxford University Press, 1996).

55. e.g. Vron Ware, *Beyond the Pale: White Women, Racism and History* (Verso, 1992); Clare Midgley, *Women Against Slavery: The British Campaigns 1780–1870* (Routledge, 1992); Antoinette Burton, *Burdens of History: British Feminists, Indian Women and Imperial Culture 1865–1915* (University of North Carolina Press, 1994). A recent exception is: Catherine Hall, 'A family for nation and empire', in Gail Lewis (ed.), *Forming Nation, Framing Welfare* (Routledge, 1998).

to look elsewhere for women's historical experiences. This has deprived the sentiments school of a sustained critique in terms of gender. An attempt to break open definitions of the family would have helped us to look at the myriad of possibilities for familial intimacy and affection which may have existed in the past.

But the concerns and obsessions of the 1960s and 1970s, when the sentiments approach emerged, limited the affective world of the family to 'nuclear' relationships of parent/child and husband/wife. These two sets of relationships, marriage and parenthood, were viewed as discrete and separate, a distinction which was almost certainly much less clearly experienced in the past. Until very recently, to be married was also to be a parent, both in reality for the vast majority of couples, and in the ways family life was generally expected to be experienced. However, today married and cohabiting couples expect to have a relationship in many ways independent of those with their children or other relatives, and this assumption has restricted the ways these histories have looked at family relationships. In Chapters 5, on fatherhood, and 7, on single women, we show how questioning these assumptions can lead to new and fruitful insights.

For example, there has been much attention to changing child-rearing practices, but this is rarely examined as an activity which shaped the lives of fathers or mothers, only as the formative experiences of children. Investigations of practices such as swaddling, wet-nursing or puritan discipline demonstrate this.[56] Similarly, work on marriage has not had much to say on the specific role and experience of parenthood. To give some examples, Edward Shorter has looked at illegitimacy,[57] Peter Laslett at the age of marriage,[58] and Phyllis Rose at the meanings of married love,[59] but there is very little in any of these works on the place of parenting in marriage. This separation of marriage and parenthood has also pervaded sociological literature, for example in Giddens's work on intimacy, which, while outlining changing ideas and practices in adult relationships, ignores questions about how children who are produced by these partnerships are loved and cared for.[60]

56. e.g. Lawrence Stone, *The Family, Sex and Marriage in England 1500–1800* (Penguin, 1979, first published 1977); Philip Greven, *Spare the Child: The Religious Roots of Punishment and the Psychological Impact of Physical Abuse* (Alfred Knopf, 1990).
57. Edward Shorter, *The Making of the Modern Family* (Collins, 1976).
58. Laslett, *The World We Have Lost.*
59. Phyllis Rose, *Parallel Lives: Five Victorian Marriages* (Chatto & Windus, 1984).
60. Anthony Giddens, *The Transformation of Intimacy: Sexuality, Love and Eroticism in Modern Societies* (Polity Press, 1992).

Yet despite all these problematic areas, the sentiments approach has continued to inspire research into the meanings of family life, with marriage attracting the most attention. John Gillis looked at changes in marriage rituals, pointing to their codification and standardization over the nineteenth century, tracing complex shifts, varying by region and class.[61] Divorce has provided another fruitful way of looking at marriage, and A. James Hammerton has used the evidence of marital relationships made public by divorce as a way of looking at changing ideas about marriage as increasing demands for genuine protection and individual rights were made by wives.[62]

Similarly, feminist historians have pointed to the importance of the first wave of feminist protesters' demands for equality in marriage, particularly in terms of property rights for wives, as a precondition for genuine companionate marriage.[63] An exploration of the reasons why these first-wave demands left unquestioned the sexual division of labour within marriage has continued. Even John Stuart Mill's elegant defence of women as equal companions in *The Subjection of Women* has been shown to have been fatally flawed by his assumption that domestic work, especially the care of children, would always be done by women.[64] Historians who have investigated domestic violence have also pointed to the prevalence and acceptability of male violence in the past, looking at ways in which domestic life, particularly on the margins of survival, contained deep conflicts between men and women.[65]

Childhood has also attracted a variety of approaches. The use of psycho-history received much attention in its early years from DeMause and others,[66] and the use of psychoanalytic ideas to reveal unconscious or symbolic meanings in historical evidence has

61. John Gillis, *For Better, For Worse: British Marriages, 1600 to the Present* (Oxford University Press, 1985).

62. A. James Hammerton, *Cruelty and Companionship: Conflict in Nineteenth-Century Married Life* (Routledge, 1992). See also Rod Phillips, *Putting Asunder: A History of Divorce in Western Society* (Cambridge University Press, 1988).

63. Mary Lyndon Shanley, *Feminism, Marriage and the Law in Victorian England, 1850–1895* (Princeton University Press, 1989); Lee Holcombe, *Wives and Property: Reform of the Married Women's Property Law in Nineteenth-Century England* (University of Toronto Press, 1983); Jane Rendall, *The Origins of Modern Feminism: Women in Britain, France and the United States, 1780–1860* (Lyceum Books, 1985).

64. Mary Lyndon Shanley, 'Marital slavery and friendship: John Stuart Mill's *The Subjection of Women*', *Political Theory*, Vol. 9, No. 2 (1981), pp. 229–47.

65. Clark, *The Struggle for the Breeches*; Nancy Tomes, 'A "torrent of abuse": crimes of violence between working class men and women in London 1840–1875', *Journal of Social History*, Vol. 11, No. 3 (1978); Ellen Ross, '"Fierce questions and taunts": married life in working class London 1870–1914', *Feminist Studies*, Vol. 8, No. 3 (Fall 1982).

66. Lloyd deMause (ed.), *The History of Childhood* (Psychohistory Press, 1974).

remained an interesting and fruitful possibility.[67] As Peter Gay pointed out, historians hold a common-sense view of human nature and motivations which has been shaped by Freud's ideas, and this has deeply influenced attempts to understand families in the past.[68] It is perhaps one of the most pervasive sets of assumptions a historian brings to pre-Freudian evidence, a filter which distances and distorts. Thus, as we investigate further in Chapter 3, one of the central themes of family history, the changes in the ways that the individual can be constructed and can construct him/herself, is closely related to twentieth-century psychoanalytic understandings of the Oedipal drama and the emergence of the rational, autonomous and male individual out of dependence and attachment.

Historians and sociologists of the family have also turned to broader issues of changing understandings of the passage of time in terms of families, drawing upon notions of historical shifts in the experience of time and work developed initially by E.P. Thompson,[69] and extending these to the ways families construct the time they spend together. Here the work of John Gillis has begun to outline changes in family rituals, in the ways families have used domestic space, and the varying ideas about mortality which permeate family experiences.[70]

From all these very different approaches, theories and constructs how can we assess the popular idea that modern families have developed a unique and important world of affection and emotion not available in the past? Clearly, this unilinear picture is seriously flawed. Crude associations of social, economic and cultural change linked in an unproblematic way with the possible kinds of emotional lives which might be experienced by families have not proved very helpful; neither has the assertion that familial love is a natural and therefore transhistorical experience. But curiosity about the inner lives of families in the past inspires great popular and academic interest and continues to provoke new research.

The increasing involvement of the state?

The idea that families are a site of social problems which are amenable to correction through national policy measures is of a fairly

---

67. For example in the work of Philip Greven on childrearing in *Spare the Child.*
68. Peter Gay, *Freud for Historians* (Oxford University Press, 1985), p. 7.
69. E.P. Thompson, 'Time, work-discipline, and industrial capitalism', in M.W. Flinn and T.C. Smout (eds), *Essays in Social History* (Clarendon Press, 1974).
70. John Gillis, *A World of Their Own Making: Myth, Ritual and the Quest for Family Values* (Basic Books, 1996).

recent date, from around the late nineteenth century. This perception of the changing relationship with the state at both local and
national levels can be traced in the popular story that society has
progressed through legal and social reforms, and this is reflected in
many historical accounts of marriage, child protection, compulsory
education and the emergence of the welfare state for families in
need of support. The reverse of this coin has been the critique by
the new right that the family has lost its power and cohesion because of these kinds of interference by the state. A third critique
was offered by Marxist feminist sociologists who argued that the
state, acting in the interests of capital, supported and shaped an
ideology of family which would provide unpaid reproductive services to society. Furthermore, these ideologies ensured that services
were provided by women, whose reproductive labour was exploited
to these ends. Measures such as state education and welfare were
thus key elements in maintaining a hegemonic family ideal.[71]

The modernization paradigm has again reappeared in these
stories, for example in ideas about children's care, beginning with
casually uncaring and instrumental relationships dominated by fears
for the souls of children and exploitation of their labour, and culminating in a society of doting and sacrificing parents backed by a safety
net of protection by a benevolent state and education system. Histories of social policy relating to the family have thus tended to focus on
issues like restrictions on child labour, control of juvenile crime, and
protection from abandonment, neglect and violence within families,
and families and reforms in these areas are portrayed as possible
only because of the development of modern industrial society.[72]

However, the idea of the state as a monolithic presence has
increasingly been questioned. Local institutions like the parish,
philanthropic and voluntary efforts, and the growing power of
educationalists, doctors and scientists were actively if not always
consistently influencing both ideas and practices of family life.
Others have further questioned this model by examining the representations and meanings of childhood – for example, Hugh
Cunningham's work on the changing popular images of childhood
in the nineteenth century, which shows the ways these ideas influenced social policies in dealing with children.[73] Margaret Arnot's

71. See, for example, Mary McIntosh, 'The state and the oppression of women',
in Annette Kuhn and AnnMarie Wolpe (eds), *Feminism and Materialism: Women and
Modes of Production* (Routledge & Kegan Paul, 1978).
72. e.g. Ivy Pinchbeck and Margaret Hewitt, *Children in English Society. Vol. II: From
the Eighteenth Century to the Children's Act 1948* (Routledge & Kegan Paul, 1973).
73. Cunningham, *The Children of the Poor.*

work on infanticide abandons the notion of social progress in order to trace the origins and consequences of representations of child neglect, and how these shaped and were shaped both within families and beyond.[74] From these approaches, we can begin to trace a more complex picture of how families and the state shaped each other.

Another area which has challenged the common-sense understandings of how the state has reached into the family is that of sexuality. Earlier work by Edward Shorter, who argued that it was the availability of waged work for young adults which liberated them from parental control over courtship and sexuality, was widely criticized for its simplistic assumptions derived from limited sources. A much more influential approach has been Foucault's analysis of historical changes in sexuality. His thesis was that as modern societies emerged, there were fundamental changes in the ways sexuality, among other things, was regulated and controlled. He turned on its head the idea that Victorian society sought to repress sexuality, arguing that from the late eighteenth century sexuality was increasingly talked about and regulated in the most intimate as well as the most public ways. Whereas in the past it had been particular sexual acts which were deemed to be acceptable or not, explosions of classification and the close examination of both desires and practices in modern societies have meant that sexuality has become a quality of the individual. Thus, while sodomy was a criminal act in early modern England, the homosexual emerged as a type of person whose identity was fundamentally shaped by a definition of a specific sexuality. The regulation of sexuality therefore became increasingly complex, as the state began to draw upon science, social science and medicine to develop new regulatory systems.

Foucault's work has sparked off much innovative research.[75] Feminists in particular have looked at sexuality and its relationship with marriage for women, particularly in the nineteenth century, in studies of prostitution by Judith Walkowitz, in medical discourses by Ludmilla Jordanova, and in feminist campaigns around sexuality by Lucy Bland.[76] For the twentieth century, further research has been

74. Margaret Arnot, 'Infant death, child care and the state: the baby farming scandal and the first infant life protection legislation of 1872', in *Continuity and Change*, Vol. 9, No. 2 (1994).
75. Michel Foucault, *The History of Sexuality. Vol. 1: An Introduction*, trans. Robert Hurley (Penguin, 1984, first published 1976).
76. Judith Walkowitz, *Prostitution and Victorian Society: Women, Class and the State* (Cambridge University Press, 1980); Ludmilla Jordanova, *Sexual Visions* (Harvester Wheatsheaf, 1989); Lucy Bland, *Banishing the Beast: English Feminism and Sexual Morality, 1885–1914* (Penguin, 1995).

done on sexuality in marriage, drawing upon a particularly rich source, the letters written to Marie Stopes in the 1920s.[77] Oral historians have also attempted to approach this subject, despite the reticence of many interviewees, and it remains an area of great public interest, as shown by television and radio series drawing upon such research.[78]

If new histories of the relationships between families and the regulation of the state have begun to emerge, current social policy research has tended to remain rooted in several familiar assumptions: that family affairs should fundamentally be a private matter separate from the state; that particular dependencies and divisions of labour within families are natural and normal; and that social services developed by the state and others are primarily presented as facilities for individuals, rather than families, with intervention generally directed at those whose relationship with families is problematic.[79] Agencies of the British state have never evolved an explicit set of family policies, and have consistently claimed that they do not interfere in family life, while at the same time reinforcing particular boundaries of family obligation based on implicit constructions of the 'normal' family. A clear example of these processes can be seen in the ways the Beveridge Report, the cornerstone of the post-war welfare state, dealt with benefits for unmarried couples:

> For pension she will have to contribute throughout her working life, and if she does not do so will not be qualified for a pension. The contributions of the man with whom she is living, if he is married to someone else, will go to secure pensions and other benefits for his legal wife; if he is not married, his contributions as a single man will go to support the benefits of married women generally.[80]

The search for stability in the face of rapid change draws heavily on a popular understanding of families in the past which, as we have seen, is highly suspect. This is not just an academic debate, but has far-reaching political implications. For example, the focus of many policy makers has been the 'problem' family and the ways in which agencies of the state can assist or disrupt families to produce healthier

77. Lesley Hall, *Hidden Anxieties: Male Sexuality, 1900–1950* (Polity Press, 1991).

78. e.g. Steven Humphries's series *The Secret World of Sex*, BBC, 1993.

79. Hillary Land and R. Parker, 'United Kingdom', in S. Kanerman *et al.* (eds), *Family Policy: Government and Families in Fourteen Countries* (Columbia University Press, 1978).

80. William Beveridge, *Social Insurance and Allied Services* (HMSO, 1942), Cmd. 6404, para. 115, p. 184.

social outcomes, but the framework often employed in this kind of research is still based on functionalism and its particular political as well as historical perspective, one which gives families and individuals within them little scope for creating and sustaining social change. Another crucial example arises from the supposedly scientific and non-political field of historical demography, which has legitimized attempts to impose a Western reproductive pattern through policies aimed at reducing the birth rate in the Third World. This relied heavily on a version of modernization, long after others had modified or even abandoned this framework, in which change was assumed to be universal and unilinear flowing toward an idealized, isolated, stable married couple and two children.[81] Demographers have tended to remain silent about the historically created relations of unequal power between the 'first' world and the 'third' world that have permitted this vision to go forward.[82]

It is also in the histories of gender relations that the stereotypes of family history must be challenged, because they underpin and justify the inequalities between men and women which are so deeply embedded in family processes and relationships. Historians of the family have been remarkably slow in hearing the feminist critique raised more than twenty years ago. As recently as 1989, a general text on the history of the family could use the expression 'the individual – his wife and family'.[83] The myths that women's natural role as full-time carers has only recently altered, that marriage used to last a lifetime, that extended families cared for several generations, have all served to cover up the many ways in which women have constantly renegotiated their place in the struggle for survival of themselves and their networks of familial relationships.

Some historians of the family have retreated from these and other political questions by focusing on the particular. Local studies have proliferated, as has biographical work on particular families. It is also significant that there has been a great deal of more speculative research into families of the early modern period, where much interesting work has informed our approach, but where it is easier to portray familial life as fundamentally different from our own. Thus it seems that challenging common-sense notions about the histories of families in the more recent past and on a wider scale has become increasingly problematic.

81. Szreter, *Fertility, Class and Gender*, p. 593.
82. Greenlagh, 'The social construction of population science', p. 27.
83. Casey, *The History of the Family*, p. 15.

In order to reach more meaningful understandings of the processes of family life, we require a more sophisticated historical knowledge about what families used to be like, and about the forces which have changed what we mean by family and which people within families have drawn upon to shape their societies. The story of the family is, therefore, not just an interesting historical pursuit, or an exploration of popular stereotypes, but is vital for developing understandings of contemporary families and society. By questioning popular ideas about how 'the modern family' emerged, we can begin to tease apart the meanings, representations and experiences of families in the past in order to weave histories which will allow for complexity, variation, and differences of power which have developed and changed over time.

But it is not enough simply to redo family history in a more complicated way. It is first necessary to unpick and remake the fundamental concepts which underpin our understandings of families. In the next chapter we explore a range of these key ideas which have framed, even while they contradict, what the family has meant.

CHAPTER THREE

Conceptualizing the family

They're no relation to me. They're only blood relations. If they want to know me, it's only for what they could get out of me.
Divorced man overheard speaking about his own sons, 1997

How is it possible to understand the story of the family historically? What tools are necessary to find and to test what we have been told by previous historians and story tellers? What can contemporary investigators seek from the past on this subject? To answer these questions means first understanding the elements, the categories, the words, in sum the ideas, through which we have understood family.

Before we can begin to unravel the family story, there is a central paradox at the heart of this chapter which must be confronted directly. It resounds throughout the book and is exemplified in the epigram above, whose apparent contradiction holds the power to shock. How can 'blood relations' not be related? How can the relationship of father and son, so central to our social organization and with such powerful cultural resonances, be so easily denied? Encapsulated in this brief encounter is the conundrum: *the family is everywhere and the family is nowhere.*

The idea of family carries a heavy emotional and practical weighting and people continue to attach intense significance to familial ties. Even when the family is not mentioned, there is often an unspoken assumption that it exists, so strongly is it implicated in our sense of ourselves as individuals and in our kinship and identity with fellow beings, not to speak of the practical arrangements of our everyday lives.

But this sense that the family is always taken for granted is rarely made explicit. Rather family is generally missing from discussions of how we experience our sense of self, of how we become and

51

remain part of wider social groupings. Indeed, present culture assumes a unique yet many-faceted, even fragmented type of person, free from all ties and able to make almost unlimited choices. Yet ultimately this freedom is illusory. For despite the divorced man's belief in his right to choose his relationships, he was still conscious of the weight of assumptions and obligations carried by the term 'blood relations' and the claims, emotional as well as material, which his sons might still have upon him.

The family, then, is a prime example of the 'absent presence' which is such a challenge to social analysis. Possibly because it could be argued that human life could not function without families, the family has been removed into a separate domain and often regarded as a natural phenomenon without need of study or explanation. This absent presence of the family in historical and contemporary discourse is reflected in the way various academic disciplines have carved up the intellectual and social terrain. Without exception a division between public and private life has been uncritically accepted which, in turn, is based on unspoken assumptions about the way these domains have been formed around implicit ideas about masculinity and femininity.[1]

This chapter seeks to rectify this by searching for underlying concepts, assumptions and approaches which have informed studies of familial relationships. The purpose of what is primarily a historical project is, first, to examine existing concepts available to historians and show both how they developed over time and how they are used today by experts and laity alike. In unpicking these concepts it then becomes possible to identify possible gaps and silences in the history of families.

These gaps point to the inadequacy of particular conceptual frameworks in specific historical contexts, some of which are explored later in our empirical chapters. In this way our case studies can be used both to question and/or confirm concepts and to see where they might need to be changed or modified. This dialogue between conceptual and empirical levels has enabled us to explore new areas and to identify relationships which have not normally been seen as pertinent to the history of families.

It is the elements of the *self, kinship, home/household* and *identity* which set the framework for our family story. At first sight this may seem a disparate group of concepts which have been used in different

1. See the essays in Joan Landes (ed.), *Feminism: The Public and the Private* (Oxford University Press, 1998) and Hilde Lindemann Nelson, 'Introduction', in Hilde Lindemann Nelson (ed.), *Feminism and Families* (Routledge, 1997).

contexts for different reasons. They have been central to various academic disciplines and common usage alike. While kinship and home/household have obvious links to the family, the self and identity do not. Yet it is the latter which have attracted by far the greatest attention in social thought, particularly the concept of the self. Our discussion inevitably mirrors these differential weightings.

We begin by looking at the meanings assigned to the *self*, a concept which has dominated modern Western culture in many forms. Yet social thinkers of all kinds have seldom looked at the self in relation to either the family or the categories of gender and age which are the basic elements of the family. Here we will be arguing the particular saliency of gender in English culture and suggesting the ways in which the self has been saturated with the colours of masculinity and femininity.

It is evident from our language that the male self is only complete and valid because it is buttressed by a shadow female self, an opposite, so often cast as incomplete or inferior.[2] The generic words 'he', 'him' and 'man' are still commonly used to denote all people, so that male is assumed as the norm and female as the exception. The boy child has no difficulty in placing himself within this linguistic frame. But the girl child has to identify with 'she', a form forced into the language and thus into her social being. She learns of dogs and 'lady' dogs, poets and poetesses, bus drivers and women bus drivers, politicians and female politicians. Women's formidable struggles in having their voices heard and considered valid have only recently been recognized.[3]

Without our even being conscious of it, these gendered associations of self have also become a key component in our understanding of the family.[4] Men and women, masculinity and femininity, have had profoundly different involvement in the ideas as well as the practices of family. These have been directly related to the way the self has been defined. To make matters even more complicated, political theorists and economists operate with a particular form of the self, an even more detached rational individual. The abstract level of this concept would seem to empty it of all human relationships; in fact it is based on a particular form of modern masculinity.

2. A similar point has been made by Joan Scott, *Only Paradoxes to Offer: French Feminists and the Rights of Man* (Harvard University Press, 1996), pp. 5–9.
   3. M.F. Belenky, B. Clinchy, N. Goldberger and J. Tarvel, *Women's Way of Knowing: The Development of Self, Voice and Mind* (Basic Books, 1986).
   4. P. Young-Eisendrath and J. Hall (eds), *The Book of the Self: Person, Pretext and Process* (New York University Press, 1987), p. 450.

Only recently have feminist approaches queried received notions of self, person and individual, but even they do not necessarily relate this analysis to the family.[5]

Kinship, our second category of analysis, has a more obvious linkage to family yet it has never been of primary interest to historians or even many sociologists. Kinship has been considered chiefly the province of anthropologists and genealogists, who have attached the strongest significance to relations of blood and the marriage bond, yet who have seldom queried what underlies their use of kinship terms or structures. The word 'kin' also has wider meanings. It is possible to feel a sense of kinship with those to whom we are emotionally and intellectually attached but not necessarily physically related. Yet neither has this wider view of kinship often been a subject of historical or social enquiry.

Our third set of concepts, *house, home and household*, relates the family to space. The period covered by this book established the primacy of the home as the centre of family life and the house as the most desirable living place separated from office, workshop and factory. In a telling use of language, the influential German sociologist Tonnies proclaimed in 1887 that 'the house constitutes the realm and, as it were, the body of kinship'.[6] But the study of home and house has mainly been in the domain of geographers, who also have taken for granted a fixed divide between public and private spheres.

The household has been used as a more technical term within demography. Demographers have been more closely tied to policy areas than other disciplines, especially in concerns with the mortality and fertility of populations. And the household, those people who share domestic space, has been more a creature of statisticians and census makers. Yet demographers, as others, have uncritically accepted categories of persons within the household. They have ignored differences in power and visibility among them as well as the actual practices of life within households.[7] Economists, too, have tended to view the household as a unitary actor in consumption, a 'black box' without differences of power or needs.

5. A few political theorists have begun to make these links. Jean Bethke Elshtain, *Public Man, Private Woman* (Princeton University Press, 1981) significantly seems to take the family as a given. Carole Pateman, *The Sexual Contract* (Polity Press, 1988) focuses on marriage.
6. Frederick Tonnies, *Community and Association (Gemeinschaft und Gesellschaft)*, trans. Charles P. Loomis (Routledge & Kegan Paul, 1955), p. 48.
7. Alison MacKinnon, 'Were women present at the demographic transition?' Questions from a feminist historian to historical demographers', *Gender and History*, Vol. 7, No. 2 (1995).

Finally, the ways in which *identity* both creates and is created within the family are explored. Postmodernists have stressed the fragmentation of identity in late twentieth-century Western culture. They focus on the ways in which we create our identities from competing categories, in particular class, race, ethnicity, language use, religious affiliation, and sexual orientation. Among these, age and gender have a particular salience because of their deep connection to reproduction and mortality.

It is often forgotten that children's first identities are almost always within a family context no matter how that is defined. They also learn to identify with groups we call family which are imaginary in the sense that they have a less clear spatial location and more arbitrary boundaries. People create their own imagined families, sometimes several simultaneously, each with a unique membership, which are likely to include some, though by no means all, of our ancestors and a living network of wider kin and intimate associates. The final section explores in depth the salience of naming practices as an example of how family identities are constructed.

We conclude that, far from being a free-standing agent, a person is cradled by the family, however that family is defined and whether it is loved or loathed. In turn, through the family, other identities are formed, whether in keeping with a 'family tradition' or in conscious opposition to it. This is not a neutral matter, for fierce passions, deep moral convictions and perhaps even the basic integrity of mind, body and soul are at stake in these processes.

The construction of the individual, self and person

The word 'self' is one of the most controversial in our language, its boundaries blurred and disputed.[8] A major problem is that all the diverse definitions of self include the capacity of human beings for self-consciousness, the ability to reflect upon who we are. This gives us both the problem *and* its understanding. The thinking subject is a vehicle for all concepts, not a concept in itself.[9] Achieving a consensus about the concept of self is virtually impossible. However,

8. J. Glover, *The Philosophy and Psychology of Personal Identity* (Allen Lane, 1988); G. Breakwell, *Social Psychology of Identity and the Self Concept* (Surrey University Press, 1992).

9. M. Carrithers, S. Collins and S. Lukes (eds), 'Conclusion', in *The Category of the Person* (Cambridge University Press, 1985), p. 284.

there is some agreement that in most human communities there is
an intrinsic connection between the idea of a person and the body.[10]
This is by no means a clear connection and, as will be seen, differs
profoundly between the categories of man and woman.

In contemporary society we make a sharp distinction between
the self in human form and all other categories. Imputing selfhood
to any other entity – animals, rocks, even machines – has come to
be dismissed as 'anthropomorphism'. Yet in many if not most cultures, self and personhood can apply to non-human subjects: pets,
ancestors, natural sources such as the wind and water, trolls, fairies,
nymphs, witches, spirits and fantastic creatures of all kinds. And
these too could be part of families, kin groups, tribes, clans or
nations. People, places and spirits can, and do, melt into each other.

In the modern West, we have a much more distinct sense of self,
one which the modern philosopher Charles Taylor has described as
giving 'off the illusion of being anchored in our very being, peren-
nial and independent of interpretation'.[11] Our understandings of
self have been largely shaped by the culture of individualism. We
increasingly emphasize the human being as a single, material unit,
just as we live alone much more often than in any other known
society.

Nevertheless, there is always a strong and necessary additional
social element recognized in the concept of the self even if this is
no longer usually seen as supernatural. The 'I' is set against the
social, whether this is done to maintain the autonomy of the self or,
on the contrary, out of a desire for integration into the social world.[12]
These social aspects of the self are first experienced within families.
As we grow up we test out the consequences of our behaviour and
actions on others in relation to a system of values learned mainly
within what are defined as household and familial groups.

The familial and social aspects of self have always included a
moral dimension, an assumption we return to with the concept of
identity. Yet it is not always clear in our culture how morality should
operate. Is it to be located only in the isolated person? How much
should reside in the community and if so among which groups,
which organizations? Whatever moral responsibility now lies with

10. B. Morris, *Anthropology of the Self: The Individual in Cultural Perspective* (Pluto
Press, 1994), p. 194.

11. Charles Taylor, *Sources of the Self: The Making of Modern Identity* (Harvard University Press, 1989), p. 185.

12. N. Rose quoted in Patrick Joyce, *Democratic Subjects: The Self and the Social in
19th Century England* (Cambridge University Press, 1994), p. 13.

individual persons, by the end of the twentieth century, the entity called 'the family' is the single institution constantly called upon to cradle that morality for the entire social fabric. Even Margaret Thatcher's famous dictum that there is no such thing as society assumed that there were families as well as individuals and placed heavy moral responsibilities on those families.

While public men, as rational individuals, might be the agents of high-level morality, especially as politicians, philosophers, scientists, or clergymen, they may also be the amoral individuals who ruthlessly pilot powerful economic institutions under no obligation to moral values or behaviour. They have also morally justified violence and killing through warfare. This contradiction is especially evident in public life today where so many men fall foul of a private moral code. At the same time groups such as children, women, the very poor, slaves, supposedly free from the shackles of the autonomy and responsibility which are placed on the individual, have often been supposed to possess a kind of 'natural morality'. This involuted thinking helps to explain the common association of women, particularly mothers, with the guardianship of family morality since it has been assumed that they were without a set of interests contaminated by the external world of greed and power.

A brief look at the way the concept of self has evolved in Western late-capitalist societies is helpful in understanding how the idea has interacted with the way the family has been perceived as well as the way it has been lived.

The religious and secular self

Judaeo-Christian, Near Eastern, Graeco-Roman and Germanic traditions have all played a part in the complicated conceptions of self, person and individual. A trace of modern individualism is particularly present in early Christianity with its emphasis on the relationship of human beings to the one God, even if that individualism was then refined and refracted through centuries of scientific and secular developments. Here it is worth noting that the individual in question is already located within a family. Both men and women were under the injunction of the very first commandment: 'Honour thy father and thy mother'. Yet the masculinity of the individual is already signposted in the Creation myth, where Eve was taken from Adam's rib and was thus already in a different relationship to God the *Father*. In the New Testament too, Jesus

Christ's appearance as the *Son* of God is indelibly marked as part of a family drama.

The early centuries of Catholicism focused on self-denial, an annihilation of self reaching its highest expression in monasticism's inner world of the spirit. Renaissance humanism moved outward, marking a clear boundary between the self and the world. Man – and it was man – was now seen as the apex of creation and the master of Nature.[13] In this rendering, man's individuality was indicated in painting by the introduction of realistic features on human figures, even individualized portraits.[14] Portraiture also reflected the patriarchal principle of genealogy upon which aristocratic and great commercial houses claimed power and a form of immortality.[15]

After the Reformation, within Protestantism, the individual was now active in mundane affairs. The everyday came to hold a more important place in the great scheme of life, and God's overwhelming concern was with the good of mankind, who were to spend their time furthering this great aim. In this endeavour, the most important text in English letters as prototype of all journeys, one of the original romances of the road, was John Bunyan's *The Pilgrim's Progress* (1678). Christian, the hero of this epic adventure, could only be a man, and a man who had turned away from wife, children and domesticity in his lone search for the Heavenly City. Only in the second volume, written several years later at the request of Bunyan's readers, does this wife, Christiana, accompanied by the children and protected throughout by Mr Greatheart, set out on the same journey. Not surprisingly, this twice-told tale, nowhere nearly as well crafted, has been quite forgotten.[16]

By the eighteenth century the literate classes had become concerned with values such as public civility and universal benevolence on the one hand and more personal privacy on the other.[17] Especially among commercial groups and the urban gentry, the setting where the self could best be examined and God's ways experienced

13. For a classic feminist reinterpretation of Renaissance studies see Joan Kelly, 'Did women have a Renaissance?', *Women, History and Theory: The Essays of Joan Kelly* (Chicago University Press, 1984).

14. Roy Porter (ed.), *Rewriting the Self: Histories from the Renaissance to the Present* (Routledge, 1997), p. 3.

15. J. Woodall (ed.), *Portraiture: Facing the Subject* (Manchester University Press, 1997), p. 3.

16. John Bunyan, *The Pilgrim's Progress From the World, to that Which is to Come*, C. Wilby, 'Introduction' (Constable & Co., 1926), p. xxxv.

17. From the seventeenth century grander houses began to introduce corridors and staircases to separate sleeping and eating quarters from more public rooms. M. Girouard, *Life in the English Country House* (Yale University Press, 1980).

was in the peace and order of the well-cared-for house and garden. Spirituality moved to the godly household with a husband/father at its head. This was a departure from the more aristocratic warrior virtues pursued in the hunting field, grand procession or lavish public entertainment. It was a shift exemplified in William Cowper's immensely popular poem, *The Task*, whose most famous lines prefigure Victorian domesticity:

> Now stir the fire, and close the shutters fast,
> Let fall the curtains, wheel the sofa round ...
> So let us welcome peaceful evening in.[18]

Yet there were also pressures for men to put themselves forward as responsible workers and public persons. Intensely religious men came to depend on women, particularly female members of their family, to act as keepers of their conscience and protectors of their spiritual self. Nor was the older Greek idea of family and marriage as only the infrastructure for the good life completely extinct.[19] In this formulation, strengthened through the influence of classical learning in the public schools, for men, theoretical and intellectual deliberation and participation as a citizen came above domesticity in the order of worth.

By the end of the eighteenth century, fall-out from the American and French Revolutions, with their emphasis on freedom and equality combined with liberal political and economic theories, ensured that the masculine individual became ever more embroiled in the public world of letters, politics and action. Similar conceptions were part of science and medicine, now developing as both a profession and a coherent body of thought.[20]

These conceptions of the rational, autonomous, public and masculine individual, the self as a source of knowledge and meaning, were part of Enlightenment philosophy and science, in particular the new science of economics which emerged in the late eighteenth century. And, to this day, within neo-classical economics the family is treated as essentially driven by one will, that of the husband and father.[21]

18. William Cowper, *The Task*, Book 4 in *The Poetical Works of William Cowper* (Chandos edn, n.d.), p. 275.
19. R. Jenkyns, *The Victorians and Ancient Greece* (Oxford University Press, 1980); F.M. Turner, *The Greek Heritage in Victorian Britain* (Yale University Press, 1981).
20. L. Schiebinger, *The Mind Has No Sex? Women in the Origins of Modern Science* (Harvard University Press, 1989).
21. P. England, 'The separative self: androcentric bias in newclassical assumptions', in M.A. Ferber and J.A. Nelson (eds), *Beyond Economic Man: Feminist Theory and Economics* (University of Chicago Press, 1993).

Men, as husbands and fathers, held parental and patriarchal authority within the family and provided links with the growing external world. These ideas flourished along with capitalist enterprise and the spread of commodity, labour and capital markets. Within the market, it was only these individuals who could enter into civil and commercial contracts.[22] In these circles, the family was relegated to a separate private domain, yet paradoxically the individual was also contained by as well as being created within a family.[23] Habermas, who has put forward the most persuasive arguments about the eighteenth-century public sphere, notes that civil society must grow from the bourgeois family, but he too leaves that family, and by implication the categories of women and children, unexplored and untheorized.[24]

The power of beliefs about sexuality, reproduction, gender and family is evident in the rise of a 'taxonomic mode of thought' which was obsessed with classifying natural phenomena into families: animals, plants, minerals as well as languages and human types. This ordering as the central principle in natural history and natural philosophy rested on an idea of kinship, systematic relationships of likeness or affinity, represented by branching diagrams that resembled family trees.[25] Familial relationships in the form of father and son, brothers, uncle and nephew were also the main model available for nascent business and commerce. 'Partnerships were in some senses *brothers* who represented each other.'[26]

For in the lively eighteenth- and nineteenth-century discussions about human development and social organization, family was pivotal. The family with its supposedly naturally given divisions between men and women, parents and children, was seen as a microcosm of

---

22. For a fuller discussion of these points see Leonore Davidoff, ' "Regarding some 'old husbands' tales": public and private in feminist history', Part I, in *Worlds Between: Historical Perspectives on Gender and Class* (Polity Press, 1995).

23. Recent studies have uncovered how the creation of rational individualism was based on reactions to religious experience among both the educated elite and the population as a whole. See Jane Shaw, 'Religious experience and the formation of the early Enlightenment self', in Porter (ed.), *Rewriting the Self*.

24. Jurgen Habermas, *The Structural Transformations of the Public Sphere: An Inquiry into a Category of Bourgeois Society* (MIT Press, 1989) and N. Fraser, 'Rethinking the public sphere: a contribution to the critique of actually-existing democracy', in C. Calhoun (ed.), *Habermas and the Public Sphere* (MIT Press, 1992), and the essays in J. Meehan (ed.), *Feminists Read Habermas: Gendering the Subject of Discourse* (Routledge, 1995).

25. L. Jordanova, 'Cultures of kinship', in *Nature Displayed: Gender, Science and Medicine 1760–1820* (Longman, forthcoming).

26. W. Holdsworth, *A History of English Law* (Sweet & Maxwell, 1966), Vol. VIII, p. 192.

society. Family as an image, as the cornerstone of the nation, was embellished through representations in cheap print form culminating in images of King George III and later Queen Victoria as father and mother of the kingdom. In all these versions, the family was seen as rooted in Nature, a realm now coming to be regarded as external to human society. The link between Nature and women and children from this period colours our view today. It enhanced the focus on the Holy Mother and Jesus as infant or young child. But the context became more secular where mother and child became a symbol of the linkage between Nature and Society.[27]

Individualism was focused on a concept of difference, the 'otherness' of non-individuals who were denied control over self ownership and ultimately full citizenship. In England, ownership of property was the original basis for claiming the rights of citizenship. Into the nineteenth century this meant ownership and control of land, wealth and other forms of moveable capital, although land remained primary. The landed elite denied common humanity with labouring people and most definitely with paupers or 'native' colonial subjects, whether the latter were conceived as noble savages or bestial demons. The idea that such as these might enjoy equal rights and inclusion in the English nation was considered outrageous, transgressing civil law and religious belief alike. Adult women within the upper classes were in a special position, lacking selfhood yet included by virtue of the position of the men in their families. By the end of the century, working men who had owned nothing but their capacity to labour were claiming citizenship on the basis of 'property in labour' which included the ability to support dependent wives and children within a properly constituted family.[28]

Self, property and the law

The basis of working men's claim to citizenship, on the grounds that they supported families, can be better understood by examining the status of family dependants within English law, an area

27. L. Jordanova, 'Naturalizing the family: literature and the bio-medical sciences in the late 18th century', in L. Jordanova (ed.), *Languages of Nature: Critical Essays in Science and Literature* (Free Association Books, 1986).

28. John Rule, 'The property of skill', in P. Joyce (ed.), *The Historical Meaning of Work* (Cambridge University Press, 1987).

which will be explored further in Chapter 5. The ultimate authority of the male individual as head and representative of a family was deeply rooted. The husband was answerable not only for his children's actions but also for those of his wife, including her debts, contracts made in her name or by her on his behalf, even her crimes if committed in his presence.[29]

In the view of the eighteenth-century jurist William Blackstone, legal liability for his wife gave a man the right to control her conduct. As with apprentices and children, this included physical containment and chastisement. In return for support at a level suitable to the husband's position, a wife owed him conjugal (sexual) rights to her body and the use of her labour. Blackstone argued that the fiction of marital unity on these terms was 'the fountain of all reasoning' and the doctrine of *coverture* was its consequence.[30]

> By marriage the husband and wife are one person in law: that is the *very being or legal existence* of the woman is suspended during the marriage or at least incorporated and consolidated into that of her husband [emphasis added].

It has recently been argued that the husband's right of physical control of his wife, far from being a consequence of *coverture*, lay at the heart of the legal construction of the marital relationship.[31] In a sense, on marriage a woman 'died a kind of civil death'.[32] Certainly the law's denial of full self ownership to married women undermined their position in the workforce. A wife could not be a partner in a business, could not make independent financial and business commitments, and there was an expectation that both her person and her labour were not freely hers to sell or give. One of the most important consequences was the husband's freedom to bequeath all his personal property to whomsoever he wished, including property obtained from his wife. All legal forms, but particularly laws of inheritance, thus both mirror and help to form familial relationships: who inherits what and how much indicates the relative positioning of family and kin.[33]

29. S. Staves, *Married Women's Separate Property in England 1660–1833* (Harvard University Press, 1990).

30. William Blackstone, quoted in Maeve E. Doggett, *Marriage, Wife-Beating and the Law in Victorian England* (Weidenfeld & Nicolson, 1992), p. 35.

31. Doggett, *Marriage, Wife-Beating and the Law*, p. 35.

32. J. Collyer, *A Practical Treatise on the Law of Partnership* (1832), p. 72.

33. J. Finch, J. Mason, J. Massen, L. Wallis and L. Hayes, *Wills, Inheritance and Families* (Clarendon Press, 1996).

It is clear that, while upholding the position of the senior man, the law's view of the family was designed to protect the interests of the family as a whole from the undue influence and naked self interest of that adult male individual. In particular, the interests of the wife's natal family were seen to be at stake. The rules of Equity Law were set up mainly to protect dependants' and especially wives' rights to property in order that *their* male line, that is their fathers and sons, were not deprived, should their husbands try to dispose of it elsewhere.[34]

The inherent contradiction between individual and family interests is only too apparent here. 'The principle of "family property" does not fit well into either market or family; it stands between them.'[35] Family and kin ties intrude on the intense individuality which marks Western political, economic and social culture. Thus, within the rules of inheritance there has been a see-sawing back and forth between supporting the testator's freedom to leave his property wherever he might wish and protecting the rights of relatives, mainly widows and children, who might be left a charge upon others, particularly the state. The ambiguities about the role of the family in inheritance systems are not new. It should be noted that in the early modern period, a model of inheritance through the guilds was sometimes used when the estates of masters were passed down to journeymen and apprentices.[36]

The denial of virtually all legal, political and economic rights of married women, including all rights over their children, remained in place until the mid nineteenth century. Changes to the law were only made piecemeal under strong pressure from feminists and legal reformers over many decades. While children were also controlled and represented by their fathers, boys had at least the potential to become full persons in a legal as well as customary sense, but with girls the possibility was more equivocal. Because it was assumed that on adulthood the control of a woman's person would pass from her father to her husband, an adult single woman's rights to citizenship appeared anomalous and a possible threat to the social order (see Chapter 8). It was only as a widow that a woman might gain some legal parity with men.

34. *Halsbury's Laws of England*, 3rd edn, Vol. 17 (1956), p. 223.

35. K. Green, 'The Englishman's castle – inheritance and private property today', *Modern Law Review*, No. 51 (1988), p. 207.

36. V. Brodsky, 'Widows in late Elizabethan London: remarriage, economic opportunity and family orientations', in L. Bondfield, R. Smith and K. Wrightson (eds), *The World We Have Gained* (Oxford University Press, 1996).

The deeply pervasive colouring which such notions brought to people's experience and their sense of self can best be illustrated by some of the contradictions and conflicts which began to gather in the late nineteenth century over issues surrounding political, economic and social rights – rights of working people in general, but especially of women with the growth of the women's movement. From the 1860s onwards, a group of issues which eventually reached the courts came to be known, significantly, as the 'persons cases'. These challenged the statutes which provided access to public office. According to liberal political thinking, entry to professions and entitlement to vote should be granted to any 'person' who possessed certain qualifications. The question became, did the status of being a woman mean that, like a child, she remained permanently a non-person?[37]

Thus these cases sought to establish whether, within the common law of the land, women could be included in the category 'persons'. Contrary to popular belief that the movement for women's suffrage was only an issue at the turn of the twentieth century, the first of such cases was raised by women in Manchester attempting to register for the vote at the time of the Second Reform Act of 1867. (Significantly, the First Reform Act of 1832 had, for the first time, explicitly referred to male persons only.) One of the most notorious of these cases was prompted by the attempt in the late 1860s by Sophia Jex-Blake and half-a-dozen of her female colleagues to gain entrance to Edinburgh University Medical School, an institution which had been all-male for the 450 years of its existence. All the women candidates had been properly qualified, but by a verdict of seven to five on the panel of learned judges, they were firmly placed as 'non-persons', and thus denied the opportunity to complete their training as doctors.[38]

Significantly the same issues were still being debated in the 1920s and 1930s in the context of public-sector rulings barring married women. Now the debate had shifted to the core question, whether it was marriage which turned women into non-persons.[39]

37. For a wider discussion of this issue see H. Moore, 'Women as persons', in her *Feminism and Anthropology* (Polity Press, 1988) and S. Bordo, *Unbearable Weight: Feminism, Western Culture and the Body* (University of California Press, 1993).

38. Albie Sachs and Joan Hoff Wilson, *Sexism and the Law: A Study of Male Beliefs and Judicial Bias* (Martin Robertson, 1978); Shirley Roberts, *Sophia Jex-Blake: A Woman Pioneer in 19th Century Medical Reform* (Routledge, 1993).

39. Anon., 'The married woman: is she a person?' (1934), reprinted in M.M. Roberts and T. Mitzuta (eds), *The Wives: The Rights of Married Women* (Routledge, 1994).

The feeling and sexual self

The anomalies thrown up by such cases demonstrate that neither women nor children were completely excluded from possessing a self. Cerebral, rational individualism had another face. In the late eighteenth and early nineteenth century a romantic sensibility arose in protest against 'the Enlightenment ideal of disengaged, instrumental reason and the forms of moral and social life that flow from this one-dimensional hedonism'.[40] Romantic expression promoted a *feeling* self created and sustained by relationships to others and to Nature. Understandably, such romantic ideas were mainly represented through the arts, particularly the novel and autobiography, that odyssey of self-discovery, all of which were part of an urban print culture.

Although in these genres the hero(ine) was unique, the story at least began in a family setting. Romantic individuality favoured sentiment and was more open to claims of femininity, and thus a potential danger to masculinity, in a way that rational individualism was not. One reaction to this dilemma was an idealized autonomous subject who made his own world – the artist, the genius who suffered alone in his garret and could only live away from both the world and a family.[41] But where did this subject come from and how did he manage to both reject and connect to the world?

It was also not coincidental that Romantic thinkers placed so much emphasis upon the child as 'father to the man'. Rousseau, Blake, Wordsworth all claimed the child as central to the self. Wordsworth's 'Ode: Intimations of Immortality', claimed as having as much influence on the nineteenth century as Freud's work did on the twentieth, saw childhood freed from all notions of original sin, the fount of all goodness.[42] The child was valued as preparation for adulthood but also for itself, as innocence, especially sexual innocence.

As an adult, that child-knowledge survived through memory. The modern idea of an interior self with a personal history became embodied in the child and that personal history, or autobiography, which started with childhood, constructed each person as a unique

40. Taylor, *Sources of the Self,* p. 413.
41. Lucien Goldman quoted in N. Abercrombie, S. Hill and B. Turner, *Sovereign Individuals of Capitalism* (Allen & Unwin, 1986), p. 1; see also C. Battersby, *Gender and Genius: Towards a Feminist Aesthetics* (Women's Press, 1989).
42. B. Garlitz quoted in Hugh Cunningham, *Children and Childhood in Western Society Since 1500* (Longman, 1996), p. 74.

particular self.[43] The inner child which remains within the adult becomes the repository of feeling, of joyousness, particularly in the body. Childhood, that is usually boyhood, was an innovation mainly of the eighteenth century, and was now the antithesis of adult manhood, particularly the economists' rational man. In particular, it was their innocence of sexuality which gave the very young their charm, but also their vulnerability, a combination which has led to the confusion and projection of sexual desire by adults.[44] The ideal woman of this period, too, was described as delicate and infantile. To an extent, children, women, black people and other 'natives' were all burdened with a similar status, locked into the innocence of powerlessness. But equally this powerlessness seemed to invite violation and threaten disruption. If such categories of people by 'nature' could never be fully individuals, could they ever claim the rights which belonged to individuals?

Paradoxically, just when innocence was being equated with beauty, morality and dependency, women were also being defined as *the sex*. And it was in this period that the notion of sexuality itself was being defined. If we accept the premise that the individual was based on difference, in particular sexual difference, then it follows that the sexual became segregated as a specific entity. It seems that in the seventeenth century it had been recognized that both men and women had carnal appetites, indeed women were often seen as sexually voracious, their appetites especially threatening.[45]

But by the beginning of the nineteenth century this view had been reversed and it was men who were seen to have a powerful innate sexual drive. Ladies, particularly unmarried genteel girls, while full of emotion to the point of being incapable of rational thought, were now seen as naturally pure, without sexual appetites. But once aroused their impulses were dangerous to themselves and to men. Lower-class, black and other native women never possessed that innocence. This unbridled sexuality was seen as the gateway to chaos and the antithesis of the rational man. In contrast the ideal masculine individual was cerebral and in control. His sexual instincts were contained by his virtuous asexual wife within the private domain of family, although as an unmarried youth Nature might force him to sow his wild oats.

43. C. Steedman, *Strange Dislocations: Childhood and the Idea of Human Interiority 1780–1930* (Virago, 1995), pp. 4–5.

44. Diana Gittins, *The Child in Question* (Macmillan, 1997).

45. R. Porter, 'Mixed feelings: the Enlightenment and sexuality in eighteenth century Britain', in P.-G. Bouce (ed.), *Sexuality in Eighteenth Century Britain* (Manchester University Press, 1982).

The psychic contradictions and turmoil these beliefs could produce for men surface in the splitting of the self as in such literary characters as Dr Jekyll and Mr Hyde.[46] It was in this period too, when the sexual had been ripped away from other aspects of social life, that a separate and continuous homosexual identity was formed, at least for men. Homosexual acts had previously been recognized and widely condemned by Church, state and community. But before the clear differentiation of public and private, when the sexual became firmly placed in the private sphere, homosexual as an encompassing identity could not exist. This may partly explain why the nineteenth-century ideal of the family was so threatened by the emerging *fin de siècle* homosexual culture and how the two fed on each other.[47] Within this schema, men vibrated between a masculinity based on logical control and animal passion.[48] The man of action represented a middle way based on adventure and mateship which the outposts of Empire in particular gave him ample opportunity to follow. But, in so doing, he had to leave family and domesticity behind.[49]

Genteel ladies could only maintain their status and that of their families within the role of wife, mother, sister, aunt, embedded in a web of non-sexual empathy for others. Within this model, a show of independence immediately signalled illicit sexuality and a fall from grace: the leaden divide between Madonna and whore. The fact that actual behaviour rarely matched these stereotypes does not diminish their hold over people's conception of self or the way such configurations of self lay behind social policies.

Charles Taylor, in his classic study of sources of the modern self, maintains that 'these two big and many sided cultural transformations, the Enlightenment and Romanticism with its accompanying expressive conception of Man, have made us what we are'.[50] What

46. For the classic case study of confusion about masculine gender and sexuality see D. Hudson, *Munby, Man of Two Worlds, 1828–1910* (Abacus, 1974) and L. Davidoff, 'Class and gender in Victorian England: the case of Hannah Cullwick and A.J. Munby', in *Worlds Between: Historical Perspectives on Gender and Class* (Polity Press, 1995).
47. For a discussion of late-nineteenth-century culture of sexual relations see Judith Walkowitz, *City of Dreadful Delight: Narratives of Sexual Danger in Late Victorian London* (Virago, 1992).
48. Ideas about moral restraint and sexual continence were, not surprisingly, complicated and often contradictory. M. Mason, *The Making of Victorian Sexuality* (Oxford University Press, 1994).
49. For this point in the Australian context see M. Lake, 'The politics of respectability: identifying the masculinist context', *Historical Studies*, Vol. 22, No. 86 (April 1986) and G. Dawson, 'The Blonde Bedouin: Laurence of Arabia, imperial adventure and the imagining of English-British masculinity', in Michael Roper and John Tosh (eds), *Manful Assertions: Masculinities in Britain since 1800* (Routledge, 1991).
50. Taylor, *Sources of the Self*, p. 393.

he does not add is how closely they have followed the outlines of perceived masculinity and femininity and the construction of the public and the private, and how they have dictated the place of the family – or its absence – in the general picture.

The sociological and psychological self

As the nineteenth century progressed, men of science, particularly nascent social scientists, continued grappling with these divisions. The evangelical and romantic background which coloured middle-class efforts to frame a 'science of the poor' focused on living arrangements and lack of domestic morality among the masses. It was mainly the utopian socialists of the 1830s and 1840s who argued against the narrow views of political economy and for a more inclusive understanding of people embedded in a network of relationships.[51]

For example, Emma Martin and a handful of other radical women actually preached in public on the subject of 'militant motherhood', a contradiction in terms to those in authority.[52] The forces of the Anglican Church as well as conservative political thinkers and even many liberals were outraged at such a challenge to the perceived natural order. By the 1850s these voices were silenced with the general failure of radical social movements.

Gradually a notion of a separate social dimension of society emerged which was specifically concerned with the family and 'women's issues' as distinct from economic and political enquiry.[53] By the end of the century, social thinkers, from the intense individualist Herbert Spencer to the communitarian Karl Marx, regarded the family as a separate and natural part of the social whole where women and children were particularly located. Emile Durkheim was one of the founding fathers of modern sociology who did most to develop ideas around individualism, a belief based on a similar model. Like most of the thinkers of the time, his life influenced his thought. According to his nephew, who lived in their household, Mme Durkheim 'created for him the respectable and quiet familial

51. E.J. Yeo, *The Contest for Social Science: Relations and Representations of Gender and Class* (Rivers Oram Press, 1996), pp. 9, 24, 39.
52. B. Taylor, *Eve and the New Jerusalem: Socialism and Feminism in the 19th Century* (Virago, 1983).
53. D. Riley, *'Am I that Name?' Feminism and the Category of Women in England* (Macmillan, 1988); J. Lewis, *Women and Social Action in Victorian and Edwardian England* (Edward Elgar, 1991).

existence which he considered the best guarantee of morality and of life. She removed from him every material care and all frivolity and took charge of educating the children. She also copied manuscripts, corrected proofs and helped edit the *Année Sociologique*, and with all "she was cheerful as well".[54]

In the twentieth century, the major developments in thinking about self have shifted to the realm of psychology, a discipline created only late in the previous century. Within psychology at one pole is the physical or material explanation, from the now completely discredited study of head shape or facial expression to the most recent findings about brain chemistry and inherited patterns of DNA.[55] At the other end of the spectrum, while overtly religious ideas concerning sin and salvation have been replaced, the non-theological but spiritual dimension is still recognized. In particular, those influenced by the ideas of Carl Jung as well as Eastern mysticism conceive of individuals only as vessels to contain the collective archetypes common to all human beings, 'transpersonal', universal and timeless.[56]

At either of these extremes, the relation of the individual person, the self, to the family is not particularly significant. For the neuroscientist, the physical body and its genetic inheritance is all. Therefore only the 'birth' mother and father and close physical relations are of any interest. On the other hand, for the committed mystic, the separate person, as the carrier of the collective archetype, relates to a communal past and present. While such views are not 'anti-family', both discount familial relationships and practices, the first because it looks only at genetic, physical ties and the second because it dissolves both individual and relationships in a wider cultural and spiritual pool. Family ties, on the contrary, focus on obligations and rights to particular, socially designated people.

Most concepts of self within psychology as well as in everyday life are located between these extremes. Since its inception, psychology has placed the autonomous individual, that is the masculine individual of liberal thought, at the centre of its concerns, and independence as the ultimate aim of the mature person. In positivist psychology, which takes behaviour and conscious beliefs as its

---

54. M. Maus quoted in S. Lukes, *Emile Durkheim, His Life and Work: A Historical and Critical Study* (Allen Lane, 1977), p. 99 n. 4.

55. Represented now by such works as R. Dawkins, *The Selfish Gene*, 2nd edn (Oxford University Press, 1989).

56. Now taken up by such writers as the widely read James Hillman. See T. Moore (ed.), *The Essential James Hillman: A Blue Fire* (Routledge, 1990).

focus, this individual remains curiously detached from a social context. This individuated self is based on cognition and/or feeling and the inner life, the essence of psychological thought. This is opposed to the personae shaped by mask, rule, role or social context. These social scripts have been left to sociologists. Thus the two disciplines neatly divide along dualistic lines, psychology the micro study of individuals, sociology the study of roles, groups, institutions and macro-level societies. The 'sociology of the family' in this programme became a small, usually low-status, sub-field, making little impact on the powerful premises of sociology as a whole.[57] Genuinely innovative thought about the family has primarily come from interdisciplinary approaches fuelled by feminist critiques, interdisciplinary because the importance of gender was obscured by the scattering of the family into various disciplines.[58]

It was mainly psychoanalytic psychology which deliberately viewed the self within a family. However, as revolutionary as Freud's thinking was, it should be noted that his emphasis on the mother-and-infant relationship echoed the previously central place of mother and child. The emphasis on the *differentness* of the father who represented an external and higher realm – society or the public world – is again reminiscent of the differentiated hierarchy of earlier religious beliefs, whose influence we have already seen in other contexts.

As is well known, in the psychoanalytic framework it is assumed that the child (basically a male child despite the belief in bisexuality in early infancy) strove to gain the mother's love in competition with the father. But the father was also loved, as well as feared for his power and ability to punish, even castrate – that is, disempower or, significantly, emasculate – the small child for the presumption of such wishes: the so-called Oedipus complex. Despite the clinical details about the importance of other members of the household and outsiders in the development of the child, it is the central triad of small (male) child, mother and father which predominates. The boy can only win manhood by rejecting the femininity of the mother to which he has been so close and overcoming his aggressive fantasies aimed at the father in order to identify with him.[59]

57. D.H.J. Morgan, *The Family, Politics and Social Theory* (Routledge & Kegan Paul, 1985).

58. A. Levy, *Other Women: The Writing of Class, Race and Gender 1832–1898* (Princeton University Press, 1991), p. 7; B. Thorne, *Rethinking the Family: Some Feminist Questions* (Longman, 1982).

59. P. Gay, *Freud for Historians* (Oxford University Press, 1985).

In England, the psychoanalytic school of Melanie Klein focused even more firmly on mother and child in early infancy before the child gained language and a sense of self. Although Klein and her followers acknowledge that it is the primary caretaker who is the main actor in these interactions between adult and infant, the breast-feeding 'natural' mother implicitly remains the keystone of the theory. Like the Freudians, for all the emphasis on the body, bodily functions and sexuality, these studies have a peculiarly free-floating and unreal quality, especially when posed apart from their clinical practice. Although psychoanalytic theories permeate twentieth-century understanding of the self, their versions of the family story often seem to have little connection with everyday life.

This abstract quality was combined with the psychoanalytic emphasis on the unconscious, on desire, and on the forces of destructiveness welling up from the psyche. This idea fitted mid-twentieth-century disenchantment with Victorian beliefs in unlimited progress through the rationality of science, technology and control over nature.[60] Some scientists, as well as popular writers, had begun to see the future as a desolate dystopia rather than leading to a utopia of peace and plenty.

Middle-class and intellectual philosophical trends such as existentialism and phenomenology built on psychoanalysis to accentuate self-reflection and the perils of the unexamined life. Their preoccupation with the self as unique left little space for immediate ties such as familial relationships. The major exponent of this trend, Jean-Paul Sartre, also saw man as divided between two worlds, the rational and the magical.[61] Meanwhile, more working-class thought in the form of the various brands of socialism on offer preserved a belief in human perfectibility. But the pragmatic form of most English socialism had limited goals. Despite concern with concrete issues such as health and housing, most socialists concentrated on reforms in the workplace and political representation. They rejected psychoanalytic self-searching as a distraction while at the same time supporting accepted views about the family. If anything they made an even more complete divide between public and private life.[62]

60. S. Kern, *The Culture of Time and Space 1880–1918* (Harvard University Press, 1983).

61. J.P. Fell, *Emotion in the Thought of Sartre* (Columbia University Press, 1965).

62. S. Rowbotham, *A New World for Women: Stella Browne, Socialist Feminist* (Pluto Press, 1977).

The postmodern and feminist self

We have seen how, throughout the past three centuries, the certainty about a unitary entity with impermeable boundaries around a singular core,[63] the 'essence' of self, has been difficult to sustain. Again and again this model has been challenged as contradictory fragments of desire, cognition, attachment, rationality collide within a single complex human being. In the mid eighteenth century, David Hume had already written, 'but self or person is not any one impression but that to which our several impressions and ideas are supposed to have a reference'.[64] Only in the second half of the twentieth century did extended notions of citizenship tied to the individual create the political and cultural climate for a more universal sense of self. And it has been since then that the contradictions inherent in this universal ideal when it is up against the actual situation of disadvantaged groups have become so obvious.

In the past decade, with the development of a 'postmodern' sensibility, belief in an undivided, rational self has again come under scrutiny. Partly this has been due to the way people have travelled and migrated to live in proximity with other cultures and other ways of thinking, seeing alternatives in film or on television, and exploring them through computer-based systems. In the West, greater affluence, increased tolerance and absorption of democratic ideas have given greater choice in the fashioning of a self.

Literary experts were among the earliest to renew interest in a shifting, fragmented sense of self. Indeed, they would jettison the word 'self' in preference to 'subject'. In English, 'subject' has a double meaning: it can be one who acts, believing that it is free, responsible and the agent of its own actions; it can also be the one who is *subject to* someone else's control and, with limited freedom, is positioned within 'authority relations',[65] for example as in 'subject of the Queen'.

Within this critique, feminists have pointed out how women have so often been placed in the second, subjected, mode: model rather than artist, muse rather than poet, 'a dwelling place *and* dweller'.[66]

63. S. Smith, *Subjectivity, Identity and the Body: Women's Autobiographical Practitioners in the 20th Century* (Indiana University Press, 1993), p. 15.

64. Quoted in Felicity Nussbaum, *The Autobiographical Subject: Gender and Ideology in 18th Century England* (Johns Hopkins University Press), p. 30.

65. Ibid., p. xi.

66. Nicole Ward Jouve, *Female Genesis: Creativity, Self and Gender* (Polity Press, 1998), p. 205.

These insights have mainly come through the study of women's writing, particularly autobiography, and have focused on the unease which women have experienced in the telling of the 'self story'.[67] Why and how has 'woman' been constructed in this way? It can be argued that the accustomed angle from which men have assumed individuality and selfhood could only be sustained by casting women in the subjected mode: the artist is characterized by his model, the poet by his muse. However, greater sophistication in understanding how a masculine viewpoint continues to be taken as the norm has not significantly shifted this way of thinking from the nineteenth-century paradigm. Nowhere has this model been better illustrated than in Henrik Ibsen's 1876 verse play, *Peer Gynt*, the basis of Grieg's famous programme music and immensely popular all over Europe. The hero, Peer, is a heavy drinker, a liar and a braggart, and has consorted with the troll king's daughter. Despite all this, his true love, Solveig, abandons her family to live in his hut at the edge of the forest (where the cultivated meets the wild). But almost immediately Peer is waylaid by his troll mistress with a hideous child she swears is his. Begging Solveig to wait for him, no matter for how long, he runs away.

Years later and after many adventures Peer returns, to be confronted by the Button Moulder who is waiting to melt down his errant soul and recast him, for Peer has lost himself by his actions. Peer begs for time to find witnesses to prove that he has, indeed, been himself all his life. In despair he comes upon Solveig at the doorway of his hut, dressed for church. Peer pleads with her to tell him 'where was myself, my sole self, my true self?' and Solveig replies, 'In my faith, in my hope and in my love'. Significantly, Peer then cries: 'My Mother! My Wife! Hide me! Hide me!' The sun rises with Peer kneeling before Solveig, his head cradled in her lap, while she sings a lullaby over him as the Button Moulder fades away and the last curtain falls.[68]

This nineteenth-century fabrication contains archetypes which are pervasive even a century later.[69] Once this is recognized it becomes clearer that in order for men to exercise and sustain a sense of themselves, women *must* find their primary self as familial. Women

67. See particularly Shari Benstock (ed.), *The Private Self: Theory and Practice of Women's Autobiographical Writing* (Routledge, 1988); L. Stanley, *The Autobiographical I: The Theory and Practice of Feminist Autobiography* (Manchester University Press, 1992).

68. Henrik Ibsen, *Peer Gynt*, trans. M. Myers (Rupert Hart-Davis, 1963), pp. 19, 80, 179.

69. See J. Solheim, 'Shelter from the storm', in T. Borchgrevink and O. Holter, *Labour of Love: Beyond the Self-Evidence of Everyday Life* (Ashgate, 1995), p. 63.

must be someone's mother, someone's daughter, someone's wife so that son, father, husband can move beyond relationships to the desired isolation which 'constantly asserts its place outside, beside, aside from other clearly configured selves'.[70] What is it about these family-based positions that men have often fled in order to define themselves? Why have women, thus firmly positioned within familial relationships, lacked the right or indeed the requirement to be fully fledged representatives of the culture? In psychoanalytic terms as well, they have not been granted the right to act and to judge themselves in terms of the development of ego and super ego, or, in other words, in more abstract, moral terms.[71]

Surely a main element in this formation has been the way 'woman' is seen as always embodied while 'man' has been able, through the short-cut of definition, to dispose of his body, to make himself other than his body. The body, that material envelope which is a symbol of potential human decay and transience, of limitation generally, is pushed underground.[72] But the body *is* part of the self, and only the extraordinary male conception of the individual could have conceived of it as so separate and distinct.[73] This insight is crucial for understanding the conceptual framework we have been discussing, for it is that space established between masculine consciousness and reason and the male body that becomes the place of philosophy and other knowledges.[74]

In this scheme the male body, when it surfaces, is seen as closed and neatly bounded. Women's bodies, on the other hand, are regarded as open and messy because of their relation to reproduction through heterosexual intercourse, pregnancy, birth and breastfeeding, the very processes which have been made the foundation for familial relationships. The emphasis for women on bodily awareness, their bodies adorned, clothed, medicated, represented, desired, despised, the ever-present awareness of themselves as women, is directly related to their primary identification *through* familial roles.

70. Smith, *Subjectivity, Identity and the Body*, p. 5.
71. Nancy Chodorow, 'Toward a relational individualism: the mediation of the self through psychoanalysis', in T.C. Heller *et al.* (eds), *Restructuring Individualism* (Stanford University Press, 1986).
72. Judith Butler, 'Variations on sex, and gender: Beauvoir, Wittig and Foucault', in S. Benhabib and D. Cornell (eds), *Feminism as Critique: On the Politics of Gender* (University of Minnesota Press, 1978), p. 133.
73. A. Phillips, *Engendering Democracy* (Polity Press, 1991), p. 109.
74. E. Gross, 'Philosophy, subjectivity and the body: Kristeva and Irigaray', in C. Pateman and E. Gross (eds), *Feminist Challenges: Social and Political Theory* (Allen & Unwin, 1986), p. 136.

But this identification is not only made with women's own bodies. It includes women's association with feeding, especially feeding small children, their responsibility for teaching those children to control their bodily functions and take on appropriate behaviour, making sure little ones are safe from hazards of all kinds, protecting and watching over the health of both children and adults in their household as well as caring for them in illness.

This intimate association of women within families with food, body waste, clearing and cleaning, taming disorder, has made them touch more nearly the forces of chaos and pollution.[75] The housewife's pre-eminent duty lies in protecting the household from the contamination of dirt, waste products and untidiness, in transforming the raw into the cooked, in transforming little savages into civilized adults. There is no masculine analogue to the concept of *housewife*. Until recently it was an expected aspect of femininity to *like to* as well as to be able to undertake these tasks. It is still generally women who peel the potatoes, wash, sort and put away socks, mop up vomit, change nappies and sheets.[76] These expectations have carried over into the world of work. For example, nurses (generally women) care for patients and administer treatments to their bodies while doctors (generally men) diagnose illnesses.

These tasks constitute a central aspect of the empathy expected of the feminine, the unwritten element missing from rational, abstract individuality. Within a culture still split between mind and body, feminists have celebrated women's, especially mothers', supposed capacity to feel for others instead of the more usual denigration of their absorption in the trivial, daily round. This capacity would make women seem especially suited for the effort to shift society into a more humane, people-based social order as much concerned with caring as autonomy.[77] However, as long as men's as well as women's relationship to both self and family goes unexamined, the danger here is a return to some notion of innate gender characteristics dressed in a new language.[78]

75. Mary Douglas, *Purity and Danger: An Analysis of Concepts of Pollution and Taboo* (Penguin, 1970).

76. Leonore Davidoff, 'The rationalization of housework', in *Worlds Between*, p. 97.

77. This position is the logical outcome of the discussion of moral development in girls in Carol Gilligan, *In a Different Voice: Psychological Theory and Women's Development* (Harvard University Press, 1982). See also A. Weir, 'Toward a model of self-identity: Habermas and Kristeva' in Meehan (ed.), *Feminists Read Habermas.*

78. This has been the criticism of some influential views which privilege mothering such as Nancy Chodorow, *The Reproduction of Mothering: Psychoanalysis and the Sociology of Gender* (University of California Press, 1978) and S. Ruddick, *Maternal Thinking: Towards a Politics of Peace* (Beacon Press, 1989). Various solutions to this

What is genuinely novel about the feminist contribution to this story of a divided world is the highlighting of the way these two versions of the self, rational or feeling, are directly related to expectations about gender and the power relationships implied. For example, the telling of women's own stories has, for the first time, focused on the experience of motherhood from the mother's point of view[79] and has begun to shift attention to women as 'selves'.

But even as women are freed from the supposition that 'anatomy is destiny', there are dangers. It is so easy to slide towards seeing women's development as individuals in the traditional masculine mode, the supposedly neutral and integrated sense of self. This is particularly so as women's commitment to paid work and opportunities for 'making it' in the public world have increased, even while the original embodied, feminine construction has been retained.

Nevertheless, the acknowledgement that gender, family and self are interwoven has opened the way to seeing the self less as a static thing which remains unchanging over a lifetime, a true essence to be sought through drugs, through individual therapy, through intense introspection and search, and more as a process.

It may be no coincidence that the last ten years has seen a decline in therapies, particularly psychoanalytic, which focus on the individual. In particular the school of 'psychology of the self', a combination of psychoanalytic object relations and cognitive and developmental approaches, upholds empathy as an alternative to the knowledge values and independence values of Western civilization.[80] In reaction to the destructive powers of science and technology this view takes into account historical and social factors as well as psychological explanations. While not necessarily explicit about the family, this approach opens the way to understanding personality development as a lifelong project. Self psychologists see all people embedded for life in a network of human relationships.[81] This approach has been accompanied by the rapid rise of both family therapy and various theoretical views of the family including

dilemma have recently been discussed, for example see Karen Green, *The Woman of Reason: Feminism, Humanism and Political Thought* (Polity Press, 1995).

79. 'Review essays: maternity and motherhood, recent feminist scholarship', *Signs: Journal of Women in Culture and Society*, Vol. 20, No. 2 (Winter 1995); see also Ellen Ross, *Love and Toil: Motherhood in Outcast London, 1870–1918* (Oxford University Press, 1993).

80. H. Kohut, 'Introspection, empathy and the semi-circle of mutual health', *International Journal of Psychoanalysis*, Vol. 63, No. 3 (1982).

81. J.K. Gardiner, 'Self psychology as feminist theory', *Signs: Journal of Women in Culture and Society*, Vol. 12, No. 4 (1987), p. 772.

a family development framework, family systems, a family conflict model and an ecology of family model.[82] The watchword is no longer 'self-development' but 'relational development'.[83]

A consequence of these trends has been renewed emphasis on the self as a 'reflexive object', that is being aware of ourselves not just as actors but as having an internal self-regulating, self-constructing ability. As families shrink in size and spend much time apart, other 'primordial associations' such as occupational groups or friends are seen to be ever more important. Intimacy becomes a matter of both choice and luck, no longer guaranteed by the thin family relationships on offer. The kernel of a 'pure relationship', based on affection and intimacy rather than duty or obligation through kinship, is thought to be paramount.[84] Meanwhile the muddled, inconsistent character of everyday life is not so simple.

Without exception, all the meanings of self discussed contain an often unacknowledged element of power. Most important is the power to define what constitutes a self and who should be admitted to, who excluded from this privilege. The family was a repository for those categories of people who were denied the status of full selfhood and whose interests were represented only by virtue of their relationship to the man designated as head. This basic conception remained largely in place throughout our period.

If this element of power is incorporated into the present understanding that parts of the self may be in conflict, that integration of a self may be different for different people, a more rounded picture emerges. It would be possible to integrate many kinds of relationships, of which the familial would be one. If self is a process, then family, too, can be understood as a collection of 'selves in process', an active interplay, with all the conflict as well as cooperation that implies.

The construction of kinship

Like the construction of individual and self, kinship is built on assumed ideas about gender derived from daily life. Kinship, too,

82. Family systems theory was first taken over from business organization. See N. Ackerman, *The Psychodynamics of Family Life* (Basic Books, 1958) and D.M. Klein and J.M. White, *Family Theories: An Introduction* (Sage, 1996).

83. J. Baker Miller and I. Stiver, *The Healing Connection: How Women Form Relationships in Therapy and Life* (Beacon Press, 1997), p. 57.

84. Anthony Giddens, *The Transformation of Intimacy: Sexuality, Love and Eroticism in Modern Societies* (Polity Press, 1992), p. 98.

is based on a division between the political, economic and legal domains on the one hand and the domestic on the other.[85] Parentage and reproduction are key components of both gender and kinship systems.[86] Anthropologists, the specialists in an analysis of kinship, have usually turned their attention to non-Western cultures and away from their own society. They did so carrying with them the assumption that there exists a separate domain of life which can be labelled kinship.[87] Until the 1950s, the ability of a society to differentiate kinship from more public domains was often taken to be the hallmark of more advanced, more civilized societies as opposed to the primitive and backward where the kinship system was seen to be all-embracing. Yet it seems from innumerable ethnographic studies that kin relationships enter into all other parts of life – whether they be defined as economic, political, cultural, artistic, educational, religious. And, in turn, these activities, institutions, ways of relating, enter into and help to mould kinship relations.

Kinship has been conceived in this compartmentalized way because anthropologists and others took their common pool of ideas from existing English culture. Their prime working tool was an abstract system of genealogies with the main focus on the individual, usually adult and male, and his forebears and descendants. These 'genealogical grids' were remarkably reminiscent of the genealogies gathered within heraldry for the aristocracy and gentry, the all-encompassing power of 'blood and semen'.[88]

Thus while kinship was talked of as a system of linkages between people, it was promoted intellectually as an abstract system.[89] The basis of that abstract grid was the assumption that *blood is thicker than water*. 'Kinship was a set of ties socially recognized to exist between persons because of their genealogical connection.'[90] It has

85. Jane Collier and Sylvia Yanagisako, *Gender and Kinship: Essays Toward a Unified Analysis* (Stanford University Press, 1987), p. 7.
86. Anna Yeatman, 'The procreative model: the social ontological bases of the gender–kinship system', *Social Analysis*, No. 14 (December 1983).
87. A few sociologists have used the idea of kin as an extension of a *family life course* perspective to widen the usual emphasis on the nuclear core. In practice this means looking at the role of grandparents, aunts and uncles, not questioning the categories which make up family. C.B. Stack and L.M. Burton, 'Kinscripts', *Journal of Comparative Family Studies*, Vol. 24, No. 2 (1993).
88. J. Powis, *Aristocracy* (Oxford University Press, 1984), p. 91.
89. S.D. Faubon, 'Kinship is dead. Long live kinship', *Comparative Studies in Society and History*, Vol. 38, No. 1 (January 1996).
90. R. Firth, J. Hubert and A. Forge, *Families and their Relatives: Kinship in a Middle-Class Sector of London* (Routledge & Kegan Paul, 1969), p. 3.

only been in the last quarter of the twentieth century that our culture-bound notion of kinship has begun to be recognised, and 'kinship structure' to be acknowledged as the manner in which a pattern of physical relationships (however these are conceived) is made use of for social purposes. It is not the 'reality' of physical relatedness but what is added to it, omitted from it, and distanced from it which becomes the actual stuff of kinship.[91] This assumed kinship structure has provided a common denominator that allowed anthropologists, colonial administrators or interested travellers to describe their particular group in comparison with others and, ultimately, against the template of the English literate upper and middle class.[92] It was our nineteenth-century naming system, widening out from the core of mother, father, son, daughter, brother, sister, which underlay these small-scale abstract models. The anthropologist, almost always a highly educated middle- or upper-class man, set out to live among totally alien people. He was regarded by those at home, and felt himself to be, a prime example of the neutral observer who had left behind all attachments, when, in fact, he carried with him the baggage of his Western culture.[93]

An often unacknowledged tension is apparent here between the pivotal place of the individual on the one hand and the genealogical relatedness of kinship on the other. In keeping with Western culture's stress on the individual, we tend to regard a person as a whole and as unique. A person's kinship assignments are regarded as only a small part of that person. Yet some are more defined by kinship and familial relationships than others. And the people thus singled out tend to be those same groups of partial and legally non-existent persons that we have seen in other contexts, women and children. For example, the role of mother defines more of a woman's person than that of father for a man. Furthermore a woman is seen, and may see herself, more fully as some *particular* person's mother, just as a child will be attached to a specific mother and father. Such relatedness of women extended even to adult single women, who tended to be defined as daughters, sisters, aunts or widows rather than as persons in their own right. But in contemporary society even women claim identity from other domains than

91. E. Gellner, *The Concept of Kinship and Other Essays* (Blackwell, 1973 and 1987), pp. 166 and 170.

92. This section depends heavily on the work of David Schneider: see especially his book, *A Critique of the Study of Kinship* (University of Michigan Press, 1984).

93. J. Okely and H. Callaway (eds), *Anthropology and Autobiography* (Routledge, 1992).

kinship; women are now also students, workers, citizens, equal before the law. And, like men, to make a whole individual, all people are ultimately expected to make themselves out of a complicated web of relationships and roles, only some of which may be defined as kin.

There is thus a paradox produced by Western culture's emphasis on descent. These highly prized and unique individuals are nevertheless born, reared and placed within a kinship network no matter how attenuated; 'individuality thus is both a fact of and "after" kinship'.[94] Relationships exist prior to individual persons and go on existing when those persons are gone. Western culture, and English culture in particular, is programmed to think in terms of descent from the distant past to the present and on to the future. As Marilyn Strathern has pointed out, 'the downward flow of time is also the downward flow of life'[95] from parents to children. Childhood now holds the key to adult reality, as seen in the previous discussion of the self.

Parentage and the passing on to children and grandchildren of physical characteristics, character, skills, as well as property, citizenship and nationality, have been privileged in English thought and usage. The social fiction of an unbroken line of honourable, preferably patrilineal, descent was what counted in establishing enduring claims of political and economic privilege. Both titles and land are passed down according to inheritance through the male blood line. This replication of one's own 'blood' may have been a way of dealing with mortality, clinging to an essence which transcends death and disintegration.

Thus the narrowest definition of kin is restricted to 'consanguinity', that is blood relations through direct descent – a line from great-great-great etc. grandparents to children. Siblings, the closest genetic tie after parent and child, are problematic, for they force the family to dilute emotional, material and financial resources.[96] In this view even marriage, which produces 'affinal' relationships, is suspect, for marriage is not a blood tie but a contract, even if it includes love and devotion.[97] What, then, is our relationship to in-laws? What, if anything, do we owe them? What do they owe us?

94. Marilyn Strathern, *After Nature: English Kinship in the Late 20th Century* (Cambridge University Press, 1992), p. 15.

95. Ibid., p. 62.

96. L. Davidoff, 'Where the stranger begins: the question of siblings in historical analysis', in *Worlds Between*.

97. J. Finch, *Family Obligations and Social Change* (Polity Press, 1989).

It is the tie between parents and children which has been imbued with ever more poignancy as people's relationship to the transcendental realms of religion, folk belief and magic has gradually disappeared. Kinship is a system which was placed within the context of nature, alien to late twentieth-century connections through advanced technology and communications. As 'Nature' seems to be constantly receding from our lives, the self becomes even more detached from the realms of both the natural and kinship.[98]

Is it possible that another type of relationship will replace kin ties? It has recently been argued that the sense of uniqueness of an individual is 'safer with friendship than with any other relationship – because friends are the people who see no contradiction in our wanting to be ourselves and wanting to be close to other people as well'.[99] Friendship has been a much neglected topic of historical and social analysis, yet it is closely related to the idea of kin. We would not claim friendship with others unless there existed a shared consciousness or sense of kinship with another person. Yet there are few formal or explicit rules governing obligations and rights between friends. Paradoxically, therefore, the uncertainty of friendship gives weight to the known obligations and expectations around family and kin even where personal choice might favour the friend, obligations formalized around ritual occasions such as family birthdays, Mother's Day and Father's Day. Friendship can be both an alternative and complement to kinship.[100]

The bonds of modern friendship have not always been so frail. The medieval and early modern systems of *patronage* meant that powerful individuals or families could befriend those weaker and dependent, offering protection, sponsorship, social recognition in return for loyalty and returned favours, such as labour where required or even votes.[101] Patrons often held positions of *stewardship* or *trusteeship* over those they were responsible for, particularly the young. Patrons and their petitioners or supporters could be kin, for example in the web of aristocratic cousinhood which once spread over the regional areas of England. But patrons need not be related

98. For example, in 1922, cousins were excluded from being beneficiaries where someone died without making a will. Finch *et al.*, *Wills, Inheritance and Families*, p. 33.

99. Graham Little, *Friendship: Being Ourselves with Others* (Melbourne: The Text Publishing Company, 1993), p. 255.

100. M. Bouquet, *Reclaiming English Kinship: Portuguese Reflections on English Kinship Theory* (Manchester University Press, 1993), p. 91.

101. C.D. Ross (ed.), *Patronage, Pedigree and Power in Later Medieval England* (Sutton Publishing, 1973); G. Mingay, *The Gentry: The Rise and Fall of a Ruling Class* (Longman, 1976).

to their subjects. For example, coming from the same locality could be interpreted as imposing certain kin-like obligations.[102]

By the late eighteenth century, this kind of vertical friendship tie was being subtly transmuted[103] by more contractual market-based relationships, notions of fraternity which had seeped into political thought from the French Revolution, and by evangelical religious groups who defined themselves through common salvation and the bonds of Christian brotherhood.[104] The most striking example of mutual obligation and support is among the Quakers, who forbade all titles and called each other *Friend*. Despite an official ban on cousin marriages, these customarily joined Quaker families by multiple marriage ties. The rich content of such ties echoes in the comment by a Quaker woman who had left the congregation on religious grounds: 'Oh I was lonely – almost all my friends and acquaintances were Friends.'[105]

The neglect and misunderstandings around terms such as patron, steward, trustee, and particularly friend, shows how important is language, the terms we use and have used in the past to denote ties of obligation, rights, expectations of material and emotional exchange and the routes they may legitimately take. It seems that for the youngest children, the person to whom they relate on a day-to-day basis is more important than the category of their carer, whether of kinship or other.[106] Even with older children, an unrelated friend of the parents who carries the fictive title of 'aunty' or 'uncle' may well be one of the most significant figures in a young person's life. For a young girl growing up in the 1930s, it was the powerful professional upper-class mentor of her father who was like a living presence in the family where the parents had come from a particularly poor and disadvantaged background. She rejected the parochial and materialistic values of her own grandparents, feeling more 'kinship' with this awesome figure who, in fact, she had never seen.[107]

102. These channels of relatedness were particularly activated during times of upheaval and emigration. For example, those Jews who originated in the same village could claim obligations as 'landsmen' during the large-scale immigration of the late nineteenth century. Similarly in the 1950s West Indians tended to identify and support those from their own particular islands. J. Rex and R. Moore, *Race, Community and Conflict: A Study of Sparkbrook* (Oxford University Press, 1974).
103. Naomi Tadmore, '"Family" and "friend" in *Pamela*: a case study in the history of the family in 18th century England', *Social History*, Vol. 14, No. 3. (1989).
104. See Davidoff and Hall, *Family Fortunes*, Part I.   105. Ibid., p. 87.
106. N. Benson and J. Anglin, 'The child's knowledge of English kin terms', *First Language*, Vol. 7, Part I, No. 19 (1987).
107. 'Charlotte's story', anonymous manuscript, 1997.

For those who would break the mould of their early inheritance, it might be necessary to find others than kin. For example, in the autobiography of the son of a poor smallholder at the beginning of the twentieth century we hear almost nothing of his parents. Rather it is the never-ending poverty and backbreaking drudgery of their lives which fill his memory. He is much more explicit about the friend to whom he turned, a youth who had already escaped to the coalfields and who offered him the possibility of work, lodgings and companionship. This young man did not necessarily love his parents less, indeed he felt guilty leaving them behind. But friendship was his route to a better life.[108] Thus the familial language of kinship, constantly invoked in daily life, while seeming to be definite and clear, is also infinitely fluid in interpretation and consequence.

The construction of home and household

Unlike the other concepts we have considered so far, the home has never been of direct interest to academics or intellectuals. It is true that, to some extent, anthropologists have considered the use of space, particularly its symbolic aspects – for example, the threshold of the house which marks a boundary between outside and inside or sacred and profane.[109] But this approach has seldom been applied to our own society. Nor has the social and psychic meaning of spatial boundaries in relation to the family been of central concern within geography, the discipline based on analysis of space.

Indeed, the place of home in everyday life means that most intellectuals and academics deliberately distance themselves from its serious consideration. Home has been the unacknowledged setting from which other, more important activities can emerge. It is both a place and a state of mind, homely (*sic*) and mundane and, as such, closely associated with family. Home implies warmth – both physical and emotional – ease, comfort and love.

In the nineteenth century the almost sacred quality of the 'temple of the hearth' became a powerful evocative image, not only in literature but in house design, and in spending resources of servants, labour and income in the lavish use of open coal fires in a deliberately wasteful manner.

108. B.L. Coombes, *These Poor Hands: A Miner's Story* (1939; Gollancz, 1974).
109. The main exponent of ideas about symbolic boundaries and the state of liminality is Victor Turner, *Drama, Field and Metaphor: Symbolic Action in Human Society* (Cornell University Press, 1975).

Then, as the dusk of evening sets in, and you see in the squares and
crescents the crimson flickering of the flames from the cosy sea-coal
fires in the parlours, lighting up the windows . . . the cold cheerless
aspect of the streets without sets you thinking of the exquisite comfort of our English homes.[110]

The nineteenth-century evocation of the thatched cottage in a
garden with roses around the door lingers in our subconsciousness.

In nineteenth-century idiom, 'when life callings have scattered
men the house is where they return to', to tie up broken links.[111]
The home prefigured the Heavenly Home where the family would
be reunited, never to be parted. Then again, the distance of colonial life was subdued by thinking of England as forever 'Home', the
Mother country which sent her sons (and sometimes daughters)
away to govern and ultimately to fight for her. The emotional pull
of this image cannot be overstated. It is ironically illustrated by the
poignant title of 'Home' given to institutions for unattached children and old people.

What has not been so obvious is that the home was made by
women, the space where femininity was maintained. A home was
not simply a house, for, as the saying goes, 'what is a home without
a mother?' It is the mother/wife who is the heart of the home. It
is her nurturing, the scent of her home baking, the hearth she
keeps always alight, that makes the home into:

> A world of care without
> A world of strife shut out
> A world of love shut in.[112]

In this formation, the wife-mother-house-mistress image often
merged with the physical symbol of the house so that it became
difficult to visualize the woman as having a separate identity from
it. In a sense she *became* the house, a sentiment echoed in working-
class culture in the expression 'her indoors'. If women made such
homes, this could be applied to all levels of society from the mean-
est cottage to the palace. Thus women, as homemakers, could, and
should, overcome the divisions created by wealth, power, education.

110. Augustus Mayhew, *Paved with Gold* (1858) quoted in Davidoff, *Worlds Between*,
p. 51.
111. J.A. Froude quoted in Walter E. Houghton, *The Victorian Frame of Mind 1830–
1870* (Yale University Press, 1974), p. 344.
112. Dora Greenwell, 1863, quoted in Davidoff, 'Landscape with figures', *Worlds
Between*, p. 41.

Home also implies marriage, and with it romantic and erotic love as well as love between children and parents, siblings, even for pets. Women even today are assumed to have a greater stake in making and maintaining that home, preserving these loving relationships. As we have seen, it is both their duty and a large part of their feminine identity. For in an urban society the opposite of the home is not so much wild undomesticated nature as the street, a place of chaos where hierarchy and order can be undermined by unregulated chance encounter. Women of the *street*, street walkers or public women were prostitutes, while idealized good women stayed at home, providing a 'fixed point' for both men and children.

The language here is telling. *Homely*, meaning plain and simple, still applied to living arrangements as well as people, began to take on negative connotations. It was then superseded by the more positive *homelike*. The home can be overly familiar (note derivation of the word) and dull, while the outside world – the street – beckons excitingly. This meant that the *homemaker*, a word only coming into general use in the mid nineteenth century,[113] had a difficult task keeping her menfolk and adult children at home. Adult men took full advantage of opportunities to explore the world beyond the home; working-class women were often forced to do so in search of work and support.[114] This was recognized in subcultures such as the early nineteenth-century Dandies, and 'Bohemians' who rejected the whole code of respectability enshrined in the idea of home and family. They favoured unconventional, even communal, living arrangements.[115]

There are other contradictions. The home also has a material and financial aspect; it is usually a unit of consumption. In heavily urbanized England, to make a home depended mainly on income, which until recently was ideally to come from the husband and father, the rationale even today for men's higher earnings. Given this model, there is little a homemaker can do to increase income. Rather activities done within the home, from cooking and interior decorating to embroidery, making music and constructing models,

113. J. Gillis, *A World of Their Own Making: Myth, Ritual and the Quest for Family Values* (Basic Books, 1996), p. 122.

114. See material on the *flaneur* by Elizabeth Wilson , 'The invisible flaneur', *New Left Review*, No. 191 (January/February 1992); Deborah Nord, *Walking the Victorian Streets: Women, Representation and the City* (Cornell University Press, 1995).

115. Ellen Moers, *The Dandy: Brummell to Beerbohm*, 2nd edn (University of Nebraska Press, 1978); J.E. Adams, *Dandies and Desert Saints: Styles of Victorian Manhood* (Cornell University Press, 1995).

are seen as non-working and given amateur status.[116] But on the whole, as the sociologist Dorothy Smith has written, 'the house constitutes a dead end. The surplus above subsistence which enters it does not pass beyond into productive activity.'[117] In addition to servicing the inmates, surplus is used in consumption to perform a display function marking the family's position. Over and above that function, homes are the containers for attachments with personalized inanimate objects as well as intimacy with other people. Family heirlooms, pictures, ornaments, books, toys have emotional value.

Unlike the home, the concept of the household is used more in official documents than in common speech. Who makes up a household – that is, shared domestic space, a common cooking pot and shared finances – has mainly been of interest for purposes of public policy such as taxation, health, or housing. It is also, as we saw in the last chapter, the unit employed in the decennial census of population and forms a grid laid over more relaxed everyday living arrangements.

Demographers, who tend to rely on formal statistical descriptions, have been responsible for much of the confusion produced by conflating family with household. This has meant that categories such as servants, long-stay visitors or lodgers have been problematic. But so also are those family relationships extending outside the boundaries of shared living space. For example, where children are sent to boarding school or temporarily put into care, they may not appear as members of the household. Yet their family will not normally define itself as childless. Then again, in the past of large families, some children slept with grandparents or others living close by.[118] Or take the two elderly sisters residing in separate flats but still doing shopping for each other and sharing some of their meals.[119] One of the main reasons for this kind of tunnel vision is demographers' almost exclusive concern with mortality and fertility

116. For an analysis of work done in the home, see C. Delphy and D. Leonard, *Familiar Exploitation: A New Analysis of Marriage in Contemporary Western Society* (Polity Press, 1992).

117. Dorothy E. Smith, 'Women, the family and corporate capitalism', in Marylee Stephenson (ed.), *Women in Canada* (New Press, 1970), p. 21.

118. Barry Reay, 'Kinship and neighbourhood in 19th century rural England: the myth of the autonomous nuclear family', *Journal of Family History*, Vol. 21, No. 1 (1996).

119. Records from Peter Townsend's study, *The Family Life of Old People* (1956) held by the National Social Policy and Social Change Archive, Albert Sloman Library, University of Essex.

and especially with the role of the nuclear family in these processes, which makes other arrangements invisible.[120]

The concept of the household has thus been used interchangeably with family, with all the disadvantages we have depicted. This is a pity, for if held independently it has the potential to highlight some of the realities of modern life with its multiple living arrangements and the presence of non-kin in the orbit of personal relationships and everyday life.

The construction of identity

Identity, the final element in our understanding of how the concept of the family and family practices have operated, has not been the province of any single approach or academic discipline. In a sense, notions of identity cling to all the concepts so far considered. Nevertheless, in late twentieth-century England, as elsewhere, unease about human beings' place in the universe as well as the mundane world has become ever more intense. Our sense of ourselves has both broken apart and taken on new dimensions. Before considering how deeply familial relationships are implicated in this search for identity, we need first to consider what identity is and how current studies of this phenomenon have been conceptualized.

At its simplest level identity builds on the notion of self. Asking the question 'Who am I?' leads quickly to the question 'Who are we?' How do we relate to a wider whole? And it is only possible to know who we are by identifying who we are not. We create identity through recognizing difference, by designating what or who is excluded or marginal, by demarcating an 'us and them'. While it follows from this that a single person may have many identities, the recognition and exclusion of particular kinds of difference gives an illusion of wholeness: a shared norm, be it physical characteristics, language, customs, beliefs or behaviour, including the use of shared spaces. For example, our sense of what it means to be English has been strengthened during times of war when our geographical boundaries, way of life and even physical existence have been threatened by a clearly defined enemy. This threat has enabled propagandists to 'manipulate patriotic sentiment to stimulate loyalty and

---

120. This approach is exemplified by Steven Ruggles, *Prolonged Connections: The Rise of the Extended Family in 19th Century England and America* (University of Wisconsin Press, 1987), p. xviii.

sacrifice and focus public attention on who "we" are and what it is we "stand for"'.[121]

From this apparently simple formulation two related questions arise. Are we given or do we make our own identities and how much choice do we have in their making? Secondly, how far are power relations implicated in choosing or being designated identities? Part of the power of an individual to take on, to reject, to mould an identity depends on a hierarchy of resources including the power of language and the legitimate voicing of that language.

Those in the most powerful positions close off the boundaries of difference. By designating themselves 'naturally' as the norm, all other groups are marked by implication as inferior. Hence men are the unmarked category in gender terms, the upper and middle strata in class terms, whites in racial terms, the English in national terms, youthful and middle-aged but neither young children nor elderly adults in terms of generation. By using the characteristics of those who do the defining as a standard to which all must conform in order to reach equality, it has also been possible to deny that differences in access to power and resources have any real significance.

This denial of difference can be traced back to the Enlightenment and the idea that it was possible to separate theoretically equal individuals from their social categories, such as race, nationality, religion or gender. The separation of the individual from his/her social environment also provided the conditions for the emergence of psychoanalysis, which 'came to occupy a for a while overwhelming cultural position because it reflected the illusory or imaginary way in which modern personal life is lived, namely as something separate, individual without relation to society'.[122] Only in this sense can we be perceived as making our own identities.

On the other hand, insights from psychoanalysis, in bringing in the unconscious and a place for fantasy and desire, can be used to produce a more dynamic concept of identity. The admission of these less rational forces has coincided with wider, more democratic access to political and, to a lesser extent, economic power, resulting from decades of organized pressure from the working

121. Sonya Rose, 'Cultural analysis and moral discourses: episodes, communities and transformations', in L. Hunt and V. Bonnell (eds), *Beyond the Cultural Turn: History and Sociology in an Age of Paradigm Breakdown* (University of California Press, forthcoming).

122. Eli Zaretski, 'Identity theory, identity politics: psychoanalysis, Marxism, poststructuralism', in Craig Calhoun (ed.), *Social Theory and the Politics of Identity* (Blackwell, 1994), p. 202.

class and from women. Taken together these developments have given recognition to diversity, a flexibility of social codes and the chance for less powerful groups to articulate their own interests. An inner search for who you *are* includes who you would like *to be*.[123] This has resulted in raised expectations about the rights to agency or at least the right for the subject to search for, to take on, to reject, to mould his or her own identity.[124]

At the same time, followers of Michel Foucault deny a core inner identity and have seen the self disappearing, leaving only a system of cognitive structures, or texts. Either way, it has been assumed that a single person may have not just one but a multitude of identities which fluctuate according to which aspect of themselves they choose to bring to the fore.

The categories of gender, class, age, race, ethnicity, nationality, religious affiliation, linguistic community and sexual orientation are believed to be paramount in the creation of identity in our society. Yet the extent to which these are imposed by others, by law or custom, or freely chosen, is by no means clear-cut. Being able to identify completely with a certain group will depend both on your sense of your own likeness to that group or culture but also on whether they accept or exclude you. This may be true even for categories with a higher degree of physical determination such as age and gender.

For example, I may be born with the bodily characteristics of a man but choose to identify myself as a woman and can now enlist medical technology to aid me. But however much I desire to be identified as a woman, I am unlikely ever to be fully accepted as such, but will rather be placed by others in the borderline category of transsexual. Age cannot in itself be altered, but the physical characteristics such as height, puberty and bodily deterioration, or customs and behaviour such as the transition from childhood to adulthood, which are expected at a particular age, are culturally and historically variable. We may or may not identify with others in our age group, but we are likely to be categorized by age and expected to conform to behaviour patterns thought suitable to that age by our culture, including legally binding rules on school attendance, age of majority and compulsory retirement.

123. Jeffrey Weeks, 'The value of difference', in Jonathan Rutherford (ed.), *Identity, Community, Culture and Difference* (Lawrence & Wishart, 1990), p. 88.

124. Stuart Hall, 'Introduction: who needs "identity"', in S. Hall and P. DuGay (eds), *Questions of Cultural Identity* (Sage Publications, 1996).

Identity and family

One of the most salient claims to inclusion is based on physical relationship. The claims of 'blood' or of 'kith and kin' can have momentous consequences for an individual's life chances. Modern states use these criteria as the basis for citizenship, now codified and enforced by law. In England passports, permission to pass beyond the boundaries of the modern nation state, only began to be required in the early nineteenth century. In the context of mass East European Jewish immigration, by the early twentieth century the first legal definitions of nationality were framed which required either British parentage or birth on British soil.

At this level, identity through family is obvious. But detailed discussions of the place of the family in creating a sense of identity are thin on the ground, the unattended stuff of individual life stories. After all, our earliest identification at birth is as someone's child, which, with other categories of familial relationship, continues to exert great influence on how we identify ourselves and are identified by others. We should not, however, take identification as fixed, for there has always been some flexibility in the ways we act out family relationships. This has been reinforced by developments in reproductive technology which 'have made explicit the possibility of choosing whom and what one desires to call family'.[125]

Nevertheless, most work on identity politics, the major contemporary focus in this area, usually 'jumps over' the family. There is little interest in the development of identity through childhood and youth. Nor is there much understanding of how family obligations, some of them legally enforced and embedded in institutions, and the enactment of family relationships enhance, constrain and mould the process of identification for adults.

This process works both ways. It could be said that the family is partially defined by being the place where basic identities are formed. We are said to 'start a family' not at marriage but by the birth of a child. That birth creates a mother and a father as well as grandparents, aunts, uncles and cousins. The births of further children generate brothers and sisters. It is impossible to repudiate these categories, although in practice people might abdicate from carrying out most, if not all, of what is expected.

125. Marilyn Strathern, 'Technologies', in Hall and DuGay (eds), *Questions of Cultural Identity*, p. 47.

Birth is only the first step for the individual. Once that child is born, it does not acquire social status until is given a gendered name. The designation Baby X or 'it' is not even fully human. It may be argued that the first social identity is that of gender. The deepest recesses of our psyches are coloured with gender resonances, almost always played out in families in the first instance. Children go on to learn and rehearse social expectations through playing at being grown-up men and women, designated work or tasks seen as appropriate to their gender. For example, until the early twentieth century, boys, who had like their sisters worn petticoats as young children, were ceremonially breeched into trousers at the age of 4 or 5 as a marker of their moving to a nascent masculine identity. Girls remained in skirts all their lives.

As they mature, children learn about and take on wider identities of race, ethnicity, class, religion, nationality. Families are the most critical site in this process of inclusion and exclusion where loyalties are shaped through habits and rituals. Particular foods first tasted in childhood, for example, hold a saliency throughout adult life, so that many English living abroad remember such treats as Marmite or custard with loving nostalgia. Ceremonies attached to rites of passage such as christenings, weddings or funerals join people together and heighten their awareness of themselves as a group. Such is the power of habit and ritual that political or religious sects who organize their members without family groupings must reintroduce them in some form.

Children's understanding of who they are has also been reinforced through parental injunctions as to which of their friends were allowed into the home, according to whether their families were black or white, Protestant, Catholic, Jewish or Muslim, 'rough' or 'respectable'. They learn that their experiences are shared by others with similar identities in groups which may be locally based, widely dispersed or which may have been connected in the past. These are the basis for the 'imagined communities' which have received much recent attention.[126]

Identification, inclusion and exclusion are not only based on difference but on the values given to one's own group and to the other. The grotesque stereotypical derogatory names for those people who, we were taught as children, are different from ourselves silt

126. B. Anderson, *Imagined Communities: Reflections on the Origin and Spread of Nationalism* (Verso, 1983).

down into consciousness never to be totally expunged. For, as the historian-cum-sociologist Sonya Rose has argued, there is a direct connection between morality and collective identity. What is moral is what we – our group – says it does. What is immoral is what 'we don't do'.[127] Morality defines and strengthens group boundaries. The moral message is part of group heritage.

The link between morality and group definition results from the way difference always carries an implicit message of power, as we have seen in the case of gender. Naked power, to be acceptable, must be made legitimate and clothed in moral terms. The act of being identified, admitted or rejected, to a family and *through* that family to other groupings, even nation states through citizenship via birth or kinship, is in itself a condition of having power or being powerless.[128]

Identity, naming and imagined families

From the above discussion it is evident that an important mechanism in the moulding of self and identity through family has been naming practices. We use names to create boundaries between belonging and not belonging. Surnames create imagined families which express our desire for unity and attachment to others. It is easier to 'claim kin' if a common name can be invoked. Modern England, a more homogeneous entity than many societies, has been relatively flexible in naming practices since a common system has been assumed rather than being imposed by Church or State.

During the medieval period the great households of the nobility and wealthy commercial clans identified people by names and titles as well as by association with places – castles, land or towns. Among these elites, masculine primacy and the blood line were well established. The heraldry of the Middle Ages flaunted genealogical attachment. But most people below this level did not have more than a nickname to distinguish them from others. Such names were often derived from their primary occupation or the place they lived in or some other identifying mark – for example, 'John of the mill' or 'Agnes with the crooked leg'. By the sixteenth century a man skilled in a trade might emerge as a Smith or Thatcher, skin or hair colouring could appear as White, Brown or Black, those who usually

127. Rose, 'Cultural analysis and moral discourses'.
128. V. Spike Peterson, 'The politics of identification in the context of globalisation', *Women's Studies International Forum*, Vol. 19, No. 1 (1996).

lived by the Lake, or in the Field or Woods took and kept their name by association. By the seventeenth century, also the period when named gravestones were introduced in churchyards, most people automatically inherited their surname from the father. Thus one of our most important keys to personal identity and sense of self, our names, is of fairly recent origin and strongly patrilineal.

In the aristocracy names have been less important than the titles associated with land and inherited through the male line. If that died out altogether a prospective husband would assume the title or name of the heiress. That name then became the patrilineal marker for *his* descendants. The untitled gentry tended to follow this aristocratic pattern in an attempt to keep name and land intact.

But naming practices reflect as well as create access to property and resources. For example, in the eighteenth century, as a growing number of families began to accumulate wealth through farming, commerce, manufacture and the professions, surnames were as usual taken from the male line. However, the vital contribution of capital and skill from the female side was acknowledged by the use of male first names taken from the mother's (or grandmother's) maiden name, particularly for younger sons. Thus can be found an attorney, Eddowes Sparrow, a farmer, Woolnough Gross, a confectioner, Chigwell Wire, a doctor, Bowyer Vaux.[129] With growing literacy and a burgeoning commerical sector, the written name in the form of a personal signature which stood in for the person came to be a key element of systems of trust for such transactions as bills of exchange and promissory notes, crucial in a society without a stable banking system or standard concurrency, but almost exclusively male as few women could legally enter into such contracts.

For the most part, such naming practices have elevated the masculine character of individuality and the masculine template of our family forms. Female first names are often male names given a feminine ending: Paul/Pauline, George/Georgianna, Patrick/Patricia, Henry/Henrietta, Gerald/Geraldine, but the reverse is never found. For men, a name at birth connotes both personhood and individuality.[130] It is notable that family names have had a different significance for men, who kept the same name throughout their lives, than for women, who have usually changed their surname. When on marriage a man becomes official proprietor of a new family, he maintains continuity with his family of birth through

129. Davidoff and Hall, *Family Fortunes*, p. 222.
130. J.S. LaFontaine, 'Person and individual: some anthropological reflections', in Carrithers *et al.* (eds), *The Category of the Person*, p. 132.

bestowing his family name on his wife and children. Unlike women, who have bodily evidence of their maternity, men can never be certain of their paternity. Giving a man's name to children born within a marriage, whatever the real circumstances of their conception, attaches them to the husband and father and enables them to inherit his property. For those born outside marriage, being denied their father's name has meant that they were also denied admittance to his family and could not legitimately inherit, as we discuss in Chapter 9.

A woman's alternative relationship to a family name is established at birth, when she is registered as a member of her father's and not her mother's family, and she does not usually pass that name on to her children, unless she remains unmarried. In the past for a child to take the mother's and not the father's surname signified the shame of illegitimacy. For example, the mother of a child born during the Second World War into a working-class community, whose father was killed in action, had no problems in giving her son her family name. By contrast a boy born illegitimately in the first decade of the twentieth century into an upper-middle-class family was given a fictitious surname and fictitious parental history by his mother, who claimed she was his aunt, in order to preserve both their reputations.[131]

A woman's loss of her family name on marriage, which to many people's surprise has never been a legal requirement but rather a customary practice, signifies and reinforces her lack of self definition and the fluidity of her family identity. If she married more than once she may have been identified by at least three names during her lifespan. Family names, surnames, identify people with a wider group of kin connected to their father, but not to their mother, and to selective patrilineal ancestors.

The idea that we may have an affinity with these people because they share our name is a powerful stimulus to genealogists and family historians who fill our local record offices. The difficulties genealogists, biographers and historians have in tracing the female line back for more than a few generations reflect patrilineal naming. It is interesting to consider how restricted a version of family is re-created through those family trees which follow only the male line. Then, too, from the nineteenth century onwards women's marital status, but not men's, has been publicly displayed through the prefixes *Miss* and *Mrs*. And until around the 1960s, the

131. Examples from oral interviews with Katherine Holden: 'Margaret', December 1993; 'David', March 1994.

middle-class convention was for a married woman to be called by
her husband's first name as well – thus, Mrs James Prescott – and
only to revert to her own name – say, Amy Prescott – on widowhood
or divorce. The consequences of these practices, both practical and
psychological, for married women's entitlement to an identity of
their own have been acute.

The convention that names are primarily established through
genetic inheritance is open to question given the high incidence of
mistaken paternity. About 10 per cent of children in Britain are
currently estimated not to be children of their putative fathers
although they and the fathers think they are and even the mother
is often not certain.[132] It could be argued that genetic relationships
would be more reliably documented if traced through the female
line. The idea that traditions may be passed on through a surname
also hides the fact that it is women who most often maintain ties
between kin through letters, phone calls, visits and arranging family gatherings. Since they have often been closest to their mothers
and mothers' relations it is this side that may actually be better
preserved.

Imagined families created through genealogy mask the reality of
familial practice by commonly excluding illegitimate, fostered and
adopted offspring. For example, in one case, the name of an adopted
child was pasted onto a family tree as an afterthought to avoid
hurting his feelings and those of his immediate family.[133] Unrelated
household members were also ignored, or their own identities were
submerged, as Chapter 6 discusses in relation to servants. Such
naming practices could be palpable sources of identity for those
privileged by being included as well as for those disadvantaged by
exclusion. Occasionally, however, the 'black sheep' or outcast of the
family who goes so far as to repudiate the family name is enabled
to follow a fuller individual identity.

A name can also link the living to each other. Claims to a common surname indicating clan membership, though of less significance in England than in Scotland, may attach to particular places
but also to kin all over the world who may have no close genetic or
marital connection but who still identify through a family name.
Widely scattered and distantly related people, dispersed as a result
of their ancestors' emigration to the British Empire, still maintain

132. Cited in: 'So you think you know your father', *The Independent* (21 July 1997),
drawing on a study by Dr Philip Elliot in 1972 which revealed that on the basis of
samples taken from 200–300 families in south-east England, 30 per cent of the
children could not have been sired by their mothers' husbands.
133. Anonymous manuscript in possession of Katherine Holden.

links with the Mother Country through the traditions and emblems attached to their family names, such as crests and mottoes, or in Scotland tartans. Significantly, these were often invented by middle-class families in the nineteenth century in order to give their name a more aristocratic-sounding pedigree.

In the past, bloody territorial and nationalistic rivalries between clans revolved around their names, most famously rehearsed in Shakespeare's *Romeo and Juliet*. The overweening power the posses-sion of a family name could hold over an individual is brought out in Juliet's speech: "tis but thy name that is my enemy; thou art thyself not a Montague. What's Montague? it is nor hand, nor foot, nor arm, nor face, nor any other part belonging to a man.'[134]

In the past, as today, we recognize that primary relationships can and do arise according to gender, ethnic, class, religion, occupa-tional or national identity. Often these are congruent with familial relationships, but sometimes they are not. These identities can both build on and override familial and kin ties. It is not unknown even now for people to speak of outsiders as 'not one of us' or 'not O.C.D.' (Our Class, Dear). Relationships, alliances, affinities should perhaps be regarded as techniques that serve as best they can to maintain and reproduce, through physical reproduction *and* re-cruitment, whatever the group, institution, establishment, house, clan, class – or family – no matter what term is used.

The particular techniques used in the construction of the family may be visualized as a combination of the following: genetic inher-itance and relationship, marriage or adoption, similar appearance, a shared name, customs and traditions held in common, emotional, material and financial interdependence, mutual affection or expec-tations of obligation and duty. This list includes all aspects of blood, contract and intimacy. Yet, as we have acknowledged, our religious and cultural traditions, Middle Eastern, Judaic, Hellenic, Roman and Germanic as well as Christian, have cast the mother–child dyad, protected and dominated by a patriarch, as the most significant as well as the idealized form of family. This was then bolstered by aristocratic and later middle-class ideas about breeding and the relation of Man to Nature, with special attention to lines of descent.

Paradoxically, these traditions culminated in the modern ideal of the person, the rational thinking individual, the unique self, at the same time that the family retains its overwhelming emotional

134. William Shakespeare, *Romeo and Juliet*, Act 3, scene 3, line 104.

and symbolic importance. Family ties seem to gain by their sheer longevity, for 'in no other institution are relationships so extended in time, so intensive in contact, so dense in their interweaving of economics, emotions, power and resistance'.[135] Even now, it is the family which has filled a need for preserving memory, the unbroken self narrative.[136] Kin, home, household – family – the stuff we are made from. Despite legal and customary norms, it is not only a question of external definitions or of rational choice, but goes deep into attachments, the tangle of desire and feelings of both love and duty.

This shining web of interdependence has made the family the ideal and often the real setting for the awesome events of birth and death, our entrance to and exit from this world. As formal religion seems less and less a container for spirituality, we turn to personal relationships for intimations of transcendental meaning. Why else would the family and familial types of relationships be seen as the most precious site of morality?

It is almost impossible, therefore, for the concept of the family to contain and uphold all that we demand of it now. As this chapter has argued, family, and thus morality, cover different assignments for different people. Each of the received meanings of self, of kinship, of home and household, and of identity, in its own way silences too many voices with unspoken assumptions of divisions between the masculine and feminine. It is little girls who are sugar and spice, who are regarded as naturally more clean and good; the little boys – and their big brothers – more naturally prone to disorder and criminality. Indeed, as more and more relationships come to be seen as contractual and therefore legitimately amoral, the family with wife and mother as its core carries an ever heavier burden in upholding both intimacy and morality.

The family, whether embraced or rejected, thus remains the central moral unity in most people's lives, despite, as well as because of, the 'disengagement and commitment-avoidance' which now seem to colour much late twentieth-century life.[137] As this book attempts to show, the margins of the family may actually be porous, its forms protean and familial relationships almost infinitely varied, but the family story continues to have an emotional and even spiritual force lacking in so many other parts of our lives.

135. R.W. Connell, *Gender and Power* (Polity Press, 1986), p. 119.
136. Young-Eisendrath and Hall (eds), *The Book of the Self*, p. 456.
137. Zygmunt Bauman, 'From pilgrim to tourist – or a short history of identity', in Hall and P. DuGay (eds), *Questions of Cultural Identity*, p. 33.

PART TWO

Families 1830–1914

CHAPTER FOUR

Social and cultural change: the nineteenth century

All comforts [are] exposed on the brink of a precipice with a loose and crumbling soil. Disease and accidents have keys for every door.

Ann Taylor Gilbert, *c*.1825[1]

In many ways the modern understanding of the family was a creation of the nineteenth century. It was those generations that so busily elevated familial relationship and cultivated the ideal of Home. The family was the counter-side to individualistic rationality; the interdependence of husband and wife a moral contract at the heart of a capitalist market society. It was both a God-given and a hierarchical interdependence, a supposed Eden where everyone 'knew their place'.

But the constituents of home and family changed over the period and were never identical for different strata in different parts of the country. The meanings and values attached to family even within the same group could be varied and often contradictory. The model of family harmony was in tension with more radical ideas about familial relations such as the beliefs of Owenite Socialists. They maintained that the enslavement of women by men made social hierarchies natural and inevitable, a view which was perceived as highly threatening to social stability in the 1820s and 1830s.[2] It is significant that, by contrast, the more overtly political Chartist movement twenty years later tempered the attack on the sexual division of labour and paternal authority to emphasize adherence

1. Josiah Gilbert (ed.), *Autobiography and other Memorials of Mrs Gilbert* (1874), Vol. II, p. 19.
2. Barbara Taylor, *Eve and the New Jerusalem: Socialism and Feminism in the 19th Century* (Virago, 1983).

to acceptable domesticity.[3] What the family was and should be was open to wide debate.

This chapter, then, considers the material circumstances, the beliefs, ideas and institutions which interacted with family life from the 1830s to the First World War. Before looking at specific absences in histories of families, it is important to establish the key areas of social, economic, political and cultural life which families shaped and were shaped by. In doing so, the conceptual frameworks and languages discussed in Chapter 3 can be put into action, drawing on the work of historians across a wide range of approaches. After discussing the broad material and cultural milieus for family life of this period, there follows a consideration of those features specific to different social classes, ranging from the upper strata to the poor, and within institutional settings.

Material life

In early nineteenth-century England, the overwhelming facts of life were still poverty, illness and death. Even the better off faced hazards of early death and bankruptcy, as Ann Taylor Gilbert reflected above. Under these circumstances, people turned to various sources of security. Religious belief, magic or fatalism might provide solace, but for practical and emotional support, patrons, kin and family, those you could expect to trust, were the primary bulwark.

By the late nineteenth century, new issues, novel technological and social arrangements had begun to reshape this vision of the family. For centuries people had measured distances by walking time or the speed at which a horse could travel. But from the end of the eighteenth century, the need to transport more materials – and people – for longer distances meant development of canals, improved roads and coaches, coastal sail, and later steam vessels, and above all, from the 1830s, that marvellous monster, the railway. And people were moving about. It might have been to the colonies or only to the next town, but any new environment widened horizons.

Improved transport and lower prices also meant more and faster distribution of information. The first penny post in 1841 and the lifting of various taxes added to the flood of printed material for the eager reading and writing public. By the 1870s, photographs

---

3. Anna Clark, *The Struggle for the Breeches: Gender and the Making of the British Working Class* (University of California Press, 1995).

became more affordable and circulated with letters to and from families, keeping memories alive and cementing friendships, even contacts between those who had never met. The telegraph now carried news and messages, both commercial and intimate, around the world in hours rather than months.

For family and friends it became easier, but also more of a duty, to keep in touch, to use such ties for mutual help and agreeable intercourse. For example, at the beginning of the century news of a death in the family could take weeks, the corpse long buried, before relatives could be alerted. But now family members could attend even distant funerals; long-standing rituals of family inclusion and exclusion were extended and altered. So too was practical assistance. In 1842, when a daughter living in London contracted typhus, her mother, living over sixty miles away, was able to rush to her bedside using the 'penny-a-mile' train.[1] Such maternal solicitude would have been impossible fifty years earlier. Even when there was no crisis, extensive visiting and correspondence, at least for the better off, widened and maintained family relationships.

If the miracle railway held both fascination and terror for the first generations, so too did its industrial base. Machinery was Victorian England's cultural icon; the entrepreneur, Manchester Man, was its hero, the wave of the future. Families and households, like communities, were often compared to both businesses and vast machines, each part working, it was hoped, harmoniously with the others to produce goods, people, the machinery of life. But there were also disruptive social consequences of machine production.

Women and children had become the first factory workers, overturning received notions about the sexual division of labour. There was urban sprawl, overcrowding and disease. These disruptive forces were countered by intense longing for a rural, pre-industrialized landscape romantically encapsulated by that whitewashed, thatched cottage, surrounded by sturdy rosy-cheeked children and deferential agricultural labourers. The tug of these two imaginary and contradictory models, the factory and the cottage, can be traced in the growing tendency for living places to be separated from sites of commerce and industry. The models were bolstered as the individual wage replaced family resources based on household production.

By the end of the eighteenth century, the common practice of young people leaving home to live and work as apprentices or farm servants in the master's (or mistress's) household was falling into

4. Aaron Smith, 'Pocket diaries 1837–1846', *East Anglian Miscellany* (1928).

disuse. Increasingly, waged day labour was more appropriate to both industrial production and the capitalist arable farming which had made it possible to feed the expanding urban masses. Service and apprenticeship had been a means of saving up for marriage. Now younger people could set up their own household and the population had grown rapidly. But there was also a feeling that it was no longer genteel or even respectable for the family and servants to muck in together in the 'houseplace', as the old working kitchens had been called. Now servants and apprentices more often ate separately. Old rituals such as the Harvest Supper with its special ales, its inclusive ribald songs, the lavish spread with master and mistress at the head of the table, had changed to a separate meal provided in the kitchen, with the farmer and his wife putting in an appearance from the newly created parlour only for the final toasts.

Changes were piecemeal, varying from industry to industry, region to region. For a good part of the century, only a small proportion of the working population was actually employed in factories. Nevertheless, those working mainly on the land diminished from over two-thirds at the beginning of the century to under one-tenth in 1900. At the same time there was a significant shift away from people making their living from a mixture of activities. Outside the textile, mining and pottery areas, most households had provided a livelihood from a combination of food raised on a small plot of land and/or keeping a cow or pig on common land, itinerant labour, domestic or farm service, trading at local markets, and workshop and home-based manufacturing using hand tools and simple processes.[5]

Gradually men, at least, took on a single, more permanent and specialized occupation. The census, which did not list individual occupations until 1851, recorded and thus also helped to create the idea of a fixed, lifetime set of skills as an important element in masculinity. When adult men did enter factories, they and their employers regarded their abilities and final destinations as more skilled and authoritative than their female counterparts. For example, the Courtauld brothers had deliberately designed their silk production, including the invention of machinery, around a division between older men as a core of highly paid skilled mechanics and overseers and a mass of lower paid, less skilled boys, girls and women.[6]

5. Shani D'Cruz, 'Gender, diligence and "usfull pride" [sic]: gender, industrialisation and the domestic economy, c.1770–1840', *Women's History Review*, Vol. 3, No. 3 (1994).
6. Judy Lown, *Women and Industrialisation: Gender at Work in Nineteenth Century England* (Polity Press, 1990).

The labour of younger children had always been used in house-hold-based production: bird scaring, wool processing, fetching water and wood, baby-minding. And child labour had been frequently used for unskilled processes in workshops and factories. As the expectation that young children should contribute to their own keep slowly waned, the belief that parents, especially fathers, should support their children, as well as husbands maintain their wives, gained acceptance. The idea of the standard family with adult male breadwinner and a non-waged housewife/mother only employed in childcare and housework (also a word coined in this period) had been especially promoted by the new Poor Law of 1834. But it was a long time becoming the norm as few working-class households were able to conform to such expectations.

The establishment of waged work as the basis of livelihood affected both rural and urban households. Although miners and agricultural labourers continued to live in tied housing provided by their em-ployers, the Truck Acts of the 1830s had made it illegal to pay for labour with food or other necessities. Cash was becoming the only meaningful means of exchange, although informal barter continued to thrive in many communities. The most obvious expression of this shift can be found in the work contract. By the 1870s, amid some-times violent clashes, the law of Workman (note) and Employer replaced the old rules of Master and Servant which had given almost total control to the master. Now the cash nexus gave formal equality before the law, a development coinciding with the formation of modern trade unions and a nascent labour movement committed to men's wages high enough to support their wives and children.

By the end of the century, the working day and week had been shortened for many; the lucky few were now able to enjoy annual holidays. More time free from work allowed more time for family activities. It also created a demand for more commercial leisure provisions such as the music hall and professional football. How-ever, married women, with their double burden of housework and work for money income, could take little part in what were mainly masculine pastimes.[7]

The structure and composition of households were also affected by the reduction of women's employment in areas such as mining, metalworking and field labour (except for the harvest) sometimes through legal exclusion as with the Mines Act of 1846. As single

7. Hugh Cunningham, *Leisure in the Industrial Revolution 1780–1880* (Croom Helm, 1980).

lifetime occupations for men became more firmly established in people's minds (if not in reality), women's work became more problematic. Historical accident had made women's presence in textile manufacture, dressmaking, millinery and the keeping of small shops acceptable. But the overwhelming sentiment among middle-class commentators was that residential domestic service was the only unproblematic wage-earning position for women, and many now had little choice but to take up this option. In the words of a contemporary, domestic servants living within the household were 'attached to others and connected to other existences which they embellish, facilitate and serve. In a word, they fulfil both essential of woman's being: *they are supported by, and they administer to, men'* (his emphasis).[8] All philanthropic institutions for girls trained them for no other occupation until well into the twentieth century.

The shift to more continuous waged work for labouring people was part of wider changes in economic life. Commercial and manufacturing trades, the professions, farming, had all expanded dramatically over this period. The single entrepreneur or simple partnership between male relatives had been the common pattern, as we have seen, as wives, who were often *de facto* partners, were legally barred from entering into commercial contracts. But by the end of this period the partnership had for many been transformed first into the business house or the private company and by the early twentieth century a few at least into large public companies. In the earlier decades, the more affluent had envisaged business and the professions as a way of providing a livelihood, setting up an 'establishment' of both family and work activities, with family the more important. Now work was becoming an encompassing part of men's identity.[9]

Financial facilities such as banks grew alongside expanding opportunities for trade with the Continent and Empire. So too did larger units, more heavily capitalized businesses and more highly qualified professionals with greater demand for their services. One of the most dramatic changes can be seen in the introduction of limited liability in the 1860s. For the first time the resources and finances of the business or professional unit were clearly to be separated from the family and household. The threat of total bankruptcy, when house, furniture and personal possessions down to the

8. William Greg, 'Why are women redundant?', *National Review*, Vol. 15 (1862), p. 451.
9. Leonore Davidoff and Catherine Hall, *Family Fortunes: Men and Women of the English Middle Class 1780–1850* (Routledge, 1994), Part II.

wife's petticoats could be swept away in the uncertain commercial climate, was finally lifted. Men, as husbands, fathers and brothers, were set free to act in the public world without endangering the livelihood of wives, daughters and sisters. Another significant indicator of these arrangements was the spread of life assurance, used mainly by men with a salary or fee income which ceased at their death, in order to make provision for dependants.

The nineteenth-century ascendant middle class founded innumerable voluntary and philanthropic societies which bridged the gap between the fierce market economy and the supposedly gentler world of home. Professional and business men, as trustees, managers and guardians, became responsible for dependants outside as well as inside their own families. In such organizations the day-to-day work was often done by middle-class women, those men's wives, daughters and other female relatives. The highest echelons, as with political office, tended to be the preserve of the gentry and aristocracy. And it was among the gentry, the untitled but landed, in their manor houses, both large and small, that new money, often brought through judicious marriage, could nestle. In these strategic amalgamations, family and kinship relations as well as patronage – or, as it was sometimes called, friendship – from the greater to the lesser played a key role.

Even the gentry had been affected by change. The legal and institutional frameworks of marriage, property and inheritance could no longer cope with the scale of new developments. Reform of the legal system was necessary to clear away more archaic forms; more flexible inheritance, marriage and divorce procedures were gradually introduced. Feminist political pressure had also been used to extend the rights of married women.[10] At the other end of the social scale, the new Poor Laws imposed an increasing burden on the poorest families, no longer dealt with by local, customary practices or eligible for 'out relief' in their own homes. Now those without means of support were forced to enter the new purpose-built workhouses, wives and children with no option but to follow the husband/father when he entered or left. Once inside, families were divided, adult men separated from women, and children separated from both parents. The shame of public failure to survive as a family unit drove some to starvation rather than enter such institutions.

10. Mary Shanley, *Feminism, Marriage and the Law in Victorian England, 1850–1895* (Princeton University Press, 1989).

For all the stress on the sanctity of the home, by the late nine-teenth century the inner life of working-class households had become the object of both voluntary societies and state organizations. Restrictions on child and female labour, civil registration of births, deaths and marriages, compulsory vaccination of children, regulation of lodging houses, registration of 'baby farms' to prevent infanticide, compulsory education, provision of social housing, mechanisms for child protection and control, and the beginnings of welfare provision with the first state pensions, were accompanied by scientific social surveys on a range of issues.[11] These measures were aimed mainly at families who were regarded as unable or unwilling to fulfil their social or moral obligations. They did not address issues of unequal wealth, power and resources either between families or within them. Combined with a rising standard of living for those in work, this contributed to the growing wedge between the 'respect-able' and the minority of the 'rough'.

Ideas, beliefs and institutions

At this time, when about three-quarters of the population spent most of their waking lives in hard manual and mental labour simply to survive, the views of their world were deeply coloured by their immediate surroundings. For those in rural areas, the natural world was a vivid reality, their beliefs embracing a pantheon of animals, trees and plants, even as they submitted to a predominantly Christian culture. For example, in mid-century Lincolnshire the practice of 'telling the bees' dictated that after the death of the family head, the new father/husband/master must take funeral food to the bees and tell them of the change, emphasizing transition from old paternal authority to new, from death to ongoing life.[12]

With migration to the towns, many of these beliefs became attenuated into fatalism, a pessimistic dependence on chance and luck. Before the mid century, a minority sought more or less uto-pian solutions to their often desperate lives in forms of communal ownership of land or productive enterprise, or by political representation through the people's Charter. For substantial numbers, however, it was evangelical enthusiasm, the open-air preaching of

11. Eileen J. Yeo, *The Contest for Social Science: Relations and Representations of Gender and Class* (Rivers Oram Press, 1996).

12. James Obelkevich, *Religion and Rural Society: South Lindsey 1825–1875* (Clarendon Press, 1976), p. 297.

Methodists, the cottage religion of Bible Christians, which salved their troubled souls and gave them some hopes for the future, if only in the afterlife. Undoubtedly, despite the numerical preponderance of non-churchgoers which so alarmed contemporary commentators, a Christian tint permeated the climate of the times, not least because of the grip of the Churches, whether established or dissenting, on the education of the young.

All denominations had been touched by the waves of evangelical zeal of the early century. Salvation was a universal possibility where the most modest could claim equality with the most wealthy or socially elevated. Both women and young people followed the white-hot call to conversion, a legitimate reason to break from constraints of family ties, of a master's authority, and obey instead a Father in Heaven. At the same time, the family had become a central feature of religious life, the home its most perfect location. In the imaginary ideal family, the earthly father mirrored that Heavenly Father, now less the glorious throne of God than a Heavenly Home where all family members could unite in perfect harmony. It was increasingly the family's, particularly the mother's, task to raise second- and third-generation 'cradle Christians'; the practice of family prayers reached a peak at mid century.

This domesticated, committed religious life flourished particularly within the middle ranks of bankers, lawyers, medical men, farmers, manufacturers and business people. In their unpredictable lives, religious attachment brought both spiritual security and practical assistance. Marriages were made within church or chapel circles, capital could be raised among fellow worshippers, as were potential customers or clients. The community of believers could be seen as an extended circle of family and friends.

In the 1840s some upper-middle-class men felt that religious feeling had become too domesticated and trivialized. The Anglo-Catholic movement emerging from the masculine atmosphere of Oxford can be interpreted as partly a search for a male-bonded culture which recovered the richness, colour and music increasingly denied to men. It offered aspects of the spiritual nourishment of Victorian femininity without the interference of women. Later these High Anglicans founded a series of Brotherhoods and eventually permitted a form of Sisterhood, the closest to a monastic life seen since the Reformation. Here members lived in single-sex groups separated from existing families. Yet their naming practices and relationships were based on a family model, as were those of the Christian Socialists who went to live in settlement houses where committed young men and women came to do good works for the urban poor in East London and other slum areas. While there were fewer Christian organizations for women established, the practice spread of lay women visiting the poor, although always, at least nominally, under the fatherly supervision of the priest or minister.[13]

Churches were giving more public recognition to the roles of women, although this was always based on their primary position as home-maker, wife and mother. The Mothers' Union, founded in 1876 as the established Church's answer to the thrusting activities of nonconformist sects, had 200,000 members by 1900.[14] It acted as an umbrella group for married mothers to meet and to ensure the dominance of Christian family values in a period of lessening church attachment. Such a widening of pastoral concerns to include the admission of poverty, ill health and bad fortune as important Christian issues marked a change in a religious impetus which was gradually being displaced by secular concerns.

The foundations of faith were being queried by the new dating of the Creation offered by palaeontologists, by the historical interpretation of the life of Jesus and, above all, by Darwinian views of evolution. These upsetting ideas were emerging at a time when a series of political and social shocks at home and in the Empire broke mid Victorian complacency: the Indian mutiny of 1857, the parlous state of the armed services revealed by the Crimean War in the 1850s, the insurrection in the Jamaican colony brutally suppressed by Governor Eyre in 1865, the depression of the 1870s which particularly affected the landed interest, the near riots of the destitute led by London's East End dockers in the 1880s and the first recognition of serious industrial competition from America and Germany.

The family as a bulwark against such threatened social and cultural disintegration was elevated as people sought for a moral order less constrained by doctrinaire religious belief. This was exemplified by the extraordinary success of Mrs Humphry Ward's novel *Robert Elesmere* (1888), which sold 400,000 copies at first publication and kept MPs avidly reading through the night, calling forth a review by Gladstone himself. The eponymous hero was a young clergyman who, under the influence of an agnostic and bachelor

---

13. C.M. Prelinger, 'The female diaconate in the Anglican Church: what kind of ministry for women?', in G. Malmgreen (ed.), *Religion in the Lives of English Women 1760–1930* (Croom Helm, 1986).

14. James Obelkevich, 'Religion', *Cambridge Social History of Britain* (Cambridge University Press, 1990), Vol. 3, p. 341.

squire, loses his faith in revealed religion and feels forced to give up his country parish. His doubts are set in contrast to his wife's deep, abiding faith in the old forms. His greatest torment, which eventually kills him, is the effect his lapse has on her and his golden-haired little daughter.

> [Robert] knew that to such Christian purity, such Christian inward-ness as Catherine's the ultimate sanction and legitimacy of marriage rests, both in theory and practice, on a common acceptance of the definite commands and promises of a miraculous revelation.[15]

Elesmere, like many others, was on the brink of jettisoning belief in miraculous revelation but clung to the morality, sense of duty and above all commitment to an idealized family. The power of these emotions is reflected in late nineteenth-century nostalgia for the paradise of innocent childhood in upper-middle-class nursery culture and the flowering of children's literature.[16]

The interrelationship of spirituality and family in the tumultu-ous final decades of the nineteenth century is well illustrated in three movements operating at different social levels. The Salvation Army, founded in 1865 and growing rapidly thereafter, captured the imagination and the hearts of the poor and unskilled. Anyone could join; salvation was the message, music the method and the street the meeting place. The conversion experience made sense of a world stalked by disease, violent death and endogenous unem-ployment. The uniformed army provided an ordered alternative family and source of power, and, for men, a redefinition of manli-ness for those whose status as household head was precarious. The appeal to women combined opportunities to preach and hold office with respect for their family role. The Salvation Army made full use of that Victorian icon, the Praying Mother. In its lexicon, drink, prostitution, the pub and the music hall equalled sin; salva-tion was home and family.[17]

Spiritualist belief and practice swept urban England from the 1860s. Its practices, the seances, the sightings in drawing rooms, and the emergence of women and later young girls as the most potent mediums, were particularly compatible with the closed family world

---

15. Mrs Humphry Ward, *Robert Elesmere* (Oxford University Press, 1987), p. 361.
16. Discussed in Jacqueline Rose, *The Case of Peter Pan or the Impossibility of Chil-dren's Fiction* (Macmillan, 1984).
17. Pamela Walker, ' "I live but not yet I for Christ liveth in me": men and mas-culinity in the Salvation Army 1865–90', in Michael Roper and John Tosh (eds), *Manful Assertions: Masculinities in Britain since 1800* (Routledge, 1991).

of the urban lower middle and upper working class. The search for
lost family members on 'the other side' provided a powerful motive.
As an editorial in a Spiritualist journal noted in the 1870s:

> Spiritualism is essentially a domestic institution . . . Spiritual mani-
> festations have been most successfully evolved in select companies,
> more particularly in the family circle, or where there is a kinship of
> spiritual development similar to true family affinity. Mediums have
> the greatest degree of power and communications are purest, when
> present in select and harmonious gatherings of which a well-ordered
> family is a type.[18]

A few decades later, women and femininity also found a home in
the Theosophical movement, which attracted mainly the professional upper middle classes with a scattering of gentry and aristocracy. Founded on a blend of Western science, spiritualism and
Eastern mysticism, the movement's influence went far beyond the
small number of members through the numerous social and political leaders who embraced its beliefs. Theosophists' conviction of
reincarnation meant that a present assignment to a male or female
body might be reversed in future, that a range of social, sexual and
familial relationships were interchangeable. The acceptance of both
masculine and feminine characteristics within the same person was
in keeping with the concerns of many searching for an intermediate way, whether they were practising homosexuals, feminists, or
just men and women uneasy with existing gender relations.[19]

The concern to prove such belief systems scientific is under-
standable, given the increasing professional dominance and cre-
dence given to formal science by the 1880s. Current assumptions
about gender and family permeated scientific and medical systems
and their professional organizations. *Anthropology* as the study of
man played a role in building a hierarchy of peoples based on the
ideas of evolution. The educated English white male stood at the
apex of civilization because of his physique and brain size. Women,
the poor and black people were considered biologically inferior,
beliefs suited to the general hardening of opinions about the physi-
ological basis of social hierarchies. On the other hand, *gynaecology*,

18. Quoted in Alex Owen, 'The other voice: women, children and nineteenth
century spiritualism', in Caroline Steedman *et al.* (eds), *Language, Gender and Childhood* (Routledge & Kegan Paul, 1985), p. 52.
19. Joy Dixon, 'Gender, politics and culture in the new age: Theosophy in England 1880–1935', Ph.D. thesis, Rutgers University (1993); Judith Walkowitz, *City of
Dreadful Delight: Narratives of Sexual Danger in Late Victorian London* (Virago, 1992).

the study of woman, had narrowed to a medical specialty solely concerned with female reproductive capacities.[20]

While individual physicians and scientists became involved in feminist causes, most of these male professionals had an antipathy to interfering in received ideas about marriage and family. The precedent of taking the male head of household's gainful occupation as the fundamental generic social category or unit of identity set by the General Registry Office in the decennial census was used without question in all social and economic investigations, an outstanding example being Charles Booth's monumental survey of life and labour in London in the 1890s.

In practical terms, medical men came to dominate over older systems such as the use of herbal medicines which had been the province mainly of women. More affluent families now consulted private doctors, others made do with services offered by the Poor Law and hospitals or relied on older methods of self-doctoring and the neighbourhood wise woman. Medical men were becoming oracles on all issues of mental and physical health, giving evidence in court, pronouncing on sanitary questions or enforcing children's vaccinations. These public roles as well as private practice were gaining for them some of the social and moral prestige formally given to the clergy. Doctors had developed particularly close relationships with married women, and could invoke fear and resentment as well as trust, even love. Medical students by the 1880s were being advised that the key to becoming general practitioners and family doctors was through the successful management of the diseases of women.[21]

By the late nineteenth century, diagnosis and administration of heroic surgical procedures in the hands of male doctors was combined with nursing care carried out by women, mainly within their own households but also by a growing number of formal and informal nurses. Skill and care in nursing the sick and dying was an expected, integral part of nineteenth-century femininity, and the tasks this entailed were becoming more onerous as knowledge about the connection of disease with dirt and about nutrition developed, even before the discovery of the role of bacteria. Cleanliness and order were seen as crucial both to health and to the respectability of the family and were the special responsibility of its female members.

20. Ornella Muscucci, *The Science of Woman: Gynaecology and Gender in England 1800–1929* (Cambridge University Press, 1990).

21. Cited in Anne Digby, *Making a Medical Living: Doctors and Patients in the English Market for Medicine 1720–1911* (Cambridge University Press, 1994), p. 254.

Patterns of family life

For all social strata, geographical mobility, shifting lifestyles, fluid household structures and many different forms of housing were the norm rather than the exception. For example, a survey of Northampton in the 1900s found 330 distinct groupings of people within households.[22] Furthermore, almost all the information we have on the way both families and households were made up is from snapshot pictures, the categories pre-determined, which may give a spurious solidity to structures in sources such as the census. But from other types of evidence it is clear that there could be much shifting in an individual's situation over relatively short periods, let alone a lifetime. People moved house and household with a frequency which would seem strange and uncomfortable to late twentieth-century sensibilities. Renting was almost universal, even middle-class tenancies being renewable after at most seven years. For all groups, moving to less expensive housing was a prime way of making ends meet.

There was also much variation in the ages at which people left home and married, while second marriages, mainly through death of a spouse, produced as many reconstituted families as divorce has done in the late twentieth century.[23] There were variations in family patterns between regions, between urban and rural areas and between the many overlapping social strata, often living cheek by jowl as the population grew.

Here we can only offer a sketch of four family settings. The first two, upper and working class, shared in some ways domestic lives where the ideal of home and family had arguably less impact than it had for the middle classes. The middle strata, which we consider next, promoted ideals of domesticity and correct behaviour in both state and voluntary societies' policies. Our fourth example, those institutions which replaced or supplemented family life, reflect their influence.

The upper strata

By the 1830s, new wealth based on trade, commerce and finance was threatening to overwhelm the traditional lifestyle of the gentry,

---

22. Bowley and Hurst, quoted in Anna Davin, *Growing Up Poor: Home, School and Street in London 1870–1914* (Rivers Oram Press, 1996), p. 42.
23. Michael Anderson, 'The social implications of demographic change', *Cambridge Social History of Britain* (Cambridge University Press, 1900), Vol. 2.

and even of the lesser aristocracy. Their code of honour had included lavish hospitality and patronage, participation in the social
and political life of the local region and, if of sufficient wealth and
breeding, of the national elite with its pinnacle in the monarchy,
the greatest House of all. Intermarriage had always been a means
of absorbing the *nouveau riche*. But now the sheer numbers called
forth more elaborated mechanisms of inclusion and exclusion, an
intense preoccupation with gentility. There grew up strict access
rituals of Society, punctuated by the events of the Season. To be
genuinely part of Society necessitated having been presented by a
patron to the Sovereign at Court, for both men and women. The
same procedure of introduction through an acknowledged inter-
mediary operated throughout lesser social circles. Coming of good
family was the only sure entry, although great wealth undoubtedly
helped to open doors.

Before reform of local and national politics in the 1880s, political interests had gathered around great houses in groups of like-
minded kin and friends. The role of the political hostess was central
to public life. In 1900, in a crisis over tax reform, one hostess tried
to negotiate a truce between her brothers and reformers on opposite sides of the tariff question. She noted that while her other
guests played bridge she made sure that 'the boys could come to an
understanding'.[24]

In such households, the public arena's primary purpose was
entertainment, formal functions to set the seal on social acceptance, for, as one hostess remarked, 'the roof is an introduction'.[25]
The complicated business of calling and leaving cards was constructed to keep distance between social levels and acknowledge
the identity of a family. Formal calls were made to mark rituals of
the life cycle, such as after marriage or childbirth, as well as the
more ordinary weekly times of being At Home to receive visitors.
Such a system put duty to family well above individual preference,
especially for girls and women.

One of the prime purposes of such formality was to oversee
suitable marriages within the group. Young unmarried women were
expected to be chaperoned and not allowed away from a family
context on their own. Marriage and family alliances were the cornerstone of the system, as witnessed by the interconnecting web of

24. Quoted in Pat Jalland, *Women, Marriage and Politics 1860–1914* (Oxford University Press, 1986), p. 238.
25. Quoted in Leonore Davidoff, *The Best Circles: 'Society', Etiquette and the Season*
(Hutchinson, 1986), p. 42.

relationships between the great Tory and Whig dynasties or within the 'intellectual aristocracy', such as the Wedgwoods and Darwins.[26] For wives and female relatives of high church dignitaries, headmasters of public schools, fellows of Oxbridge colleges (first allowed to marry in the 1890s), diplomats and armed service officers, or those who had simply 'married a country house', calling and entertaining connected to the annual rituals of these various institutions were an intrinsic part of their role. It was their duty to run an establishment worthy of that position. Private familial activities were relegated to nursery, schoolroom and bedroom, while all domestic work was done by servants.

It is no wonder, then, that these houses could resemble less a haven than a military headquarters where social strategies were launched, rivals sighted and routed, a literary or musical lion captured as a drawing card to evening entertainment, and where the dinner party was the zenith of the system. The battleground may have been drawing and dining rooms, the weapons troops of servants, ball gowns, the beauty of a daughter, the net worth of a husband, the acquisition of a famous chef, but the final aim of demonstrating social position was well understood.

Despite huge disparities in wealth and household plant, the regulation of social behaviour was in some senses common to all family practices. The introduction of the young to their social sphere, the making and breaking of financial as well as marital reputations, the ostracizing, if necessary, of those who were defined as 'not one of us', whether done from behind the lace curtain, via gossip over the teacups, over the backyard fence or in the street doorway, was not so very different from what was done in the grand ballroom. Such practices were an endemic part of family identity and moral duty, militating against the more personal, emotional and nurturing aspects with which we now define family. Among the very wealthy and socially powerful, they had become the most important aspect of family life, dominating the layout of houses, the use of time and manifold resources.

Working-class families

Family reputation was also a vital working-class asset at all social levels, for self-respect as much as for being able to raise credit, if

26. Noel Annan, 'The intellectual aristocracy', in J. Plumb (ed.), *Studies in Social History* (Longman Green, 1955).

only with the corner shop. Those without capital or even skill to fall
back on, without political power, and represented by no organizations, were the most vulnerable, whether from trade recession, personal tragedy, illness or desertion, any of which meant disappearance
into the abyss, a favourite Victorian metaphor. The overriding necessity to find income meant a settled family life could be delayed or
disrupted by the need to travel for work. Men, if sufficiently skilled,
could use their membership of trade unions or Friendly Societies
to find lodgings and employment while on the tramp. But for the
main tide of immigrants, women as well as men, flowing into larger
towns or new areas of work as when the Welsh coalfields opened
late in the century, kinsfolk and former neighbours were the main
avenue to finding shelter and work in the new surroundings.

Such networks could extend around the globe in the great exodus
to the colonies and Empire. And some occupations were intrinsically itinerant: soldiers, sailors, merchant seamen, domestic servants,
building labourers, laundry workers, brick makers, fish gutters, and,
above all, harvesters, flowed in and out of regions, houses, families
as the seasons and exigencies of employment dictated. Those who
moved frequently were less able to build up knowledge of the local
community and networks of charitable support. Not coincidentally
the most rootless and feared were the navvies, travellers and gypsies, the latter a dark-complexioned people who, it was believed,
stole property or even the precious blond, blue-eyed English child,
the heart of the family ideal.[27] Thus, for the majority, family or
personal relationships – neighbours, friends, accidental contacts –
based on trust and/or mutual interest were crucial ballast in the
perilous journey of their lives.

Although for many working-class people formal marriage was
neither affordable nor desired, young people of both sexes usually
sought reasonably stable unions. But the custom of self-help weddings, where troth was plighted by such rituals as jumping over a
broomstick or exchanging rings, was declining. Increased pressure
from reinvigorated Church authorities encouraged the equation
of marriage lines with respectability. Practices such as wife sale,
immortalized in Thomas Hardy's *The Mayor of Casterbridge*, where
a woman would be led to market by her husband with a halter
round her neck to be given to another man for token payment,
had become outrageous to middle-class opinion. Yet these transfers

27. An exploration of the meanings of darkness and lightness, particularly linking
darkness with gypsies and with evil, can be found in Emily Bronte's *Wuthering Heights*,
Vol. 1, Ch. 4, where Heathcliffe is called a 'gipsy brat' by Mrs Earnshaw.

could sometimes be negotiated at the wife's instigation. Similarly, jumping over the broomstick backwards to end a relationship had been one of many flexible practices which fitted the instability of working-class life and could be especially useful for women.

Formal marriage was also increasingly enforced by state authorities and charitable organizations attempting to separate the married from more casual cohabiters. Legislation such as the Contagious Diseases Acts of the 1860s, where special police rounded up suspected prostitutes, began to winkle out 'professionals' from the woman who might have more casual affairs, or on/off long-term commitments. Evidence shows that the meanings given to marriage and coupledom could differ to the point of mutual incomprehension. In a well-known trial of 1870, Harriet Hicks, when asked whether she was still a prostitute, replied, 'No, only to the one man', meaning her common-law husband.[28]

While rising real wages during the 1880s meant fewer wives and mothers had to find waged work, the unwillingness or inability of husbands and fathers to provide steady maintenance remained a central problem for household stability. Many men subscribed to a code of masculinity which stressed the responsible and kindly husband and father, but wives and mothers had few real sanctions to enforce maintenance. A wife's home was technically her husband's; her income belonged to him. Only late in the century could a woman sue for a maintenance order following proven separation, but this was a difficult and costly business. Then, too, married women and widows had no direct access to trade union or Friendly Society funds since it was the husband's membership which determined their eligibility. This conception of the sexual division of labour within marriage carried over into social insurance legislation well into the twentieth century.

In parliamentary legislation, case law, charity work and political discussion of the family, concern with maintaining women's dependent role was matched by recognition that a stress on manliness exhibited by breadwinning and support of dependants was the surest way to lock men, particularly young men, into steady work. Going to sea, or the safety valve of the Empire, might siphon off the worst of masculine restiveness, but the responsible working man supporting his wife and family was seen as the backbone of society by conservatives and radicals alike. These underlying fears surface in Charles Booth's statement:

28. Quoted in Judith Walkowitz, *Prostitution and Victorian Society: Women, Class and the State* (Cambridge University Press, 1980), p. 203.

The club loafer of Piccadilly and the unkempt and ill-clad vagabond sleeping away the summer day on the grass of St James Park are often influenced by much the same desire – to attain the advantages of the associate life without the cares of housekeeping.[29]

It was recognized that the wife was the central point around which family and household rotated. The common custom of husbands and adult children 'tipping up' their weekly wage to wife/mother indicates that it was she who organized consumption and negotiated credit, often desperately trying to tie spending to resources, both labour and money. She often had to fund supplementary earnings, practising skills of the informal economy, especially pawning, to make up routine shortages. It has been estimated that wives and children contributed about 25 per cent of household income, although much depended on what was available in the local area. But even where men's wages were good and work steady, the standard of living depended on many other factors, especially the wife's health, strength and skill. For example, in a steel town like Middlesbrough with little work even for juvenile males, much less girls and women, high wages for adult men could not counteract the toll of illness and accidents from the heavy labour in the steel mills. Particularly in such regions the intensely male, work-oriented culture meant that even organized labour took little interest in domestic issues such as provision of water supplies which would have contributed much to family welfare in the long run.[30]

Family propriety was used as a vital resource by working-class wives: for credit, gaining access to work and the respectability demanded by charities. Clothes were a vivid and visible sign of status. 'My mother was a dressmaker and she always kept us nicely dressed and no one knew we were poor', recalled the child of a woman who was supreme at making things do.[31] Even where living space was cramped, the front room was often kept apart for ritual occasions such as wedding parties and funerals. A decent funeral was vital as a source of family identity and pride, supported painstakingly by weekly payments for burial insurance, drawing together the whole court or street.

Where clothes and furnishings were unavailable, food became the crucial item to preserve health, even life, as well as evidence of care and a certain standing among others. In a society where

29. Charles Booth, *Life and Labour of the People in London* (Macmillan, 1892), Vol. 1, p. 206.
30. Trevor Lummis, *The Labour Aristocracy 1851–1914* (Scolar Press, 1994), p. 140.
31. Thea Thompson, *Edwardian Childhoods* (Routledge & Kegan Paul, 1981), p. 105.

starvation was still possible, meals signified safety and comfort. The putting of food into the children's stomachs was the ultimate test of motherhood, as preparing food acceptable to the man was the ultimate test of wifehood. Irate exhausted husbands on returning from work for their tea might throw the precious meal on the fire as a grand gesture of disgust and masculine prerogative. The status given to food is illustrated in the language of the Sunday dinner which dominated the working week in the urban, wage-oriented household. An East Londoner recollecting a 1900s childhood poignantly portrayed its role in denoting respectability: whether or not his mother had any real Sunday dinner to serve, she always rattled the plates for the other tenants to hear at the appropriate time.[32]

Wives and mothers often fed others before themselves, sometimes existing on 'kettle broth', dry bread sopped in water or tea, even when pregnant and breastfeeding, thus leaving a terrible legacy of undernourishment and illness, not only for themselves but for future generations. Numerous pregnancies, miscarriages and still-births, plus the burden of living, but frequently ailing, children, aged young women quickly when accompanied by chronic malnutrition, appalling housing conditions and constant worry about making ends meet. This was a recipe for the deadening of emotion. Robert Roberts, who grew up in late nineteenth-century Salford, observed how 'kindliness, sensitivity, intelligence' were stifled, the 'too much sacrifice' that turns the heart to stone.[33]

Thus families were at once crammed together and set apart, with little opportunity for sustained emotional support, and it is surprising that more did not turn to physical assault. It is difficult to assess the place of domestic violence, its incidence, and who was responsible. But there is evidence that it was not unusual. In particular, wife beating was an accepted part of many working-class communities and children were also frequently beaten – but there were limits. In the past these had often been set by neighbours through public ridicule such as performing 'rough music' outside the perpetrator's house.

Women could also defend each other, as in this account featuring the daughter of a small farmer, married to an engineer who

---

32. Ellen Ross, *Love and Toil: Motherhood in Outcast London, 1870–1918* (Oxford University Press, 1993), p. 20.

33. Robert Roberts quoting his mother, who observed her neighbours from her position as corner shop keeper, in David Vincent, *Poor Citizens: The State and the Poor in Twentieth Century Britain* (Longman, 1991), p. 21. See the classic 1915 study of Margaret Llewelyn Davies (ed.), *Maternity: Letters from Working Women* (Virago, 1978).

must have been earning good wages, with five children. He was a heavy drinker who unmercifully beat his terrified wife and children over a period of many years, particularly picking on his young son whom he laid into with his metal-buckled belt. He also kept them short of money and his wife often had to rely on her mother to supply food and sometimes even rent. The following story, told by her much younger half-sister who did not herself witness the event, has an almost folk-tale quality and may even be apocryphal, but it indicates the warning signals to violent men which may have circulated in local communities.

One night Mary Ellen arrived at her parents' farm and begged them and her brother to go back with her. Her husband, who had already beaten her, was fighting drunk and she had locked the children away from him and slipped out.

> They went back with her, to find Jonah lying on the sofa so dead drunk that nothing, seemingly would ever waken him again. But Grandma Stringer woke him. She asked her daughter for a stout sheet and a darning needle and strong thread. While they stood around wondering what she was up to, she unbuckled that cruel strap. Then, with the men's help, she got the sheet underneath the unconscious Jonah, and firmly sewed him up, looking as though she wished it were his shroud. She sewed him up so tightly that he could not move hand or foot, and then, taking the strap she set about him. She beat him till, in his agony, he rolled off the sofa on to the flagged floor, but still she struck at him. She went on and on. He was very much awake by this time and begged for help from his wife, from his father-in-law and brother-in-law. But Grandma ordered them fiercely not to lift a hand.

She called him a bully and threatened to have the law on him if he ever laid a hand again on 'my girl and t'childer'.[34]

Mothers found mutual aid from their own mothers, mothers-in-law, aunts, siblings, older children, neighbours and, at times, husbands. Neighbours felt some responsibility for doing something about maltreatment of children. They would intervene to feed children who were hungry. A few sources indicate that women might even breastfeed each other's babies on occasion, not difficult when so many women were lactating over much of their adult lives.[35] The

34. Margaret Penn, *Manchester Fourteen Miles* (Caliban Books, 1979), pp. 50–1.

35. Margaret Arnot, 'The uses of childhood? Gender and alleged neglect and cruelty to children in England 1840–1880', unpublished paper given at 'Childhood in Question' Conference, University of Essex, 1997. Robert Roberts recounts that while his mother was serving in the shop, the waiting customers might give him the

'dowager' or ex-baby lost the privileges of breastfeeding and sharing the parents' bed as soon as the next baby arrived. Crowded space and a sparse purse meant that older children might be farmed out to neighbours, grandparents, older siblings for shorter or longer periods and such arrangements could become permanent. They could be sent off to the countryside or alternatively to the big city to 'claim kin'. Home and family, even mother and father, were less fixed concepts for some working-class children than for their middle-class counterparts.[36]

A typical case was Thomas Morgan, youngest of thirteen children of whom five had died. One sister had been sent away to truant school for stealing a kipper. He recalls he had 'one decent sister' who became a hospital nurse, but his aunt, whose husband was a 'big sea captain', had adopted her and had been able to afford to send her to college while he, who had been sent to a charity school because he was a cripple, had left home at about the age of 12, like his other siblings.[37] Such sickly youngsters, unwanted children, youths who did not get along with parents or siblings, or those who had no support, could simply disappear onto the streets; they do not appear in the census. We only know of their existence because of the fascinated fears they aroused among commentators and in literary and artistic representations. Their image was held up to respectable working-class and middle-class children for compassion but also comparison. The very names used to describe them are pitted against family and nation: 'street arabs, urchins, scaramouches, guttersnipes, a "wild race", nomadic, a multitude of untutored savages – even English Kaffirs and Hottentots'.[38]

From mid century legal changes and new initiatives, combined with a rising standard of living, gradually transformed the experience of many working-class childhoods. Children were less often treated like smaller versions of adult criminals. Although considered inherently sinful by some, especially if the child was working class, their wickedness was regarded as amenable to discipline and retraining in moral surroundings. For girls this morality was usually centred on sexuality; laundry work regimes were a favourite method

---

breast to quiet him. Robert Roberts, *A Ragged Schooling: Growing up in the Classic Slum* (Fontana/Collins, 1978), p. 15. See also the case of Jane Bishop (1877), *Central Criminal Court Sessions Papers*, 3rd Series 1876–77, pp. 365–9. Reference thanks to Margaret Arnot.

36. Davin, *Growing Up Poor.* 37. Thompson, *Edwardian Childhoods*, p. 21.

38. Anna Davin, 'When is a child not a child?', in Helen Corr and Lynn Jamieson (eds), *The Politics of Everyday Life* (Macmillan, 1990), p. 43.

of washing away the sins of female street waifs. The second half of the century saw the establishment of many institutions such as the National Society for the Prevention of Cruelty to Children, Dr Barnardo's Homes, and the Church of England's Waifs and Strays Society. Orphanages were for those children, by no means all of whom were without parents or other family, who had, for whatever reason, come to be without temporary or permanent support.

The most momentous shift for all children was the introduction of compulsory education starting in the early 1870s. While previously many had picked up some reading and writing skills, the Board Schools were the biggest state intervention in ordinary people's lives yet experienced. At first parents and others in control of children's time and labour were unconvinced about the benefits of this education. Harsh and sometimes humiliating punishments meted out by teachers were often resented as unfair by adults and pupils alike. There was some unease, too, at the introduction of school meals in the 1900s, by men as casting doubt on their abilities as earners and by women on their capacity as food providers. Compulsory education also increased burdens for mothers faced with keeping up new standards of dress and obedience in their children. Truancy officers, school medical services, sanitary inspectors and district visitors expected and could enforce these standards, but often without giving financial or material underpinning. This was compounded by the loss of children's earnings and help at home.

Even with more education and higher real incomes, well-off working-class people still had little in material terms to hand on to their kin to ease their passage through life. Over their lifetime, with loss of youthful vigour, their earning capacity waned. Personal relationships remained their greatest resource as well as their heaviest burden.

Middle-class families

By the second half of the century, the less well off among the middle class, such as the many small shopkeepers, were being joined by new white-collar occupations, often recruited from the children of artisans and small farmers. The family life of school teachers, clerks, police, railway staff was oriented to respectability. With only minimum help from servants, their resources were often tightly stretched. Shopkeepers had to prove probity to attract credit and customers; white-collar workers had to dress, speak and bring up their children with an education which had to be paid for in money as well as forfeited contributions to the family income. Isolation, and an acute consciousness of social status, enhanced the saliency of domestic life. These families were the backbone of the temperance movement; church or chapel provided social networks, leisure pursuits and a place for courting.

The toll on health and spirits in keeping up standards was considerable, although warm, even claustrophobic, family relations could result. H.G. Wells, born in 1866, son of an unsuccessful small shopkeeper, was one of three surviving children. His mother, a former lady's maid, 'feared us terribly before we came and afterwards she loved and slaved for us intensely, beyond reason'. Looking back, he saw her 'engaged in a desperate single-handed battle with our gaunt and dismal home, to keep it clean, to keep her children clean, to get them clothed and fed and taught, to keep up appearances'. She also helped in the shop when her husband was off to his beloved cricket, her only recreation being the 'large and confused work basket' with its never-ending overflow of mending.[39]

Those with more substantial wealth focused on creating their version of the home. The duty to work, the necessity for men to provide an income to support an establishment of both productive enterprise and home life, was often contrasted to aristocratic gentry habits of living off rents and assets. Middle-class masculinity needed to elevate the despised notion of work, distinct from the older traditions of sport, politics and civilized leisure. In this scene, the 'family of love' became a rationale for devotion to the sordid working world.

This home entailed intense preoccupation with furnishings, decoration of rooms and gardens, with the appearance, behaviour and language of household members and the minutiae of social interaction within and outside the family. Within this endeavour, women were assigned a critical role. By the 1860s the position of wife, or, failing that, adult sister, daughter or niece, as mistress of a household had become the only route to recognition and assured genteel status for ladies. In these circles, the preparation and serving of food, particularly to visitors, had intrinsic significance with a stunning proliferation of linen, glass, china, silver, or more likely silver plate. Food, like household linen and clothing, was segregated according to the categories of servants, children, family and visitors. So too was the use of space in the house, with specific

39. H.G. Wells, *Experiment in Autobiography* (Gollancz, 1934), Vol. 1, pp. 63, 71.

rooms set aside for study, music, entertainment and the social duties which were women's prime occupation.

By the 1840s the creation of residential suburbs in cities and towns, and the piecemeal but increasing physical separation of houses from commercial, manufacturing or professional activities, meant that husbands and fathers spent less time with other family members. Among wealthier families the practice of sending boys to boarding school became more common, while the growth of men's clubs and organizations resulted in many people, at least from adolescence onwards, spending much of their lives in a single-sex atmosphere. Never before or since had there been such strongly drawn boundaries between masculinity and femininity, men and women.

In this climate, where manhood and womanhood, adulthood and childhood were so sharply contrasted, where power and re- sources were heavily concentrated with adult men, vexations and explosions behind the façade of loving devotion were endemic. Tensions over control of finances and material resources, conflict between parents and children, sibling jealousies and simmering sexual passions, fissured the smooth surface of family life. The shift from a discipline backed by belief in spiritual salvation to a more secular morality placed even more pressure on family relationships, for example struggles over the father's authority (see Chapter 5). Despite exhortations to loving care from those with power, pun- ishments could be harsh, some bordering on the pathological. Domestic violence was by no means confined to the lower orders, as middle-class sources would have us believe.[40]

Constant references to 'the little woman', such as the child-bride Dora in Dickens's *David Copperfield*, and the ideal of child-like fem- ininity in songs, drawings and popular stories, were in contrast to the mockery made of the independent 'strong-minded' woman, lacking feminine appeal and destined for lifelong spinsterhood, a label especially projected onto feminists. This emphasis on the strong older man and weak younger woman is in keeping with porno- graphic preoccupations with pre-pubescent girls and the under- tones of father–daughter attraction which surface in sources of the period. It may also be related to the wide expected and often actual

---

40. A hint at these issues is found in the two-year-long correspondence about mothers' control of their daughters, 'The whipping of girls', in the *Englishwoman's Domestic Magazine*, cited in Deborah Gorham, *The Victorian Girl and the Feminine Ideal* (Croom Helm, 1982), p. 77; see also James Hammerton, *Cruelty and Companionship: Conflict in Nineteenth-Century Married Life* (Routledge, 1992).

age gap between husbands and wives. The higher the social level the wider the difference in ages for married couples,[41] and although a husband needed to establish himself before taking on the support of dependants, this does not explain why he would so often take on a much younger bride.

The middle classes were characterized by strong bonds between siblings, brothers and sisters who grew up together and stayed close all their lives. In large families, elder siblings exercised quasi-parental affection, and authority, over younger. Young adult un-married brothers and sisters, together with younger siblings of the parents, provided an intermediate generation between elderly parents and the youngest children in the standard large family. As adults, sisters often took over housekeeping roles supported by their brothers in a financial and emotional bond not dissimilar to the conjugal. Such sibling relations could be amplified by financial interdependence through family partnerships between brothers and brothers-in-law, uncles and nephews. A pattern of two brothers marry-ing two sisters or a sister and brother marrying the brother and sister in another family was not uncommon; against popular present beliefs, cousins did marry each other.[42]

By the third quarter of the century, the ferment over divorce and married women's property legislation, the open and often vehement debates about feminist issues, the laying bare of the double standard of sexual morality in discussions about the control of prostitution and the movement for 'social purity', the establish-ment of women's organizations as auxiliaries to Church, chapel and political parties, all led to a questioning of relations between husband and wife. In practical terms, the introduction of larger shops such as the department store, catering mainly to women, had enlarged middle-class women's social opportunities outside the family. In the earlier period husbands had been more heavily involved in domestic affairs, but now more segregated and elaborate homemaking, entertaining and fashion were creating a legitimate place for wives as consumers in the public arena, the development of London's West End being a striking example.

41. In a sample by Leonore Davidoff from the Colchester census of 1851, it was found that while working-class couples might be close in age, with a substantial minority of wives a little older than their husbands, in the lower middle class the average age difference was the husband four years older than the wife, rising in the upper middle class to an average of six years.

42. Leonore Davidoff, 'Where the stranger begins: the question of siblings in historical analysis', in *Worlds Between: Historical Perspectives on Gender and Class* (Polity Press, 1995).

Husbands generally continued to pay for and own purchased goods, since under common law wives were allowed to pledge their husband's credit according to his accustomed status. But consumer purchasing was becoming more impersonal, beyond men's direct supervision. The danger of frivolous femininity was seen as a threat to masculine prerogative while shopkeepers grew increasingly restive under a system which often left them unable to call in accounts from angry husbands.[43] Men's sense of being threatened by such independent action by married women heightened unease over women's education and other feminist issues. Masculine disquiet can perhaps be seen in the increasingly paramilitary trappings of many men's organization of the latter part of the century, from the Volunteer movement and territorial army through cadet corps for boys. But there were also deeper tensions haunting married couples in this period.

Sexuality and the fertility transition

Undoubtedly one of the most stressful areas of family life centred around sexuality and procreation. Since the end of the eighteenth century a blanket of silence had surrounded these topics in genteel circles so that it was impossible to air opinions except in stilted medical language.[44] More open debate had only begun with the campaigns around prostitution and the Contagious Diseases Acts in the 1860s and was furthered by the notorious trials of Annie Besant and Charles Bradlaugh for publishing information on contraception a decade later, followed in the 1880s by that of Oscar Wilde for his avowed homosexuality.[45] Press exposure of the deliberate purchase of an under-age girl had also provoked near hysteria about a traffic in 'white slavery'. Realistic fears about the epidemic of venereal disease were elevated to a crusade by feminist revelations about the double standard which allowed husbands to infect wives and cripple unborn children, fears which fed eugenist anxiety about racial degeneration in the 1900s.

The belief in the inheritance of character and intelligence informed most thinking, both professional and lay, at this time, and

43. Erika Rappaport, 'A husband and his wife's dresses: consumer credit and the debtor family in England, 1864–1914', in Victoria de Grazia and Ellen Furlough (eds), *The Sex of Things: Gender and Consumption in Historical Perspective* (University of California Press, 1996).
44. Mason, *The Making of Victorian Sexuality.*
45. For a perceptive discussion of these issues see Walkowitz, *City of Dreadful Delight.*

fears about the passing on of 'bad blood' in the forms of criminality or alcoholism as well as disease were widely discussed. Ideas about racial purity were being explored, especially in the growing eugenics movement, just as serious doubts were being raised about the health of the British 'race', no longer so dominant throughout its Empire. The investigation following the defeats suffered in the Boer War in South Africa was a particularly unwelcome shock, exposing British manhood as a mass of underbred physical weaklings. Scientists and medical men warned that the right types were not breeding in sufficient numbers, and feminists were blamed for attacking the heart of family relations – marriage and motherhood – thus deterring middle-class young women from performing their proper function.

These public discussions should be seen in the context of private beliefs and behaviour. From mid century, upper-middle-class couples had been having smaller families. Family size had been steadily, if unevenly, falling from the average of six living children (many families had over ten), to three or four by 1900. The change coincided with a decline in childhood mortality; that is, more children survived once they were past the critical first year, for infant mortality remained high until the 1900s. There is no doubt that throughout the second half of the century many couples delayed marriage, which in itself cut the possibilities of producing large families. Within marriage it seems a combination of abstinence from intercourse and *coitus interruptus* (withdrawal) was being practised. Jose Harris supports this view by citing the massive advertising of birth control devices in popular almanacs and illustrated Malthusian guides.[46] It is possible that some families who gained commercial or professional success may have done so partly because they had fewer children.[47]

Unease about supporting large numbers of children at an expected living standard, which lay behind this change, may be glimpsed in a series of newspaper debates on marriage. These reveal contradictory pressures – on the one hand to maintain standards as a social duty, and on the other to follow what was seen as the natural, moral desire to marry and produce the inevitable quiverful of children. Significantly the starting point was an article

46. Jose Harris, *Private Lives, Public Spirit: A Social History of Britain 1870–1914* (Oxford University Press, 1993), p. 91.

47. Simon Szreter, *Fertility, Class and Gender in Britain 1860–1940* (Cambridge University Press, 1996); for the effects of family cultures on social mobility see Daniel Bertaux and Paul Thompson (eds), *Between Generations: Family Models, Myths and Memories* (Oxford University Press, 1993).

in *The Daily Telegraph* in 1857 on prostitution. The difficulties of the 'Young Man of the Period', a selfish creature out for a good time and exposed to temptation, coalesced around the proper time to marry. More affluent readers of *The Times* had followed in 1858, responding to a leader: 'Can you live like a Gentleman on £300 per annum'. The debates rumbled on through the century. In 1888 a *Telegraph* leader, in response to the feminist Mona Caird's attack on marriage in the *Westminster Review*, had elicited 27,000 letters; the correspondence filled three columns every day for six weeks. For *Telegraph* readers, the demands of decency as much as gentility tipped the balance against marriage when 'income does not always increase as rapidly as children'.[48] These discussions in the press took place alongside the coverage of the Jack the Ripper 'sexual drama', at a time when attention was intensively focused on prostitution and male sexuality.[49]

A complicated web of factors induced people to curtail their sexual behaviour. For those with capital and an ongoing enterprise, there had been a movement away from recruiting clerks, managers and even eventual successors only from family members; large numbers of younger brothers, sons and nephews could no longer be sure of finding a berth with relatives. Reform of the Civil Service, armed services and professions had contributed to the shift from approval of family connections in recruitment to unease about favouritism or, as it was coming to be negatively labelled, *nepotism*. Then, too, these young men were more expensive to educate, in private or boarding schools rather than apprenticeships. Even their sisters were beginning to require better education, and a small minority of young women began to have opportunities which did not include marriage and/or motherhood as an option at all.[50] In addition to the heavy costs of supporting and educating children throughout their youth, standards of housing, furnishings, servants and vehicles were rising; in J.A. Banks's well-known phrase, the demand for the 'paraphernalia of gentility' was ever more costly.[51]

By the 1900s, the combination of a more educated population, a higher standard of living, more stable urban communities and

48. John M. Robson, *Marriage or Celibacy: The Daily Telegraph on a Victorian Dilemma* (University of Toronto Press, 1995), p. 51.

49. Walkowitz, *City of Dreadful Delight*.

50. Alison MacKinnon, *Love and Freedom: Professional Women and the Shaping of Personal Life* (Cambridge University Press, 1970); see also Martha Vicinus, *Independent Women: Work and Community for Single Women, 1850–1920* (Virago, 1985).

51. J.A. Banks, *Prosperity and Parenthood: A Study of Family Planning Among the Victorian Middle Classes* (Routledge & Kegan Paul, 1954).

lower mortality also allowed for a more settled, family-oriented atmosphere among the lower strata. Some people in some areas began to desire and conceive fewer children. To this day, historians do not fully understand these changes but most now agree they arose independently in different locations and were not simply a case of working-class people following behind a middle-class precedent.[52] Numerous offspring had been regarded as inevitable: for the religious they were given by God, while for many others children had been desired as insurance in old age and/or evidence of a man's virility. Now bearing and rearing large numbers were beginning to be viewed first with compassion and later as in bad taste, as evidence of unrestrained lust. Such a momentous change was spread over several generations and unevenly distributed. For example, highly paid miners in communities with little waged work for women married relatively young, and produced large numbers of children.

Whatever the cause, this fundamental shift to limiting births within marriage affected all aspects of life both inside and outside the family. Control over an individual's life, for women as well as men, seemed possible as it never had before, although the price paid in self-restraint and forgone sensuality could be high. It seems that married women experienced fear of the outcome of sexual activity while at the same time expecting lovemaking to be enjoyable. But now it was becoming possible for choice as well as duty and fate to decide a person's sexual life story, whether homosexual or heterosexual.[53]

Institutional life

While many families were shaping themselves around the domestic ideal, a growing number and variety of formal and bureaucratic institutions were created based on the opposite premise. The early nineteenth century was a period when a range of hospitals, schools, orphanages, clubs, gaols and workhouses had been built. Early

52. John Gillis, Louise Tilly and David Levine (eds), *The European Experience of Declining Fertility: A Quiet Revolution 1850–1970* (Blackwell, 1992); Szreter, *Fertility, Class and Gender*.

53. For a discussion of the debates around sexuality and reproduction in marriage in the early twentieth century, see S. Szreter, 'Victorian Britain 1837–1963: towards a social history of sexuality', *Journal of Victorian Culture*, Vol. 1, No. 1 (1996) and Lucy Bland, *Banishing the Beast: English Feminism and Sexual Morality 1885–1914* (Penguin, 1995).

informality in relatively small buildings with easy access both in and out now gave way to large walled premises amidst deliberately bleak surroundings, with inmates segregated according to age and gender. This shift is clearly illustrated within the army. Traditionally soldiers had been billeted in pubs or private homes with local women supplying laundry, cooking and sexual services. Army reforms brought in stricter discipline within purpose-built barracks, separating service personnel from civilian life by both physical and social barriers.

Many of these institutions were founded with an emphasis on everything that the family was not. Their regimes would be tough, without emotional or physical mollycoddling (a molly had been colloquial for homosexual or effeminate). The point of such regimes may have been to save money by mass catering and accommodation but it was also to create a distinctly masculine atmosphere without feminine warmth and care. This meant minimal fires, cold water for washing and only the most basic food. Beds, if any, were hard pallets, rooms sparsely furnished, discipline harsh, and being able to take it a sign of strength and masculine pride. The ultimate in physical and humiliating punishments routinely used in these institutions was public flogging (not outlawed in the British Navy until the 1940s). Most of the inmates were working class, although boys' boarding schools, with their fagging system and rituals of beatings by staff and older boys, meant that upper-middle-class men's personal and social development was also deeply marked by an absence of family experience. Within all these settings, the level of legitimate bullying, cruelty and violence would now be considered as unacceptable physical and sexual abuse.

By contrast, living-in arrangements for girls and women were to be as much like a family as possible. Punishments were more often deprivation of food and privileges and verbal humiliation, although rough handling could be common where the clientele was working class. Older women and girls were often made to act as little mothers or sisters to the younger in the numerous but always small private boarding schools which came and went.

The Girls' Public Day School Company, formed in the 1870s, was riven with conflict as to whether the girls would receive a similar, if watered down, regime to the boys. Feminists claimed schools should prepare girls for 'a fair field and no favour' when they went out into the world, but they were pitted against parental, and other, expectations that the fate of the girls was to marry and run a home. School mistresses therefore assumed that natural femininity should be given prime attention in surroundings as homelike as possible. Girls in institutions such as Barnardo's Village Homes, in contrast to the large barracks for boys, were housed in small units, each with a cottage 'mother', where they were trained in domestic tasks for their fate as servants and mothers. Tensions between the domesticated aims of those who founded and ran all-women institutions and the demands of operating along business lines within a competitive public situation were intense and proved the downfall of some.[54] All institutions were single sex or at least divided into clearly separate male and female sections. Within these settings, age and class hierarchies meant that the poor, who formed the lowest echelons, were treated like children while middle-class staff, no matter how young, held parental authority. Raw Oxbridge undergraduates in their late teens and early twenties flocked to the settlement houses in London's East End to teach, lecture and cajole the adult local population on issues of family life, religious beliefs and morality.

The shared beliefs underlying the various institutions for boys and men are evident in the experience of Arthur Harding, born in 1886, in a London slum. His family could not afford to feed him or contain his energies. At the age of about 9, when he was sleeping rough, he was picked up and sent to a Barnardo Home. He then spent a period of equivalent discipline in the army, from which he was ejected for being under-age. Eventually sentenced to a year in prison, he soon after became one of the earliest Borstal boys, a range of experiences with remarkably similar conditions. It is striking, however, that despite these long spells, he kept in touch with his old haunts, mates and some family, thereby confounding the commonly held stark distinction between inmate and family member.[55]

The overlap between the two models was present in that ideal of bureaucratic hierarchy and rational efficiency, the army. As the army became more professional in the later decades of the nineteenth century, the new type of soldier was to be less brutalized and seen as needing the civilizing effects of domesticated feminine attachments. Yet the soldier's duty and masculine persona was as a fighting man, not a responsible husband and father, made clear in the level of pay which was sufficient only for a single man. While officers had always been allowed marriage, a selected minority of private soldiers were now allowed to marry and provision was made for their

54. Vicinus, *Independent Women*.
55. Raphael Samuel, *East End Underworld: Chapters in the Life of Arthur Harding* (Routledge & Kegan Paul, 1981).

wives and children. But the major mechanism used to solve this paradox was the imposition of a familial ideal whereby officers acted as heads of the regimental 'family', dispensing fatherly rewards and punishments. These could be heavy and arbitrary, particularly when informal and where the non-commissioned officers might play the part of a bullying elder brother. Officers' wives, and sometimes sisters or daughters, acted in a maternal, philanthropic capacity. Meanwhile the wives and children of private soldiers found themselves incorporated into military discipline. Soldiers' wives earned money, compulsorily, by doing laundry, cleaning and cooking; their married quarters were set standards of housekeeping and regularly inspected; their children were given schooling and medical services but their behaviour was monitored and the whole family were expected to attend church parade. Any soldier who married without permission could expect no help and no quarter.[56]

It may be a truism, but it is still worth stressing that over the scant 85 years covered in this chapter, immense changes had taken place. By its close on the eve of war, England had become the greatest world power ever known, London a leading centre of wealth, social and cultural life. Much of the general population was enjoying a standard of living unimaginable to their parents' and grandparents' generations. The terrible and desolating effects of chronic malnutrition, backbreaking labour and continuous childbearing were beginning to be mitigated. All sections of the population had been affected by the fall in infectious disease and lower death rates. This is not to deny an abysmal level of poverty for those at the lowest levels of society, and the gap between the rich and the very poor, now exacerbated by differential birth rates, was if anything greater than ever.

Nevertheless, this was a more stable, settled, prosperous yet hierarchical nation with almost a half century of rising expectations. In this atmosphere, entrenched ideas about respectability, gentility and duty depended a great deal on family reputation, often pressed beyond personal preferences.[57] These families now also existed in a setting of larger institutions; no longer did the Church have a monopoly of public life. Businesses, schools, local and national government offices, even theatres and sports facilities had expanded and become more professional, more distanced from personal lives.

56. Myna Trustram, *Women of the Regiment: Marriage and the Victorian Army* (Cambridge University Press, 1984).
57. Standish Meacham quoted in Lummis, *The Labour Aristocracy*, p. 137.

Homes were more often now located in residential enclaves. Against this background, personal networks of family, patron or friends had begun to shrink in scope and importance. Continued migration, and particularly emigration, pulled family members apart. But, in another sense, family connection and family claims had never been so vital.

These families were expected to focus upon the male head, the breadwinner, the representative in the public world. In the following chapter we examine the way men were conceived in this role and the way they reacted to it, particularly as fathers. Our second in-depth view of this period takes up the hidden but necessary network of services which sustained everyday life as well as the ideals of home and family. The work provided by family members themselves, the role of wives and mothers, of children, has had some, if limited, attention. Here we rather turn to the subterranean world of domestic service and lodging, without which many families would not have survived, but which also provided kinds of family in itself.

CHAPTER FIVE

Fathers and fatherhood: family authority

The father's right to the guardianship of his child is high and sacred.
Lord Justice O'Hagan, 1875[1]

A good father and husband up to a point, he left the responsibility of the whole family to my mother.
Mrs Layton, a working woman, 1860s[2]

The exercise of power in the intimacies of family life has become a central concern for family historians, and fatherhood lies at the heart of familial dependencies and interdependencies. However, despite its centrality, fatherhood as a topic of historical study has been particularly neglected. This absence can be explained partly because, as we saw in Chapter 3, men have on the whole defined themselves as autonomous individuals, as actors in the world, not requiring any acknowledgement of the web of domestic and intimate relationships which has underpinned their public personae. There has also been a deep reluctance to consider men as gendered beings, their experiences as fathers thus escaping analysis in these terms. Men have largely remained the standard, opaque subject whose positions of authority did not require explanation.

When we reverse the lens to examine the shifting meanings and experiences of men as fathers, we can see that they have not formed a single social group, and were not equally powerful in these processes in terms of class, 'race', or other social inequalities. This also reveals that men's familial relationships were not only central to

1. *Symington* v. *Symington* (1875), *LawRep* 2 *ScApp* 426.
2. Mrs Layton, 'Memories of seventy years', in Margaret Llewelyn Davies (ed.), *Life as We have Known It, by Co-Operative Working Women* (Virago, 1977, first published 1931), p. 7.

their constructions of their own identities, but reached out beyond and between families and the 'public' worlds of work, religion and politics.

In this chapter, the place of fatherhood and the experiences of fathers are investigated mainly within the nineteenth century. Despite the range of families' responses to social and economic change examined in the previous chapter, the idea that fathers had natural rights, so clearly set out in the first remark above by a judge in the House of Lords, was to prove highly resistant to change. Fathers occupied positions of great authority in families, based on their control over property, income and other material resources, and sanctioned by a wide range of laws, religious symbols, metaphorical hierarchies and social practices. By revealing these relationships of power and obedience, we can deepen our understandings of family processes, and the relationships between families and society in general.

The second statement, by a working-class wife and mother, indicates that fatherhood, and its responsibilities, was not simply an unchanging framework of natural rights. Fathers' positions varied between social groups and over time. As the century progressed the authority of fathers contained growing contradictions, as women, children and other dependants found new ways to resist or bypass them.[3] At the same time changes in society at large loosened the relationship between fatherhood and other more 'public' positions, particularly as enterprises became less familial and as work became increasingly distinct from domestic life.

The particular focus of this chapter is the nature of fatherly authority and how it was exercised and negotiated both within families and in other contexts. Definitions of authority combine the ideas of power or right to enforce obedience with moral or legal supremacy, including the right to command, to give an ultimate decision and the power to influence the conduct and actions of others. Other meanings of authority in terms of knowledge are also resonant in the context of fatherhood, such as the entitlement to be believed and to be an expert. The origins of paternal authority can also be traced in the idea that authority comes from one who originates, begets or gives existence to things: a father, an ancestor, or God as creator. Until the late nineteenth century it was generally believed that men provided the active element in the conception of

3. Ellen Ross, *Love and Toil: Motherhood in Outcast London, 1870–1918* (Oxford University Press, 1993), ch. 5.

a child, with the mother a passive, nurturing vessel for a pre-formed embryo, which meant that fatherhood was closely associated with an exclusively male power of creating life. These definitions of authority explicitly link power and knowledge with the generation of people and things, specifying a male creator. As we saw in Chapter 3, men were also understood to have the capacity to create and define their own sense of identity as autonomous individuals. Thus personal authority within the family can be linked to much broader relationships of power, particularly over identity, language and knowledge.

Three extended examples are used here to examine the ways these forms of authority were experienced and understood: a very public legal contest gives us an insight into power struggles within the Agar Ellis family, showing the shifting rights and duties of fatherhood; an autobiography by Roger Langdon and his daughter spanning three generations illuminates how fathers and children understood their relationships, showing changing ideas about fatherly care; and an autobiographical account of family life by John Pearman draws attention to the links between the private and public, exploring the interconnections between men's domestic, economic and political identities.

Rights and duties of fathers

It was in the courts that the legal rights and duties of fathers were codified, and the definitive case of Agar Ellis, which began in 1878 and rumbled on for over five years, set out the limits of fathers' rights for the nineteenth century, and was still used as a precedent long into the twentieth.[4] In this dispute the deeply rooted spiritual authority of fathers is articulated. But tensions between these ancient rights and new legislation to protect mothers and children also emerge, showing a weakening of fathers' absolute authority. The close intertwining of marriage and parenthood underlies these conflicts, as was exposed when this family failed to reconcile a mother's role of nurturing her children, and a husband's right to submission from his wife.

Thus the case began with a dispute between a husband and wife, The Hon. Leopold and Harriet Agar Ellis, over the religious education of their children. Harriet came from an aristocratic Catholic

4. *In re* Agar Ellis (5.8.1878) *LawRep 10 ChD* 49; *In re* Agar Ellis (Appeal) (8.8.1878) *LawRep 10 ChD* 63; *In re* Agar Ellis (23.7.1883) *LawRep 24 ChD* 334.

family, and had reached a pre-nuptial agreement with Agar Ellis, a Protestant, that any children could be raised as Catholics. They married, and produced a son who died as a child, and then three daughters. Three of the children were baptized as Catholics, but trouble began as the second and third baptisms took place against the express wishes of their father. Harriet continued to raise her children as Catholics, attending mass and having the children confirmed; Leopold continued to object until finally the children began to refuse to attend Protestant church despite being punished by their father for disobeying him.

The first court action began when the three girls were 12, 11 and 9 years old. Mr Agar Ellis went to Chancery to have the children made wards of court, demanding that they be sent away from home to live with a Protestant clergyman, removed from the influence of their mother. Mrs Agar Ellis petitioned that she had rights of custody, under a specific Act, the 1873 Custody of Infants Act, and that the girls would find that attempting to change their faith would 'violate their consciences and thus materially injuring their moral sense'.[5] She argued that they needed maternal care, had never lived away from home, and that she had always been entrusted with their education by their father.

The Vice Chancellor in 1878 ruled against her, commenting thus:

> I am very sorry to find that she has thought herself justified in going to such an extent as this, that she had set at defiance the authority of the father over the children, and has so far instilled these principles into the children, seeming to have entirely forgotten that by the laws of England, by the laws of Christianity, and by the constitution of society, when there is a difference of opinion between husband and wife, it is the duty of the wife to submit to the husband . . . The principles of this Court are the principles of common sense and the principles of propriety, that the children must be brought up in the religion of the father. The father is the head of his house, he must have the control of his family, he must say how and by whom they are to be educated, and the Court never does interfere between a father and his children unless there be an abandonment of the parental duty.[6]

Quoting another judge, he added:

> any engagement by a father to have his children brought up in another religion than his own, however absolute, is null, and he is at liberty to revoke it, and to insist that his children in his lifetime

5. *In re* Agar Ellis (1878), p. 52.   6. Ibid., p. 55.

shall be brought up in his religion, and to direct by his will that they should be so after his death.[7]

Mrs Agar Ellis appealed this decision, but again lost, the Lord Chancellor adding that:

> the law has made him (the father), and not us, the judge, and we cannot interfere with him in his honest exercise of the jurisdiction ... recognising the father's undoubted right as master of his own house, as king and ruler in his own family ... He ought to discard and we have no doubt will discard, all thought of personal dignity or personal supremacy or of triumph in a personal struggle ... and we, pronouncing what we deem the law to be must leave the matter to his sense of parental duty and to his conscience.[8]

There the matter rested until the second daughter, also called Harriet, was 16 years old. She petitioned the court with her mother, asking for permission for them to have a holiday together against the wishes of her father. Since the earlier case, she had been living away from home. Her father had finally acquiesced in allowing her to practise the Catholic faith unhindered, but he had only permitted her to see her mother once a month, and required all correspondence between them to be seen by someone nominated by him. A letter from Harriet to her mother's solicitors was quoted:

> I write again to ask you to apply to the Judge for leave that I may spend my vacation with my mother, as you know for this last two years I have been moved about from place to place, and have only had part of one vacation with my mother, which the Judge ordered. The people I am with now are very kind to me, but they want to go abroad in July and are unable to take me with them. Father has no place to take me to, and with one exception has never spent a vacation with us in over four years. I am always amongst strangers. I am longing to see some of my relations.[9]

Her father strongly opposed the petition on the grounds that prolonged contact with his wife 'would tend to create a great prejudice in the child's mind against him, and might result in entirely alienating her affection from him'.[10] After some unsuccessful attempts to negotiate with Mr Agar Ellis, a judge in private ruled in his favour, and Mrs Agar Ellis and her daughter took the decision to appeal.

---

7. Ibid., p. 61/2, quoting *In re* Browne, 2 *Ir.Ch.Rep.* 160.
8. *In re* Agar Ellis (Appeal) (1878), p. 75.
9. *In re* Agar Ellis (Appeal) (1883), pp. 318–19.   10. Ibid., p. 319.

The legal arguments for the appeal were complex, but the underlying principle of the sacred rights of fathers was upheld, because: 'If the principles laid down by the Appellants were to be adopted by the Court, they would produce a revolution in the relations of father and child.' Although the father's insistence was 'strange', it was not actually cruel or morally dangerous, so the court had no power to interfere.

The Master of the Rolls put it thus:

> The law recognises the rights of the father because it recognises the natural duties of the father. Now the natural duties of a father are to treat his child with the utmost affection and with infinite tenderness, to forgive his child without stint and under all circumstances ... which, if he breaks, he breaks from all that nature calls upon him to do; and if he breaks from these duties, the law may not be able to insist upon their full performance.[11]

Lord Justice Bowen added:

> I do not believe that a court of Law can bring up a child as successfully as a father ... Fancy the position of a child, with its father living, which the Court endeavours to bring up by judicial machinery, instead of leaving it to be brought up by parental care. ... to interfere further would be to ignore the one principle which is the most fundamental of all in the history of mankind ... If that were not so we might be interfering all day and with every family.[12]

Thus Mr Agar Ellis retained control over his children, and his wife's relationship with them, until they reached the age of 21. The judges were obviously unhappy about his parenting, indicated by their repeated requests that he consider his 'natural' duty of affection towards his daughters. But they did not wish to interfere with the established rights of fathers without much more serious reasons than the wishes and desires of wives and children.

What all the judges involved in this dispute agreed about was the absolute authority of fathers over their children, an authority which was derived from nature, and confirmed by religious and civil practices. A father was master of his household, the king and ruler of his domain, and thus he was immune from interference by any other authority. This absolute right was modified only in the most extreme circumstances. Only by threatening in some gross way the moral upbringing of their children would fathers have their rights curtailed by the courts. The most notorious example had been the

11. Ibid., p. 327.   12. Ibid., p. 338.

poet Shelley, who lost all connections with the children of his first marriage after declaring that not only was he himself an atheist, but that he would raise his children as atheists.[13]

Thus the most significant duty of fatherhood was seen as the imparting of Christian faith to one's children. The right of fathers to determine the religious beliefs of their children was of very ancient origin, extended in the seventeenth century to include the power to appoint guardians to ensure religious orthodoxy after death, superseding any rights of mothers. The consolidation of Protestant belief through the family was also closely tied to rights of citizenship and property until Catholic emancipation in 1829, and echoes of these tensions are still evident in the Agar Ellis case.[14]

But throughout the nineteenth century, the spiritual training of children was increasingly seen as a concern of mothers as part of their domestic roles. Middle-class women had been elevated to a position of moral superiority in the family because of their exclusion from the contamination of public life, and thus were increasingly seen as better suited to impart religious and moral values to children, especially very young boys, and girls of any age.[15] The explicit representation of God's authority by fathers in the practice of family prayers was giving way to more informal family religious practices, as we saw in Chapter 4, and thus a powerful reinforcement of fatherly authority was in decline, further undermined by the gradual secularization of society. It is in this context that the Agar Ellis disputes about faith between husband and wife, and father and children, can be interpreted.

Another vital historical legacy was the tight interrelationship between marriage and parenting. Marriage had from ancient times been seen as necessarily leading to parenthood, and even where no offspring were born to a couple, children were frequently informally adopted or fostered into families. A father's authority over all of his household was intertwined with his authority over his wife, and the submission of both wife and children was seen as essential to his position, as we can see by the comments of these judges. The problem Mr Agar Ellis had with his children was mainly expressed as a difficulty between him and his wife, and the children's defiance of his demands to alter their faith was seen by him not as their own

13. *Shelley* v. *Westbrook* (17.3.1817), *37 ER* 850.
14. James Obelkevich, 'Religion', *Cambridge Social History of Britain* (Cambridge University Press, 1990), Vol. 3, pp. 317–18.
15. Leonore Davidoff and Catherine Hall, *Family Fortunes: Men and Women of the English Middle Class 1780–1850* (Hutchinson, 1987), pp. 340–1.

act, but as a deliberate provocation by his wife. The judges were forced to collude with this view, although their remonstrations for Mr Agar Ellis to be more reasonable can be seen as attempts to remind him of his duties to his children as separate from his dispute with his wife. However, the needs and wishes which the children expressed were not considered important enough to influence the final judgement.

By the 1880s, there was serious concern about the weak position of women as mothers in the face of this uninhibited authority of fathers. There had been limited attempts to give mothers some rights of custody, leading to the passing of the two Custody of Infants Acts of 1839 and 1873, reflecting the importance attached to maternal care for children, especially infants, as women's domestic roles were growing in prestige. These Acts did not help Mrs Agar Ellis, because she and her husband had not separated, and thus the provisions of the Acts could not be applied. Mothers, therefore, held no legal rights over their children's upbringing within marriage. The comments in this case show that extending any rights to women or children within 'intact' families was seen as highly dangerous to the family as a social institution.

This can be seen most vividly in the widespread apprehensions expressed when divorce was reformed in 1857. It was feared that if women had rights to care for their children, they would desert their husbands in droves, that marriage was often so precarious that only the threat of losing their children kept wives within it. On the other hand, concern was expressed that husbands were able to use their rights over children to compel wives to tolerate cruel or immoral behaviour in the marriage. If a woman left her husband to protect herself, she might never see her children again. As one judge commented, 'a wife should not be compelled to do violence to her feelings as a mother by parting from her infant child, when she was not in fault'.[16] Under the new divorce procedures custody was normally given to the 'innocent' party, and this meant that while adulterous wives continued to automatically lose custody, adulterous husbands began to find their children removed from their care. For the first time, a father's behaviour as a husband began to affect his rights as a father. But despite growing concern about the position of mothers, particularly pressed by the widening feminist movement,[17] if marriages were not broken by separation or

---

16. *Bazeley* v. *Forder* (1867), *LawRep 3 QB* 564.
17. Jane Rendall, *The Origins of Modern Feminism: Women in Britain, France and the United States, 1780–1860* (Lyceum Books, 1985), pp. 228–9.

divorce, fathers continued to rule the lives of their wives and children with very little legal interference, as Mrs Agar Ellis and her daughters discovered.

One of the key reasons for the minimal impact of these early reforms was the control that husbands and fathers exercised over the material resources of families. Married women had no rights to property or even their own earnings before the Married Women's Property Act of 1870. Although wealthier families did provide for their married daughters and sisters through the legal mechanisms of marriage settlements and trusts, very few married women had personal control over their own capital, much less the resources of their husbands, and thus few were able to provide for their children independently. Poor women knew that female wages were rarely sufficient to support dependent children, and thus faced severe hardship as the alternative to the dependency of marriage. Women without supportive fathers, uncles or brothers found it particularly difficult to break away from abusive husbands because of financial dependence.

Caroline Norton was perhaps the best-known victim of this dilemma. She was a journalist and author, active in literary and Whig political circles throughout the mid nineteenth century, whose marriage acrimoniously broke down in 1836 with her husband successfully demanding financial support from her earnings, and keeping her young children from her for many years. As a wife without sufficient grounds for divorce, she had no access to any kind of court proceedings herself. Instead she lobbied through her political connections, writing pamphlets and articles demanding changes to the law of married women's property and child custody. At the centre of her plea for change was the argument that women needed protection from those few husbands who abused their powers:

> A woman may bear cheerfully the poverty which anomalies in the laws of property may entail upon her; and she may struggle patiently through such an unjust ordeal of shame [i.e. a divorce or accusations of adultery] . . . but against the inflicted and unmerited loss of her children she *cannot* bear up; that she has not deserved *that* blow, only adds to its bitterness; it is the master feeling of her life; the strong root of all the affection of her heart . . . It is the one power of a husband against which she has not power of remedy.[18]

18. Caroline Norton, *A Plain Letter to the Lord Chancellor on the Infant Custody Bill* (Bruce Rogers, 1922, first published 1839 under pseud. Pearce Stevenson, Esq.), p. 11.

Her influence on public opinion and Parliament was significant,
not least because while she argued for greater rights for women,
she did not challenge dominant ideas about women's place as sub-
missive wives and nurturing mothers.[19]

In contrast to the courts' willingness to support fathers' rights,
it was practically impossible to force fathers to provide for their
children, as the only existing legal framework for doing so was
based on the Poor Law, which only obliged men to maintain their
families at the very lowest subsistence levels. Lord Eldon stated the
law thus:

> You may go to the Court of Kings Bench for a *habeas corpus* to restore
> the child to its father; but when you have restored the child to its
> father, can you go to the Court of Kings Bench to compel that father
> to subscribe even to the amount of five shillings a year for the main-
> tenance of that child? ... Is it an eligible thing that children of all
> ranks should be placed in this situation – that they shall be in the
> custody of the father; although looking at the quantum of allowance
> which the law can compel the father to provide for them, they may
> be in a state little better than starvation?[20]

Even wardship proceedings in Chancery depended on the availability of capital sufficient to provide an income for a child made a
ward of court, and wives and mothers rarely had access to this, even
those from wealthy families. At the other end of the social spectrum, the reform of the Poor Laws in 1834 in effect removed any
obligation of fathers to maintain illegitimate children, tightening
even further the relationship between marriage and parenthood.[21]
Its punitive workhouse test, which forced families claiming poor
relief to live in the workhouse, where husbands, wives and children
were forcibly separated, used the social shame of failing to provide
as the only real sanction against improvident fathers.

Thus there was simply no mechanism to back up the duty of
fathers to provide for their children, despite the fact that, within
families, only adult men had legal control over property and income. Only with the formal breakdown of marriage was specific
maintenance of children enforced, initially through the divorce
courts. This was supplemented by the Matrimonial Causes Act, 1878,
which was aimed at protecting working-class women from violent

19. Mary Poovey, *Uneven Developments: The Ideological Work of Gender in Mid-Victorian England* (Virago, 1989), p. 81.
20. *Wellesley v. Duke of Beaufort* (1825), *38 ER* 243.
21. Anna Clark, *The Struggle for the Breeches: Gender and the Making of the British Working Class* (Rivers Oram Press, 1995), pp. 187–95.

husbands, giving local magistrates' courts powers to award a mother custody of her children, and to order that the father pay maintenance for them. However, in practice, the local magistrates seemed to have adopted a highly paternalistic role, eager to bring reconciliation, rather than formalize separations.[22]

Limited as they were, these reforms had the long-term effect of gradually separating parenthood and marriage, and of highlighting the interests of children over those of either parent. At the same time wives began to gain rights over property, of protection from violent and abusive husbands, and recognition of their crucial contributions to the upbringing of their children. With these changes, fathers' rights were necessarily undermined, although this process was often imperceptibly slow. Mr Agar Ellis's case was the last of the big Chancery battles in which a father's word overruled all. In 1886, the Guardianship of Children Act was passed after vigorous feminist campaigning, which explicitly put the interest of the child on an equal footing with parental conduct, and gave wives an equal right to custody.

In analysing a case such as this, there is no straightforward relationship between the reports of a legal dispute and the many other competing ideas about fatherhood, much less the daily experiences of family life. It is necessary to place these cases and debates in wider contexts through other sources such as advice literature, discussions in the press, fiction, biography and autobiography. From these it emerges, for example, that questions about the custody and care of children after their parents separated were often resolved for middle- and upper-class couples not through the courts, but through private legal agreements drawn up by family solicitors.[23] Such separation agreements usually gave custody of young children and girls to mothers, and older children, especially boys, to fathers, and arrangements about schooling, place of residence, and maintenance were commonly included. These agreements were not legally binding, as no arrangement concerning children would be enforced by a court if it interfered with the father's rights, but this did not deter the many separating couples who used them to avoid the public scandal which resulted from divorce procedures.

Thus the formal processes of the courts were far from being in the vanguard of any changes in the authority wielded by fathers,

22. A. James Hammerton, *Cruelty and Companionship: Conflict in Nineteenth-Century Married Life* (Routledge, 1992), pp. 39–41.
23. Lawrence Stone, *Road to Divorce: England 1530–1987* (Oxford University Press, 1990), ch. 7.

but rather reflected social shifts, often long after the initial debates were aired. Each piece of reforming legislation was followed by more explicit and wider provisions necessary to push a reluctant judiciary into new precedents. Thus, the law changed only after many individual men, women and children had already rejected or revised older legal models of family life. A single court case can show how the authority of fathers was deeply rooted in social institutions which were highly resistant to change, but it is also important to look beyond this into the ways these structures were negotiated by families in their daily lives.

Changing ideas about fatherly care

By using other sources it is possible to turn away from fathers in situations of family conflict, to look at more harmonious descriptions of fathering. It is also possible to move away from the upper- and middle-class families found in court disputes to the stories of working-class families, through the many surviving autobiographical accounts.

Using such autobiographies to explore family life necessarily involves a complex process of interpretation, as the stories presented in them are never simple descriptions of what happened. Autobiographies represent a writer's attempt to shape his or her world to fit the picture she or he wishes to present within the structures and meanings available to him or her. While autobiographers usually strove to be truthful, myths and consequent silences were built into every account of family life.[24]

One such writer was Roger Langdon, born in 1825, died in 1888, who wrote his autobiography in the early 1860s while working as a railway stationmaster in Devon, with additions by his daughter Ellen nearly forty years later.[25] From their stories it is possible to find many important elements of fatherhood in working-class family life at this time, and to trace some of the changes in the expectations and interpretations of fathering which appear between the two generations of fathers here.

24. David Vincent, 'Introduction', in *Bread, Knowledge and Freedom: A Study of Nineteenth-Century Working Class Autobiography* (Methuen, 1981); Jean Peneff, 'Myths in life stories', in Ralph Samuel and Paul Thompson (eds), *The Myths We Live By* (Routledge, 1990).

25. Roger Langdon, *The Life of Roger Langdon Told by Himself, With Additions by his Daughter Ellen* (Elliot Stock, 1909).

Langdon began by describing his own parents thus: 'My father had enough to do to make both ends meet, and how he and my mother slaved and toiled to keep out of debt.'[26] His father was a parish clerk:

> a power in the village, and used his stick accordingly... [he] thoroughly believed that the stick was a cure for all complaints... I do not wish it to be understood that my father was a wrong-headed man, far from it; for I am sure that he possessed some of the finest qualities that adorn human nature. He possessed in the very highest degree, the qualities of truth, justice, honour and honesty of purpose; he considered it an exceedingly bad practice to owe anything to anybody, so he rose very early in the morning and took rest late that he might maintain his children, in what he termed 'poor independence'.[27]

Roger was one of ten children, and, like all his six brothers, he was sent out to work from the age of 8, having the misfortune to be employed on a farm as an assistant to a violent and vicious ploughman. 'I was thrashed and kicked and beaten most unmercifully by this brute',[28] who came close to killing him more than once. However, he was unable to tell his parents, because they desperately needed his income. 'It was not the parents, but the age that was to blame.'[29] He could stand no more when, at the age of 14, he ran away from home to find work in Jersey.

Thus, as a child, Langdon experienced the failure of his father to keep poverty at bay, to prevent his economic exploitation as a child and to protect him from the violent abuse he suffered. In this account of childhood we encounter one of the fundamental duties of fatherhood: the protection of children and other dependants from the vicissitudes of life. By leaving home and doing better by himself, Langdon demonstrated his father's inadequacies, but he was also unwilling to blame him for these shortcomings, recognizing the constraints within which his family lived.

Langdon's best memories of childhood were associated with his friendship with a father-substitute, as his own father's energies were clearly directed elsewhere. The local curate was the one who stimulated his interest in reading and learning:

> [he] would tell us of all the most interesting things that were going on in the outer world, and of which we should never have heard without him. And when the dear man stood there in our midst

26. Ibid., p. 13.   27. Ibid.
28. Ibid., p. 29.   29. Ibid., p. 34.

telling us all these stories, his face beaming with goodness and kind-
ness, and his hair as white as snow, I think I almost worshipped
him.[30]

Thus even when 'natural' fathers were not available to provide
and protect, father figures often stepped in, whether relatives like
uncles or grandfathers, teachers and clergymen, or masters and
employers. When Langdon found his first job in Jersey, he lived
with his (childless) employer and his wife who treated him much
like a son. Transitions from childhood to adulthood were thus
often smoothed and managed by other men acting like fathers.

An even more obvious transmission of adult knowledge occurred
when children worked with their fathers, which many did for shorter
or longer periods. Fathers were also responsible for the entry of
their adolescent children, especially but not exclusively boys, into
a trade or other long-term adult employment, and success as a
parent was measured by the degree to which children could be set
up in life. Other family members, especially mothers, but also
wide networks of friends and kin, were drawn upon to help in the
process. Finding suitable work for daughters was complicated by
the need for fathers to find employment which would not damage
a girl's reputation as well as to protect her from predatory male
employers. For children to grow up to be a credit to their parents,
to be financially secure, to be respected members of a community,
to become good parents themselves, these were significant goals for
fathers however scanty their resources.

Langdon became a father himself after he found secure employment with the railway as a signalman, and was able to marry, his
wife setting up a small school for neighbouring children in their
home at the railway station They had eight children, two of them
girls, and he portrays the relationship between himself and his children as much more intimate and caring than those he experienced
as a child. This can be seen by the significant shift in Langdon's
lifetime in ideas about the styles of disciplining children. Langdon's
father and his foreman were both obviously accustomed to using
harsh physical punishments against children. But while the use of
force by the ploughman was recognized as abusive and excessive,
even if never directly challenged, the beating of children by fathers
was seen as normal, so normal that Langdon draws the links between his father's use of the cane against his own children and his
public position in the village. However, by the time that Langdon

was a father himself, such beatings were no longer considered quite so acceptable, although corporal punishment was still common.

In common with other autobiographers of this period, Langdon does not mention his own disciplining of his children, but it is clear that he placed great value on having companionate relationships with them in a way his father had been unable or unwilling to enjoy. The heavy responsibilities of fatherhood were tempered by the pleasures which he was able to find in the company of his children. Because of the nature of his work as a signalman and then stationmaster, Langdon's work and home life were not strictly separated, and he had the time as well as the financial security to enjoy being with his family.

We can see this in Langdon's hobbies and interests, which were central to his daughter's memories of childhood, opening doors to adult (and often exclusively male) knowledge. He made mechanical models, including a magic lantern, and studied astronomy, showing her the planets and stars with his home-built telescope. He knew about electricity and photography as well as teaching himself Greek, and his daughter described his teaching of the catechism as 'pretty unorthodox and advanced'. She remembered her times with him thus: 'if we had gone to the dullest place in the world I should have been quite as happy so long as father was with me, for on all occasions he was just the same age as his children'.[31]

However, not even the security of a railway job could prevent familial disaster. His eldest son died as a teenager in a train accident at his station, a terrible blow which turned his hair white, and the death of his youngest son in 1888 was a 'fearful blow... After this time father never appeared to be very well, and before long his health entirely gave way.'[32] His deep grief at the deaths of his sons shows how important his children were to him, and how crushing his failure to protect them from accidents and illness.

In other autobiographical writings and in poetry, there are frequent expressions of mourning at the loss of children of all ages, however frequently parents faced these losses.[33] J.H. Powell, another working man, wrote about the death of his daughter Marion, at the age of seventeen months: 'to me it seemed like the parting of life from love – the decay of hope – the separation of the soul from the body'.[34] In expressions of grief we can trace fatherly feelings of care, concern and affection combined with regrets at their powerlessness to protect their children from misfortune.

31. Ibid., p. 80.   32. Ibid., p. 84.
33. Vincent, *Bread, Knowledge and Freedom*, pp. 56–9.
34. J.H. Powell, *Life Incidents and Poetic Pictures* (Trubner & Co., 1865), p. 28.

Mothers had very different places in their children's lives. In working-class families, they generally had the responsibility of providing meals, clothes and comforts, sometimes from the most meagre of resources. Their care and concern was seen as vital to survival, perhaps ultimately even more important than the contributions of fathers. Langdon's mother held less public authority, but seemed to find other ways of eliciting obedience and respect, perhaps connected to her careful allocation of food and domestic comforts. His 'dear good mother' commanded instant obedience without a blow.[35]

He was also clear about the unconditional nature of motherly affection, as shown when he comments on the effect of his leaving home:

> Of course I could not realise how very deep her grief must have been, being only a male. We as men love our children, but our love at best cannot be measured or weighed against the deep and constant love of a mother for her child.[36]

He, like many nineteenth-century working-class writers, presented a romantic, idealized picture of his mother, while his feelings towards his father are portrayed as much more ambivalent, combining respect with an element of fear and distance.

From the story of Roger Langdon we see the authority of fathers largely in a benevolent light, as protecting their children and transmitting knowledge of the world. To carry out these duties, it was very widely accepted that men required the authority to command obedience and respect from their children. Without these, a father could not enable his children to survive and develop into adulthood. In the stories of children themselves there remained a reluctance to condemn the ways their fathers sought to exercise authority, even many years after childhood, as Roger Langdon himself demonstrates in his narrative of respect for his father, and condemnation of 'the times' for his failings.

This unquestioned power gave men great freedom to choose and develop the kinds of relationships with their children which they felt appropriate, within the norms of their class, ethnic or religious group, and community. Abuse of this power was, therefore, difficult to name, to uncover or to ameliorate. The sexual exploitation of children by their fathers, as abusers themselves or through others, was the most hidden of all family secrets, and there remains

35. Langdon, *Life*, p. 12.   36. Ibid., p. 49.

very little evidence to the historian of these kinds of relationships. From the Langdon family story, we see that a sense of fatherhood as moving towards a kindly benevolence towards children can also mask the underlying continuity of the authority which fathers could exercise.

Public and private identities

Fatherhood can also be viewed through a wider lens. Being a father carried social meanings which extended beyond domestic life, and fatherhood acted as a crucial link in the interrelationships between the many public worlds which men occupied and the private worlds of their families. The role of breadwinner in the world of work had profound effects on domestic relationships, as did the gradual untangling of work from domestic life. The ability to provide for dependent wives and children was also increasingly a central element of masculine identity, although this was mediated by class, region, ethnicity and occupation. Such an identity formed the basis for the demands by working-class men for a widening of political rights, achieved in the Second Reform Act of 1867.

To look at some of these connections, we turn to the story of John Pearman, born 1816, died 1908, a police inspector based at Eton College. He wrote his life story around 1880 after retiring, describing his years in the army fighting in India, and then his married life, interspersed with a radical political polemic.

Pearman was an unusual autobiographer in that he wrote as a husband and father about his familial relationships, while most other working-class writers limited their family stories to their childhoods. He seemed to need to articulate the troubles of his family in a way other autobiographers chose not to discuss. He describes his marriage thus:

> What is Marriage but a life of trouble and Care and in most cases of the Poor a Great deal of poverty My own married life as been a life of much care having to raise eight Children out of eleven borned. ... Well the early part of my married life was I suppose much the same as other peoples some times a few sharp and hot words with the Wife but soon over ...[37]

37. John Pearman, *The Radical Soldier's Tale, John Pearman 1819–1908*, ed. Carolyn Steedman (Routledge, 1988), p. 217.

He went on to describe the division of responsibilities in his household:

> I would always be Master of the home and I spent the money as I found my wife was not up to the mark in laying out money to the best advantage but this never led to any words . . . But she as a very bad fault that is Ingratitude . . . it did not matter what you gave her in the way of money she never was thankful for it. I never spent a shilling from the home but that she never took into account Perhaps had I been a man otherwise I mite have been better thought of as then she would have had to work to bring something to help to maintain the Children. But I knew she had enough to do to keep the house and the Children straight and this she did much to her great Credit for the Children was always clean and fit to be seen and I must do her justice the Children was taught no bad ways nor did they see any.[38]

Pearman, as Master of his home, was the breadwinner, and he expected that his wife would be grateful to him because he had relieved her of the burden of paid work, although in fact wives of police officers were prohibited from working at this time. The division of labour for the breadwinning model is set out here, the husband earning income and the wife caring for house and children, with her most valued tasks being the public display of respectability and the moral training of the young.

This division of domestic labour and responsibility was only possible for those few working-class families with secure and reasonably well-paid work for the head of the household. We saw that even Roger Langdon with his railway job had a working wife. At crucial stages of the family's existence, especially when there were many young children who could not contribute, most could not survive on a single wage. But many families did aspire to do so, seeking to free hard-pressed wives from the extra burden of waged work, and to allow children to escape exploitation in the labour market, which could damage their prospects by breaking their health and restricting their education.

The benefits to husbands and fathers who could sustain the breadwinner role were significant. Husbands gained complete control over the income of the family, and could choose how much to allocate to the household rather than for their own use. However, Pearman went even further by insisting on controlling his wife's spending, commandeering even this area of domestic authority. This interface between the earning power of husbands in the

---

38. Ibid., pp. 218–19.

public world of work and the private spending needs of families was highly contested ground, and women used a wide range of tactics to maximize the resources they could command.[39] Many husbands left the household budgeting to their wives, whose skills in this area were highly valued, not least by cold and hungry children, and, like Pearman, felt entitled to gratitude for any restraint in spending their earnings on themselves. The definition of a 'good husband and father' focused on the generosity of financial contributions to the household, rather than their presence in the family as carers and helpers.

Standards of domestic life and comfort were undoubtedly higher when wives could concentrate on providing them, and breadwinners expected domestic comforts by virtue of their earning power. However precarious their income, they commanded the best when they were at home: the best food – men being given the largest share of any meat at mealtimes – the special chair by the fire, quiet and orderly children, and leisure time, as in this description of his father by Frank Steel:

> he would settle into that old mahogany-and-horsehair chair, so well worn and moulded to his convenience, and read – and discuss his readings with my mother, who sat knitting or sewing after clearing the tea-things away.[40]

As workplace and household became more and more distinct, men left most domestic matters to their wives, and by the late nineteenth century the popular stereotype of the husband who had no idea how to boil an egg or a father who was unable to change a nappy began to emerge. These arrangements were never universal, as we have seen with Pearman's intimate concern with domestic spending. Many chose to be 'family men', willing to help their wives at home, and enjoying the company of their children. Pearman wrote:

> And I must say the early part of my married life was mostly happy I used to save some money every year so as to give them a days outing sometimes 2 day and go to Sandhurst and this gave me more pleasure than anything I ever had . . . it lives in my minds eye and I can even enjoy the Sight now when I think of it and picture their happy young faces and that I think is the real blist of a married life . . .[41]

39. Ellen Ross, 'Survival networks: women's neighbourhood sharing in London before World War I', *History Workshop Journal* (1983).

40. Frank Steel, *Ditcher's Row: A Tale of the Older Charity* (Sidgwick & Jackson, 1939), p. 41.

41. Pearman, *The Radical Soldier's Tale*, pp. 218–19.

He also took his responsibilities as a parent very seriously, seeing this as the most significant area of conflict in his marriage:

> [sharp words were] always about the Children a Wife can be to much of a mother and indulge the children to every folly I must say this was the case with my wife. She is a most hard working woman and in the whole a Careful woman. . . . But no affection ought to make us blind to the faults of the Children or the mother. We may accept them as part and parcel of the beloved but we ought not to ignore them or Call them good . . . the Children loved beyond reason is a lasting fault of the Parent. We must do our duty in order to love them. such love is passionless. Duty gives neither kisses or caresses . . .[12]

We can see that Pearman had very definite ideas about how his children should be raised, and would not give way to his wife's softer approach. He believed that it was necessary for children to be disciplined and that childish desires should be contained in the interests of the child. He asserted that it was only men who were capable of controlling their feelings to the degree necessary to achieve this. Thus, while leaving the day-to-day care of children to wives, husbands could continue to insist that their own wishes about the ways children should be treated were carried out.

Pearman was in a good position to enforce his will, because he lived and worked in the same place. However, the increasing separation of men's work from their domestic lives which occurred as the breadwinner model took hold, meant that their authority over wives and children could be undermined in the many day-to-day decisions and practices of family life which took place when fathers were absent. While mothers might threaten 'Just wait till your father gets home' to impose control, they had in fact a whole range of material and emotional opportunities as parents which men were increasingly denied, whether by choice or by circumstances.

Pearman was not a distant father. He was intimately concerned with the upbringing of his children, but this closeness is entangled with an explicit demand for obedience. The successful assertion of his authority over his children and his wife was a necessary element, along with protecting and providing for them, of social respectability, of economic independence and, increasingly, as the basis for political rights in the public world.

But for Pearman, despite his mastery over his household, success was precarious, and this crisis, both in his family and in his sense of identity as a man, cruelly exposed his vulnerabilities:

42. Ibid., p. 218.

But I had many trials as a father . . . [it was] the end of August 1867
when one morning after Breakfast John Could not stand and was
very ill and in a little time after Lizzie was the same . . . they had got
the Scarlet Fever and in a few days more . . . the Wife was ill and not
able to give the Baby the Breast . . . the Head Master he sent for me
when he said he should like me and my Family to leave the College
until we were all well as he could not have the Students back while
such a bad case of Fever was in the College . . . Dr Gooch and Pearle
both said I must not move them but a few miles as the Children
could not stand a Journey of long distance . . . Now here was a trial
for a man to move my Wife and Children, Almost said Death to some
of them . . .

We started at 10AM . . . my wife tapped on the Fly window we
stopped John was taken worse. I looked at him and he poor Boy was
like Death the motions of the Fly had made him feel sick I rolled the
blanket round him & took him out when he was very sick at this time
a Gentleman Came up on Horseback and said do you know whats
the matter with that Boy. I did not answer him as the Boy was Vom-
iting he said he as the Scarlet Fever I replied I know that. He then
looked into the Fly and said (Inspector I had my uniform on) they
have all got the Fever were are you taken them I replied unto
Winkfield he said no that you shant I replied that I shall and Put my
son in the Fly again and was about to get on the seat myself when
he said what is your name I am the Doctor of Winkfield and must
know . . . I remained at Winkfield until the 5th November when I
returned with my Family again to Eton & thank God they continued
to do well & again got strong.[43]

Pearman tells this story of being forced by his employer to risk the
lives of his wife and children, and, after securing with great difficulty alternative accommodation and transport, facing a public
challenge by the Gentleman at the roadside. It was not just compassion which the Gentleman lacked, but respect for a man carrying
out his social responsibilities. As Pearman struggled to care for and
protect his family, he was also asserting his right as a man to do so.

This right had been expressed by many working-class men in
political terms since the days of the Chartist movement. Demands
for political reform and the extension of the franchise in 1867 were
focused on exactly what kinds of working men should be able to
vote, and it was those who had achieved independence, who could
support a family without resorting to charity or the Poor Law, who
showed sobriety, prudence and responsibility, who were thought
most acceptable as citizens and voters. The reforms themselves were

43. Ibid., pp. 220–4.

largely designed around ways of locating such men through a house-holder qualification which would show that a certain standard of living and respectability had been achieved.[44] Underlying these ideas was the breadwinner model, which gave a man responsibility and authority over a household, i.e. his wife, children and any other dependants. Only by successfully supporting these dependants was a man deemed fit to participate fully in political life, and thus marriage and fatherhood became increasingly associated with citizenship.

John Pearman was an exceptional autobiographer, in that he articulated feelings about marriage and fatherhood which few other working-class writers thought were important or appropriate. He was also exceptional because he implicitly linked his position as a husband and a father to his radical politics. His experience on the roadside confirmed and reinforced the development of his re-publican and anti-clerical views. Immediately following this story, he wrote:

> Returning again to the will of God I offtimes think what as he done for those poor people that live in poverty of the worst sort from birth to Death and no Cause of their own. . . . Well again we will look at our Parlement men they make Laws so as to keep 3 fifths of the whole people very poor so as the very poor may work and keep the other two fifths some in Comfort and some in splendour . . . some times they are Drove by the will of the people to a little for them but they rangle for a long time and then they leave some hole or corner to themselves.[15]

Like many demanding reform in 1867, he argued that men like himself were entitled to citizenship and equality based on their ability to support a family by their labour, rather than ownership of property or membership of an elite class. Success in the struggle for survival of his family, and resistance to those who threatened them, provided one of the few available proofs of his political as well as his personal worth.

From these diverse sources, it can be seen that the authority of fathers lay at the heart of their lives, linking and consolidating their positions within families, in communities and the nation. As we saw in Chapter 3, men were able to construct themselves as free-floating individuals, disconnected from these 'private' familial contexts. Fathers were seen as male individuals able to generate independently

44. D.G. Wright, *Democracy and Reform 1815–1885* (Longman, 1970), pp. 77–84.
45. Pearman, *The Radical Soldier's Tale*, p. 225.

their own sense of self, at the same time as being begetters of the next generation. However, the pervasive influence of individualism in understandings of the self has masked the continuing importance to masculinity of the successful exercise of authority over women and children.

When under threat, as in the case of Leopold Agar Ellis, fatherly authority had to be bitterly defended because it was such an important indicator both of adult masculinity and of full participation in society. The historical roots of this familial power were of such ancient origin, and such an integral part of social structures in the nineteenth century, that formal assertions of control by fathers were virtually impossible to challenge. But the ways this authority was defined and bounded were changing as children's needs were increasingly highlighted as being central family concerns.

Roger Langdon sought to protect his children from the harsh adult world he had survived with difficulty himself, and his capacity to do this meant that his involvement with his children was very different from that of his own father. At the same time, family life was becoming more closely associated with a female world of nurture, and as women began to assert rights both as wives and as mothers, the authority of fathers was gradually undermined and subverted. John Pearman's struggle to retain control over his domestic life, both with his wife and with external forces ranged against him, reflects these growing tensions.

And yet, long-standing social structures and cultural practices which underpinned the authority of fathers were in some ways reinforced by these changes, through the model of the breadwinner and its associated privileges, and a new definition of citizenship which relied on domestic respectability and the dependence of wives and children. Fathers' rights were thus simultaneously undermined and reinforced by legal and political reforms. A society in which the authority of fatherhood could be openly challenged remained unimaginable, and men as fathers continued to be able to determine how their children should live and grow up long into the twentieth century.

CHAPTER SIX

Domestic service and lodging: doing family work

Some places you knew you were the maid. Another place you'd go and they were just all right. You didn't think you were a maid, you just lived with them you see.

Yorkshire servant, 1890s[1]

I have many times felt sorry to observe that she [the landlady] had gone beyond her means in making a pie or tart merely for the satisfaction of asking me to have a bit.

London journeyman builder, 1820s[2]

Until the Second World War almost all upper- and middle- and some working-class families relied heavily on paid domestic help, and the majority of working-class women worked in some kind of service position at some time during their lives. Residential domestic service was the largest single employer of women and girls well into the twentieth century, peaking in the 1890s, in the region of 1,400,000, an estimate of one in every three young women between the ages of 15 and 20, not to speak of the roughly 60,000 men and boys. Exact figures for the number of households employing servants are misleading for reasons which are discussed later in this chapter. Nevertheless, it can be stated that the majority of the population had the experience of either having been 'in service', living in a household with servants, offering services as a landlady or receiving them as a lodger. Over a life cycle a person may have been in several of these positions. Yet oddly the service relationship has never been regarded as an integral component of history, either of the economy or the family, possibly because it so clearly exemplifies the blurring between home and work, private and public.

1. Essex Oral History Archive No. 268.
2. John Burnett, *Useful Toil: Autobiographies of Working People from the 1820s to the 1920s* (1974; Penguin, 1984), p. 285.

Another reason for this absence may be that analysing domestic service 'undresses' the upper and middle classes. The issue of service has been productive of tensions and conflicts within families, which go to the heart of gender and class hierarchies in ways which have been – and are still – hard for those with most power to acknowledge. To preserve the privileges of status and deference demanded clear boundaries between servants and family members, for these boundaries were in reality constantly being breached and put under strain. This was particularly the case in a society such as mainland England with few differences based on racial, ethnic, religious, linguistic characteristics, in contrast, for example, to the Empire abroad.

In the nineteenth century the class and gender order inherent in service positions was much more visible than it is today. The language of the period is illuminating. Unless a man was living at home with his wife, mother, sister or other female relatives he would, if possible, pay someone to look after or 'do' for him. What did 'doing' for someone entail? It meant having the house – including outside steps and surroundings – cleaned, clothes washed, ironed and mended, meals cooked and served, coal fetched, fires lighted and tended, bathing water carried to and from bedrooms, chamber pots emptied, errands run and messages carried. It might also entail 'people work': listening to grievances, being the repository of secrets, lying to save face, giving emotional support and sympathy. Only with wives were sexual services a legitimate part of the bargain, yet these too might often be included.

Adult men, by virtue of their masculinity, had access to at least some of these services. But unless they could assert their familial rights as husband, father, son, brother or uncle, they had to pay in cash as master to servant(s) in their own home or as lodger to landlady and her helpers. Femininity was partially defined as being a server, foremost as wife, then as mother. But since similar skills and labour could be 'sold' as a servant or landlady, women would often gain their livelihood throughout their lives in servicing roles, however named, paid in a combination of cash wages, board and room. The *position* of being a wife, a servant or a landlady differed, but the daily round was remarkably similar.

Considerations of class as well as gender predicted who was served and who was the server. Middle- and upper-class women demanded services based on their wealth and status. Their way of life depended on round-the-clock attendance on the house and its occupants. Household arrangements through the nineteenth century were increasingly complex. Many hands and much energy were needed to keep furniture, carpets, curtains and knick-knacks clean, for elaborate meals and visiting rituals, and for fashionable, intricate clothing to be cleaned and mended. Even where it was realized that much domestic work resulted from complicated expectations of etiquette, particularly for formal dinners, it was felt that family and civilized social life would collapse without it.[3]

But simply supplying basic requirements was hard drudgery. Both a full hod of coal and a jug of bath water weighed around 30 pounds, often to be carried up numerous flights of stairs. Until the 1850s perambulators were uncommon and nursemaids were expected to carry babies and toddlers, often for hours at a time; the average middle-class 18-month-old child weighed about 26 pounds.[4] Where servants' labour was unaffordable, members of the household would have to do the tasks themselves and the level of living was simplified. Wherever possible people would buy in help, at least for tasks such as scrubbing floors, jobs termed, significantly, 'the rough', 'the black' or 'donkey work'. Much of the mid-century debate about having sufficient income to marry centred on what a wife could be expected to do in the house and yet maintain health and respectability if not gentility.[5]

The genteel might be reduced to taking in P.G.s (paying guests), fostering children, running a boarding house or, if they were unmarried women, taking positions as paid companions or governesses, whose duties, though primarily social or educational, could involve physical care. On the other hand, some working-class households were able to pay for help, a very young girl for baby-minding or the weekly washerwoman, although they usually relied on relatives or neighbours in return for other favours in a type of barter. This chapter, then, attempts to unravel some of the tangle of family life and servicing roles.

It was a tangle that troubled commentators throughout the nineteenth century, as exactly who was to be included in a family and a household shifted meaning. The office of the Registrar General struggled constantly with the problem of definitions, particularly around the edges of the nuclear core. In 1863, he pronounced:[6]

3. August Webster, *A Housewife's Opinion* (Macmillan, 1879).

4. Calculations made with assistance from the Castle Museum, York. See Leonore Davidoff and Ruth Hawthorn, *A Day in the Life of a Victorian Domestic Servant* (Allen & Unwin, 1976).

5. John M. Robson, *Marriage or Celibacy: The Daily Telegraph on a Victorian Dilemma* (University of Toronto Press, 1995).

6. Census 1863, Vol. LIII, p. 33.

> The family in its complete form consists of a householder with his
> wife and his children; and in the higher classes with his servants.
> Other relatives and visitors sometimes form a part of the family; and
> so do lodgers at a common table who pay for their subsistence and
> lodging.

But when considered through records of past lives rather than official
categories, experience refuses to fit so neatly and the boundaries
between master/mistress and servant, landlady and lodger, appear
less clear cut. An elderly widow might provide some resources such as
house room and perhaps food in return for help with cooking and
housework, plus a small cash contribution. But it is almost impossible to decide in such cases who was dependent on whom. Was this
a servant/employer, a landlady/lodger, an older and younger set
of friends, or, if kin were involved, a familial relationship? What
matters is that this was a relationship of *interdependence*. The older
person had companionship and help, the younger companionship,
food and lodging, and both gained some meaning in their lives.

By thus starting with what was actually done within households
as well as who did it, a more vivid, nuanced picture emerges. Difficulties in sorting out categories of kin, servant, lodger, which
have so bedevilled historians, might more fruitfully be viewed as a
window onto nineteenth-century social, cultural and family life.

The service relationship: masculine and feminine domains

The near universality of a service relationship between people is
difficult to grasp from a late twentieth-century perspective. Service
in a household or establishment other than that of one's birth had
been the common experience until the nineteenth century. Service
to a master or mistress, to King and country, and to God all figured
in accepted world views. The superior expected attendance and
deference as a matter of unquestioned right. Not until the nineteenth and early twentieth century were such expectations eroded
by novel forms of work, for men at least, and by evolving ideas
about individuality, independence, equality and democracy.

By the late nineteenth century adult men were assumed to be
both responsible for and served by female dependants, a growing
contradiction as women themselves gradually gained rights as individuals. Only after 1875 could a wife be legally deemed competent
to bind herself as a servant without her husband's permission and

with a right to her own earnings.[7] Conversely, the independence linked to masculinity meant that male servants, so obviously another man's (or, worse, woman's) creature, felt increasingly uncomfortable with their position. The terms 'flunky', 'menial' or 'lackey', when applied to them, implied they were not engaged in real work, and hinted at their lack of masculine prowess.

In keeping with notions of appropriate masculine and feminine roles within families, most male servants worked outside as gardeners and in the stables. They might also occasionally do heavy jobs inside, along with the boot-boy who cleaned shoes, knives, carried coal and was a general factotum, but who usually left service by his late teens. By the mid nineteenth century, except on farms, women and girls were mainly employed indoors, but were sent out on errands as it became less viable for genteel women to do their own shopping. As other opportunities for men, such as school teaching, arose, by 1900 only the wealthiest could afford male servants such as footmen, whose eighteenth-century-style costume, the livery, with its powdered wigs and knee breeches, was symbolic of their ornamental status. In grander establishments male servants were required to be at least six feet tall and have well-formed legs, sometimes with a bit of extra padding, to show off the livery. Women servants did not wear uniform until around mid century, when plain print frocks, now worn only for morning work, began to be replaced in the afternoon by the black dress with ornamental apron and cap for 'front stage' rituals in public areas of the house. Uniforms differentiated servants from family members and demonstrated the social position of the household. While most women had forsaken indoor caps by the late nineteenth century, maids had to continue wearing them well into the twentieth century, by which time they had become a resented badge of servility.

Although we think of nineteenth-century middle-class households having at least three specialized servants, few could afford such an establishment. However, the rapid increase in the number of households with an income of £100–£300 a year by the 1870s meant that a general maid became more affordable, sometimes with occasional outside help.[8] In households with numerous children, the housewife had always done a good deal of work herself, including sewing, cooking and childcare, but she could also make use of older daughters and other female kin. Such a mixture of paid service and

7. James Patterson, *Notes on the Law of Master and Servant* (1885).
8. T.M. McBride, *The Domestic Revolution: The Modernisation of Household Service in England and France 1820–1920* (Croom Helm, 1976), p. 50.

unpaid household assistance is illustrated in the life of Mary H., born in 1876. As a young girl she went by the day as companion-guardian to a mentally ill neighbour, also doing morning and evening household tasks at home. In her teens she was variously a paid living-in nursemaid, and helped her married sister and then an aunt with their new babies in return for room and board only. Back in London she became a house/parlourmaid, later promoted to head housemaid, and in her twenties married a tram conductor, when, as his wife, keeping house, she received set housekeeping money.[9] As Mary shifted between categories it was not the nature of the tasks, nor even simply the level or means of payment, which would have designated her at different times either as family or servant, but rather a mix of factors, such as her class, the sense of duty and obligation created by kinship ties, feelings of affection and the terms of the marriage contract.

The middle- and upper-class vision of service was ambivalent. At one level it stressed the familial nature of the relationship, at least officially. Servants, whatever their age, were regarded much like children in their duty to obey, to give loyalty and deference. In return they were owed basic maintenance. The term 'maid', derived from 'maiden' which originally meant a young girl, applied to all menial female servants. Indeed, in many smaller households a servant scarcely more than a child who, like Mary, might be kin or the daughter of a neighbour or friend, looked after children too young to be of help, or would substitute for the labour power of older children after they had left home.

Census takers were themselves confused about who was and who was not a servant. Edward Higgs has highlighted the problem for the mid century, when the occupation of 'servant' and 'relationship to the head' are both listed, so that it is often unclear whether the person named is in daily service in another household or a servant in the listed household.[10] Extending this critique with data from other sources, a study of mid-century Exeter concludes that the notion of servants in the classical sense may need to be revised to incorporate rather than exclude those servants related by kin. Jane Hinton was the servant of Ann Hillier but she was also her niece, daughter of Ann's brother. Although the kin relationship is thus close and the servant's surname is the maiden name of the female head of house, the kin link is not apparent in the census, and

9. Anonymous manuscript, courtesy of Anna Davin.
10. Edward Higgs, 'Domestic service and household production', in A. John (ed.), *Unequal Opportunities* (Oxford University Press, 1986).

would probably only have been acknowledged by the family if their class backgrounds were also similar.[11]

In the latter part of the century, as occupational designations hardened, government officials felt further pressure to distinguish between private, familial roles and the waged economy. Boys and young men could continue to be assumed to be helpers or informal apprentices in the productive enterprise, but girls were more problematic. As the Registrar General noted in 1861, 'the wife and grown up children (Order 4) perform at home for the bulk of the population the same duties as the persons in Order 5 (servants); but they are not paid directly in money for their services as they form a part of the natural family'.[12]

The separation of home and work dictated that, by 1871, Order 4 consisted entirely of women, embracing 'the majority of the women engaged in the most useful of all occupations, that of wife, mother and mistress of a family',[13] and through 1881 these two orders were separate. But in 1891 there was still uncertainty and it was considered that the daily occupations of daughters and other female relatives at home who had been classified as unoccupied should now be recognized as in domestic service, although it was admitted that 'as in many other questions of statistical classification, there is much to be said on both sides'. Yet by 1901 the conclusion was reached that it would be better to revert to the method of 1881.[14] This wavering has been a stumbling block to labour historians as they have tried to trace domestic service as an occupation. But perhaps it should rather be a warning to query the category 'servant' and even the category 'occupation' since it points to the fundamental uncertainty over hard divisions between paid work and family exchanges of labour.

Similar ambivalence is also reflected in the quasi-familial legal status of the service role, especially after the 1870s when the major contract of employment had shifted to the impersonal 'workman and employer' away from the previous total control of the 'master and servant' contract. Yet in controlling a daughter's choice of

11. Di Cooper and Moira Donald, 'Households and "hidden" kin in early nineteenth-century England: four case studies in suburban Exeter, 1821–1861', *Continuity and Change*, Vol. 10, No. 2 (1995), pp. 273, 275.

12. Census 1861, Appendix (1863), Vol. LIII I, p. 231. Note that Order 4 consisted of 'Persons engaged in the Domestic Offices or Duties of Wives, Mothers, Mistresses of Families, Children, Relatives (otherwise not returned)' – a catch-all category but by definition mainly female.

13. Census 1871, *General Report*, LXXI (1873), p. xli.

14. *Census General Report* (1893–94), CVI; *General Report* (1904), CVII.

marriage partner, a father could still use the device of suing for the loss of his *daughter's* domestic services.[15] Legal exemption from the Truck Acts, which since the 1830s had forbidden payment in kind rather than cash, meant that by the second part of the century domestic servants were more obviously segregated from other wage earners since they continued to live in their employers' households, were paid partly with board and lodging, and were expected to be available at all times.

Terms of service

The *personal* control of the servant's labour and time singled out the relationship and coloured the contract, as did the intimate nature of the work, caring for the bodies and the personal possessions of the employer and household. The contract bound servants for all their time, as well as much of their life course. Grounds for dismissal without wages in lieu of notice included 'wilful disobedience to the lawful orders of the master', given notoriety in cases such as the rightful dismissal of a maid who left her master's house against his orders to visit her dying mother. Hannah Cullwick did not even try. In the 1840s, as a teenage nurserymaid to eight children, she was prevented from going the three miles to her home to be with her younger siblings after her parents died within a few weeks of each other: 'I thought it was no use tho I ax'ed to go and all my strength seemed gone.'[16]

Employers stressed loyalty and harmony: the servant as part of the family. Nursemaids and nannies epitomized this ideal, as in the language of this memoir:

> The very best type of old servant . . . her stern exterior scarcely concealing an undying loyalty and faithfulness to 'the master' and 'the mistress' and their offspring. Whose whole life was a labour of love, untroubled by self or any other kind of questioning; who was loved in return and whose heart it would have broken to leave us.[17]

Lack of other employment opportunities and the power to enforce these expectations put the servant at the mercy of the employer's whims as well as external strokes of fate, such as the death or

15. J.W. Smith, *Laws of Master and Servants* (Wilson's Legal Handy Books, 1960).
16. Quoted in L. Davidoff, 'Class and gender in Victorian England: the case of Hannah Cullwick and A.J. Munby', in *Worlds Between: Historical Perspectives on Gender and Class* (Polity Press, 1995), p. 120.
17. John Raynor, *A Westminster Childhood* (Cassell, 1973), p. 86.

bankruptcy of the master/mistress. Not unexpectedly, then, servants stressed contractual elements, looking for high wages, good conditions, fair treatment and the right to move on to improve their situation. Career servants knew the advantages of never staying in one place for too long, the reverse of the old family retainer image. Faithful service gave no guarantee of support in illness and old age; elderly servants without kin or friends were disproportionately represented in the workhouse. Legally, they were only entitled to reasonable wages, food and accommodation while employed.

In a period when the social hierarchy was coming into question, personal services were justified as both a necessity and a requirement of civilized society, the means by which the better off contributed to the social order. A late nineteenth-century newspaper correspondence on domestic servants claimed that 'the highly educated class or "head" of the social body should occupy itself in doing *its* proper work of *thinking* for the welfare of the hands and feet which serve it'.[18] This sentiment survived, pervading the memoir of a 1920s upper-middle-class child who was taught that 'it is a privilege and a necessity for members of the ruling classes to have servants to run their homes, thus leaving them free to run the world and improve it'.[19]

Part of that self-proclaimed duty of setting an example to the lower orders was to be achieved by maintaining a certain standard of living and of behaviour and training young servants in household affairs and genteel manners. However, much of this rhetoric was often honoured in the breach rather than in practice. Rituals of gentility were meaningless to many servants in terms of their own lifestyle. The rites of inclusion and exclusion in At Home days, where middle-class women would hold open house for selected acquaintances, were incomprehensible to many working-class women, who derisively termed them 'tea-fights'. Nor were they impressed by the social manoeuvrings implied in the practice of calling and card-leaving.[20] A woman in service in the 1900s recalled:

> And the funny thing was, they used to leave their cards on a tray on the hall table, I think it was – I don't know why but one of her own card and two of her husband's – visiting-cards – so that each lady

18. *Sydenham and Penge Gazette*, 1892.
19. Ursula Holden, 'Maids', unpublished manuscript by permission of the author, 1996.
20. See L. Davidoff, *The Best Circles: 'Society', Etiquette and the Season* (Hutchinson, 1986).

would leave three. Goodness knows why. They were collected and anything very important they used to leave there so that people could see it. It was all so shabby.[21]

In larger establishments it was easier to maintain distance with a complicated organization as if by invisible labour, emphasized in the quarantining of servants behind a green-baize-lined door, keeping the sounds of housework and preparation out of the unruffled employer's quarters. Servants unavoidably meeting other household members might have to curtsey or even sometimes turn their faces to the wall as if they did not exist.

Servants, children and other inmates of middle- and upper-class households shared domestic routines. Especially in large aristocratic and gentry houses holding up to twenty or thirty kin and visitors with *their* servants, control over numbers was kept by the strict ordering of daily life. The day, the week and the year were divided up in an exact, unvarying pattern, often framed by church on Sunday, and punctuated by ritualized holidays. Weekly menus for the average household followed the well-trodden rotation of Sunday joint, cold on Monday, mince on Tuesday and so on, with designated puddings to match. And then,

the spring cleaning took place at a given date, no matter the temperature; down quilts disappeared into a huge camphor chest and white quilts appeared on every bed in the house. At the same time, all the windows were dressed in white lace curtains.[22]

This way of life was seen in direct contrast to the seeming disorder described in a rough London area where rubbish filled the streets, windows were always closed, meals ran into each other, and beds flowed into all the rooms, with smells, crush and messiness everywhere.[23]

Behind such divisions was the realization that upper- and middle-class identity itself was at least partly defined by servants and the institution of service. Although servants were themselves representative of the 'polluting poor', one of their key functions was to separate and protect their employers from that disordered world as well as from the potential disorder and detritus of their own genteel daily life.

21. Essex Oral History Archive No. 105.
22. Dorothy Thompson, *Sophia's Son: The Story of a Suffolk Parson 1841–1916* (Terence Dalton, 1969), p. 110.
23. Alexander Patterson, *Across the Bridges, or Life By the South London Riverside* (Edward Arnold, 1911), p. 11.

Servants and childhood

The contradictions and tensions arising from servants' presence in the houses of the upper and middle classes are particularly evident in the relationship between servants and children. Nannies were there to free mothers for social roles expected of upper- and upper-middle-class wives; the mechanics of daily infant and child care were left to inferior others. In an 1890s memoir of an upper-class girl:

> to me she was the perfect mother. I would not have liked her to dose me, bath me, comfort me or hold my head when I was sick. These intimate functions were performed by Nanny or by Annie our nursery maid. . . . I did not like mother even to see me in the bath.[24]

As one nurse put it, 'their mother was their mother but it was we who had the makin' or the marrin' of them'.[25] Whether the nurse was loved, hated or simply endured, the split was a potent part of these children's psychic make-up.

Upper- and middle-class children learned about their own place within the world from watching, listening to and interacting with servants. Parents showed how being 'one of us' was what servants were *not*. Servants' language was ridiculed, their rooms and bodies smelled 'frowsty' – unsurprisingly, given their heavy work and the limited washing facilities allowed. Servants might be expected to address even toddlers with the title Master or Miss, but they were called either by their surnames, titles such as Nanny or Cook, or if lower servants by a generic first name.

The distance between children and servants depended on the income and social position of the head of the household. Despite the famed British Nanny, numerically, a caretaker was more likely to be a girl or young woman near in status to her charges doing more than just childcare. While many servants became attached to children in their charge, generating mutual affection and loyalty, the children sensed that they were potentially part of the order-giving class. Young maids struggling to fulfil care-taking duties without an adult authority could be made miserable by the teasing and hampering of children nearly their own age, as in the pit-trap dug for the unsuspecting nurserymaid on the daily walk.[26] The unstable

24. Mary Lutyens, *To Be Young: Some Chapters of Autobiography* (Rupert Hart-Davis, 1959), p. 15.

25. Essex Oral History Archive.

26. L. Davidoff, 'Above and below stairs', *New Society*, 26 April 1973.

boundary between childhood and adulthood, determined by class rather than age, is evident in the composition of some households. A girl of 14 or 15, her undernourished body still far from puberty, was expected to do a full day's work, to put her hair up and lengthen her skirts. Yet she might be living under the same roof as the daughter of the house, of a similar age but still regarded as a child in the schoolroom, hair down her back, skirts still only to the knee, yet physically tall, well built and most likely past first menstruation.

Children might only be admitted to the front of the house at ritually fixed times, such as the 5 p.m. parental visit in the parlour with clean clothes, brushed hair and best behaviour. Servants, often working in dark, underground parts of the house, shared some of the youngsters' physical space, including the back stairs and back passage, the latter a nursery euphemism for anus, exit for waste products and object of disgust. Like the children, servants were not supposed to initiate conversation or action, especially on their own behalf. This might give a sense of fellowship against the common power of the master/father, mistress/mother. Middle- and upper-class memoirs recall nostalgically the atmosphere of the warm kitchen where children could sample more flavoursome food than their bland nursery fare. Servants offered a window on the world unlike their own protected atmosphere. Maids were a fascinating source of forbidden topics: birth, sex, adventure, whispering stories about their courting escapades, enlivened by the characteristic smell of hair oil, patchouli and body odour.

Servants also played a part in teaching the unwritten rules of gender behaviour and attitudes. Girls were told that little ladies do not whistle, slouch or sit on steps and boys were admonished to be little gentlemen while being allowed more latitude in language and activity.[27] Boys picked up masculine attitudes and skills from male staff along with the special deference accorded them by female servants. Girls in less elaborate households might learn domestic tasks from the servant. Whatever the social level, the presence of an extra person with a somewhat different point of view and relation of authority could enrich children's sense of themselves and their identity. This fascination with another, often illicit world was counteracted by their ultimate loyalty to their own family and class culture. Children of the household could show off to servants their

---

27. The neglected role of female servants in boys' boarding schools is investigated in Peter M. Lewis, 'Mummy, matron and the maids: feminine presence and absence in male institutions 1934–63', in Michael Roper and John Tosh (eds), *Manful Assertions: Masculinities in Britain since 1800* (Routledge, 1991).

superior skills, education, clothing, possessions. At the same time, parents and elders sincerely admonished their children to be polite to servants 'because they cannot answer back'.[28]

For children raised in the Indian or African colonies the expectation of both care and deference was greatly enhanced where servants were natives, a race apart, where the adults who waited on the miniature Sahibs were eternal Boy and Girl. Within English culture generally, both subliminal and conscious expectations of servants and their childlike status coloured middle- and upperclass views of the peoples in the vast domain over which the Mother Country held dominion.

Dynamics of power in domestic service

Employers expected obedience, meekness, deference and competence in those who performed personal services. Through superiority of wealth, social position and often age, they could demand these qualities and punish those who failed them. Servants might be family members, but they were primarily *hands*, not people. A terrified 12-year-old in full uniform waiting table at dinner seemed to do everything wrong, and was punished by being kept in on Sunday and given a 'a good hiding' (illegal since the 1860s) when she fell downstairs carrying a full tray.[29] Some masters and mistresses also demanded emotional support and personal attachment. Perceived failure in any area could mean a denial of a 'character', the reference necessary for obtaining another post, a potent weapon in the hands of employers. Since most servants worked alone and lived in the home of the employer, they tended not to compare wage rates. The few attempts to organize them into unions failed completely.

Despite the advantages of their position, employers often had reason to fear their servants. It was hard to hide the most intimate secrets from those who came into the bedroom every morning to open the curtains, bringing tea or a breakfast tray. There was fear of pollution from servants, contamination by those who did the family's dirty work, resulting in, for the wealthy, separate servants' laundry and linen, bathing and toilet facilities. Yet these very people prepared food, made the beds, bathed the babies, touched every

28. Davidoff, 'Above and below stairs'.
29. A. Harvey, 'Domestic service recollections collection', Leicester County Record Office.

item in the house. Common phobias reflect similar anxieties; the maid (sometimes rightfully) accused of stealing her mistress's clothes and possessions, or of persecuting the mistress, was a recognized manifestation of wealthy women's paranoia. Servants had their own methods of revenge against unfair treatment, using familiar weapons such as sulking, mishearing orders, semi-deliberate spoiling of materials, wasting time, 'the sullen dumb insolence and petty irritations'[30] bemoaned by employers.

Family rows and dramas often depended on having servants as audience, but servants were also witnesses in the legal sense in separation and divorce cases. Grounds for cruelty included a wife being insulted in the presence of her servants, her authority over them stripped away by a vengeful husband.[31] An experienced older servant could wield considerable power over a young novice mistress; the old family retainer could become a crusty domestic tyrant. Above all, employers feared becoming physically and mentally dependent on servants in illness or old age.

This combination of power, dependence and fear may account for the silence or at the best trivial attention to domestic service both at the time and by twentieth-century commentators and historians. In nineteenth-century novels their presence is generally only indicative of the status of the household, much like the mention of clothing or furniture.[32] However, tensions between servants and employers emerge in fictional form, quintessentially in Henry James's *Turn of the Screw* where an evil footman and declassed governess gain total power to corrupt the innocence of the two children of the family left in their care.

Governesses in particular were an object of intense, even symbolic ambiguity and unease. They received journalistic and literary attention far beyond their actual numbers, for becoming a governess was considered the only semi-respectable position for distressed gentlewomen. The horrified reaction to the independence and subliminal power of Charlotte Brontë's governess heroine in her 1840s novel *Jane Eyre* when it was first reviewed was a prime example.[33]

Neither servant nor family, the governess occupied a marginal social, and often physical, space in the household. Not quite a lady,

30. Margaret Powell, *Below Stairs* (Peter Davies, 1968), p. 156.
31. A. James Hammerton, *Cruelty and Companionship: Conflict in Nineteenth-Century Married Life* (Routledge, 1992), p. 128.
32. Mary D. Smith, 'Downstairs from the upstairs: a study of the servants' hall in the Victorian novel', Ph.D. thesis, Harvard University (1966).
33. Miriam Allott (ed.), *The Brontës: The Critical Heritage* (Routledge & Kegan Paul, 1974).

other servants might despise her but the family could also choose whether or not to include her. Spending her days and often her nights in the company of children, she was never fully an adult. But for that very reason she was in danger of usurping the mother's role. And there was an underlying possibility that, at least if she was young, she might become a romantic, if not sexual object for men in the household (see Chapter 8). Becoming a governess was, by definition, almost always through force of circumstance rather than choice. Their lives were often lonely with a high incidence of mental and physical breakdown. Florence Nightingale's first 'home' which provided nursing care was for ex-governesses.[34]

Although personalities of both parties could play a significant role, ultimately much depended on the obviously unequal social expectations and resources available to servant and employer. Among many landed families there was a belief that working for them was a privilege in itself. Conditions, especially wages, were not important; but their staff had rather different views.[35]

Some flashpoints emerge in the sparse records. A main source of dissatisfaction was food. Not only was it often insufficient, some employers deliberately gave inferior quality to mark their social distinction – it was 'good enough' for the servant. Servants often complained of positions where the bread 'is doled out by the piece and the milk by the drop' or where 'the meat was cut as if for the cat'.[36] Another source of bitter annoyance was having their own names disregarded for a generalized servant designation. It may not be coincidental that the most frequent of these for women, 'Mary Anne', had been a synonym for prostitute as well as female genitals.[37] The 'John Thomas' for men servants was used as a euphemism for penis, the ultimate tool or creature of the master, and both names carry these connotations in some parts of the country to this day. In smaller households, the servant might be called by her first name and eat with the family, but when visitors came she would revert to her surname and a meal in the kitchen.[38]

34. See Jeanne Petersen, 'The Victorian governess: status incongruence in family and society', in Martha Vicinus (ed.), *Suffer and Be Still: Women in the Victorian Age* (Methuen, 1973); Kathryn Hughes, *The Victorian Governess* (Hambledon Press, 1993).

35. Merlin Waterson, *The Servant's Hall: A Domestic History of Erddig* (Routledge & Kegan Paul, 1980), p. 189.

36. McBride, *The Domestic Revolution*, p. 54.

37. Thanks to Sue Hodges for the information on 'Mary Anne'.

38. Trevor Lummis, 'Historical data and the social sciences', Open University Cassettes, D 301 06–011, 1974.

There was resentment, too, over the lack of privacy even for older servants whose rooms and belongings were open to inspection, especially if anything appeared missing from the house. Personal photographs and other mementoes were often banned from servants' bedrooms. Under the rubric of moral guidance employers could dictate what clothes servants might wear, overseeing both uniform and street clothes. When family and visitors were conspicuously lazy and capricious, drank heavily, refused to pay creditors, or had adulterous affairs, the homilies about servants' duty produced much cynicism. Being summoned to daily family prayers and reminded to accept their duties according to their station in life and do their work not just to please but in singleness of heart[39] could ring hollow indeed.

Some of the most corrosive memories of service centre on rules forbidding any kind of singing, dance or music, or other expressions of an independent personality, although as a treat a maid might stand in the doorway and listen to a lady play and sing. A 15-year-old kitchen maid was instantly dismissed without a character because she had dared to play a tune on the drawing-room piano while her employers were at church.[40]

The practice of servants kneeling to remove the employers' boots and shoes, as did the wife or daughter in some establishments without servants, was another ritual humiliation experienced as 'desperately degrading'.[41] In the exaggerated play around dominance and submission of Arthur Munby and his servant, later wife, Hannah Cullwick, both power and erotic dynamics are evident in his training her to embrace lowliness and demonstrate her love for him by kneeling before her Massa, to remove but also to lick his boots, as well as scrub the pavement on her hands and knees while he looked on.[42]

Struggles over the control of the servant's time, labour and person were endemic. Men servants could use the power of their masculinity to demand more independence. In the vexed question of time off, as an 1890s commentator said, 'men servants can get out for the best of all reasons, that they insist on it'.[43] Women, particularly young girls, were easier to restrain, accustomed to a subservient and caring role. Even the Girls' Friendly Society, an organization

39. *Family Prayers For a Fortnight with Forms for Particular Days by a Lady* (1856).

40. S. McCurdy, *Sylvia: A Victorian Childhood* (Eastland Press, 1972), p. 72.

41. Male servant in Essex Oral History Archive No. 268.

42. Davidoff, 'Class and gender in Victorian England', p. 133. Note that in the famous pornographic novel, 'Walter's' *My Secret Life*, the hero still in his teens was inflamed with lust when the maidservant was ordered to kneel and remove his boots.

43. Davidoff, 'Above and below stairs'.

purportedly formed by ladies to protect servants, had to tread carefully, fearing the accusation of making girls independent and interfering between them and the employing family.[44]

With many servants there was inherent conflict between loyalty to their own family and friends and the family or household of the employer. For some, like the young girl born in the workhouse and whose foster parents had rejected her, the shopkeeper's family where she worked for forty years became her own, the children of the household her children, negating the very low wages paid.[45] Conversely in very large households the older servants could 'adopt' youngsters, protecting them, instructing them, finding them extra food and privileges. However, in both such cases, as with any deeply emotional as well as material involvement, the quasi-familial role could be exploitative and harsh, manipulative and even violent, rather than loving.

For many youngsters the first place away from home, the abrupt shift from crowds of brothers and sisters to the cold loneliness of the single-servant place or the ostracism and ridicule of their lowly position in a multi-servant establishment, meant a trial by homesickness. Servants usually left their own families for economic reasons, to send part of their wages home, to 'get their feet under someone else's table', even occasionally to have experience of an external authority. 'Me father wouldn't let me come under him; he thought I would be better with a stranger', commented the son of a farm bailiff.[46]

Yet especially for young, inexperienced girls, their relatives were the only protection against exploitation and abuse. In a study of a market town in 1851, three-quarters of servants had been born inside a radius of ten miles, just near enough to allow them to visit their own families on foot on their day off.[47] But many employers deliberately sought servants from some distance precisely to keep such contacts to a minimum. Preferably the servant had no relations at all to interfere. In the late 1860s, Mary Ann Wilson, at the age of 14, had gone from the London Workhouse to service in a suburban family. Her employer later complained: 'this girl's aunt seems to wish to have her which makes her indifferent to pleasing her mistress. Her brother has visited her and still further unsettled her.'[48] Young servants could find themselves caught in difficult

44. Girls' Friendly Society, *An Appeal to the Mistresses of Elementary Schools* (1882).
45. Essex Oral History Archive No. 19.   46. Essex Oral History Archive No. 26.
47. Sample from the 1851 census of Colchester, L. Davidoff.
48. South London Metropolitan School District Records (1868–71), GLRO [L]. SMSD/179.

situations between employers and strict, unforgiving parents. A teenage housemaid trying to avoid persistent sexual advances from the master did not dare return home to her narrow-minded, punitive widowed father, who would have undoubtedly blamed her and turned her out. The only solution was to leave her situation on the grounds of illness.[49]

Many servants felt strongly about being cut off from their own families and social milieu, a deprivation which narrowed their lives and stunted their opportunities:

> It's very difficult to get others [employers] to understand that it was your sister and you wanted to see them . . . And we couldn't get the same days off and that's really why we weren't able to see each other. It's a terrific sacrifice when you look back on it. I mean we lost touch with some.[50]

Employers were in even more of a dilemma about their servants' possible marriage. Adhering to family values and the sacredness of the marriage bond, they could hardly openly object, but in private they grumbled. A mid-century Birmingham widow begrudged her own peace of mind to the cook who wished to marry: 'we see there is not much consideration nor gratitude in servants; she must know how I have been circumstanced and still am'.[51]

While male servants expected to have wives and children of their own, female living-in servants had to pay others to board their own children. The panic over baby farming in the 1870s, where mainly illegitimate infants were fostered *en masse* with an ensuing high mortality rate, revealed a large proportion of domestic servant mothers.[52] Wet-nurses whose own babies had thus been disposed of, or who had died, sold their breastfeeding capacity to ladies who could not or would not breastfeed themselves, the ultimate expression of contractual yet intimate service by the less well off to the more wealthy.

Seeking an opportunity of meeting a husband was even more frowned upon; courting gave overt messages of independence and sexuality. Many employers tried to strictly enforce a 'no followers'

49. Essex Oral History Archive No. 129.
50. Essex Oral History Archive No. 283.
51. L. Davidoff and C. Hall, *Family Fortunes: Men and Women of the English Middle Class, 1780–1850* (Routledge, 1994), p. 389.
52. Margaret L. Arnot, 'Infant death, child care and the state: the baby-farming scandal and the first infant life protection legislation of 1872', *Continuity and Change*, Vol. 9, No. 2 (1994).

rule, only permitting female relatives and friends to visit with the odd exception of a brother or father. This was partly based on realistic fears about the invasion of their property, theft, the outflow of food and other good things through the kitchen. But there was also an underlying unease about admitting that the trusted servant's primary loyalty lay outside the employer's household.

One of the latent functions of very strict and full timetables of household tasks was to keep servants' hands and minds occupied in the employer's interest and prevent them slipping out to visit friends and potential suitors. As a result, many young women servants had fewer contacts and less knowledge about men than those with other occupational experience or who had remained in the family home. Proportionally they seem to have been over-represented as mothers of illegitimate babies.[53] Some evidence suggests that twentieth-century ex-domestic servants were less likely to practise birth control successfully than their more knowledgeable worldly counterparts in other occupations.[54]

Just as the experience of service could have various meanings, positive, negative or indifferent, for both servant and employer, so could the consequences (not forgetting those who went through both positions). A minority of young servants later became specialized as cooks, nannies, lady's maids or housekeepers in larger establishments or gained ascendancy in smaller households. Most, however, left service eventually to marry and could then only return as part-time or casual help. A few maintained the personal ties from their service days, especially with the children of the household. Some found their horizons widened through having witnessed new ways of furnishing, decorating houses and gardens, systematic ordering of tasks and timekeeping, with different priorities from the hand-to-mouth survival tactics of their own childhoods. But without material and financial resources to support such aims, disillusion could follow.

Some ideas might be passed on to their own children, together with ambitions for their advancement. The daughter of an ex-nurserymaid recalled that she 'brought them up like the nursery'. Her mother kept them from playing in the street, and punishment was guilt, refusal of a kiss at bedtime rather than the swift slap or shout. Becoming a nursemaid in her turn, she considered herself

53. John Gillis, 'Servants, sexual relations and the risks of illegitimacy in London 1801–1900', in J. Newton, R. Rapp and E. Ross (eds), *Sex and Class in Women's History* (Routledge, 1983).
54. Diana Gittins, *Fair Sex: Family Size and Structure 1900–1939* (Hutchinson, 1982).

middle class 'because we were brought up nicely', while another ex-nanny felt 'she couldn't live in a muddle now'.[55] But others turned against the system, striving to keep their own daughters from going into service: 'How could we have allowed ourselves to be ordered about so, and for that wage?'[56]

The legacy for employing families was both practical and symbolic. Upper- and upper-middle-class women in particular were unable to survive in anything like their accustomed lifestyle without servants or at least the help of female kin – who took up the role of ubiquitous female companion and unwaged dogsbody. Servant help was also vital in a period when large numbers of children were the norm. The elaborate system of social etiquette and household paraphernalia was rocked by the roughly 400,000 servants who left during the First World War never to return.

The notion that middle- and upper-class men, both as masculine beings and as members of their social strata, inherently deserved to be served was woven even more deeply into the psyche of all, socialist and conservative, agnostic and Christian believer alike, whatever the official rhetoric. Dependence and duty, the watchwords of the Victorian and Edwardian era, were at the heart of the service relationship as they were within familial relationships – dependence and duty within the social and gendered station to which you had been called by fate or God.

Thus residential domestic service was a two-way street. For the few career servants, it meant self-respect and lifetime support, in return for hard work. For the many it provided a livelihood of sorts, often with better food and accommodation than in their own overcrowded, poor homes. And there was some form of familial relationship too for potential outcasts of society: the borderline feeble-minded, the homeless, would find a place in working-class households, as servants in lodging houses or in the lower ranks of servants in larger institutions such as schools, hospitals and some large estates, although too often they were exploited, turned into drudges, the butt of ridicule, open to violence and sexual abuse. Meanwhile, the employing class benefited with an unprecedented level of personal service and companionship, provided by a pool of deferential inferiors who could also provide intimate care for the children, the ill and elderly, performing some of the drearier, less savoury tasks that this involved.

55. Essex Oral History Archive Nos 116 and 59.
56. Interview quoted in L. Davidoff, 'Mastered for life: servant and wife in Victorian and Edwardian England', in *Worlds Between*, p. 33.

Lodging

Landladies provided those same services of intimate care and companionship to lodgers, but their position as householders gave them considerably more power than servants. Predominantly older women who contracted to 'do' for lodgers, landladies had much in common with mothers living with adult sons and daughters. In her own establishment, as wife/mother, or in the absence of a husband as household head, a landlady could view lodgers as part of her family, who like other family members gave financial support. Yet lodgers, like servants, were also liminal figures at the boundaries of families, eluding any clear categorization, whose status as family or non-family did not depend simply on either financial transactions or kinship connections.

Residential domestic service and lodging had many features in common. In lodgings, people paid for service in the house of the landlady; in their own homes they paid a servant, but sometimes the two positions could overlap. In the latter part of the nineteenth century, when Hannah Cullwick was between service places, she might move in with friends and help to pay for food in cash and/ or do extra cleaning, wash curtains or whitewash a scullery in return for her keep. But if in a town where she knew nobody, she looked for lodgings, often found by simply knocking on a door. Her arrangements with her 'landlady' at these times *also* involved cash payment augmented by her helping in the house.[57]

In the eighteenth century, it had been common for even wealthy people, at least in towns, to huddle in a couple of rented rooms and live mainly in coffee-houses or ale-houses, the latter providing the necessary 'good address',[58] but by the mid nineteenth century lodging was more negatively regarded. In the words of the Registrar General: 'the possession of an entire house is strongly desired by every Englishman; for it throws a sharp well-defined circle around his family and hearth – the shrine of his sorrows, joys and meditations'.[59] However, it was clearly not possible for every Englishman to rent, let alone own, an entire house. Mobility of the population meant a constant demand for lodgings, particularly by young unmarried adults. Itinerant workers brought into an area needed

57. Davidoff, 'The separation of home and work?'
58. M. Dorothy George, *London Life in the Eighteenth Century* (Penguin, 1965), p. 100.
59. Introduction to General Report, *1851 Census Great Britain: Report*, BPP LXXXV (1852–53), p. xxxv.

somewhere to live. Later in the century, with the growth of seaside towns and cheaper holidays, demand for short-term lodgings grew. Not all lodging implied a cash arrangement. An enquiry by the Manchester Statistical Society in the 1860s discovered that about half the lodgers listed were not actually paying any rent, though it is unclear whether they were kin or friends.[60] In the 1900s, a mother of eight children took in an old man who had been living with his drunken son. He had a greenhouse and gave her the produce in addition to 2s. 6d. a week and she nursed him until he died.[61] An unmarried brother lodged with his sister, paying 10s. a week 'all found', that is lodging, food and attendance.[62]

Investigators and census takers tried to separate those eating with the family but who sometimes bought their own food from those renting living space. But in 1851 the Registrar General was forced to admit to the

> difficulty of defining in an Act of Parliament, the degree of connec- tion between the head of a family and lodgers who reside under the same roof. For in the Census of 1831 it had been stated that: 'those who use the same kitchen and board together are to be deemed members of the same family', but 'even then remains the question whether a single person inhabiting a house solely or lodging but not boarding in another man's house is to be deemed a family.' This admits only of an unsatisfactory reply that it cannot be otherwise.[63]

Some census enumerators used the category 'lodging house keeper' to designate a household head with one or two lodgers and no other declared occupation, but others did not. The distinctions between innkeeper, lodging house keeper and other occupational titles is unreliable. Furthermore, while innkeepers, who were pre- dominantly men, had a separate category for their wives in the occupation of 'innkeeper's wife', there was no category for the husbands of lodging house keepers. Since they were predominantly women, this once again emphasized men as household heads, women as helpers.

The drive to eliminate all living arrangements in which depend- ants were not under the control of a recognized head of household resulted in some of the earliest state interventionist legislation, the Common Lodging Houses Acts of the 1850s, although, significantly,

60. Raphael Samuel, personal communication.
61. Essex Oral History Archive No. 141.
62. Essex Oral History Archive No. 283.
63. Census 1851, *General Report*, p. xxxiv.

these did not apply to private hotels and houses let to the upper and middle classes.[64] The elevation of the male household head is also evident in the extension of the property-based franchise in 1867 to include every man (but not woman) who had occupied the same lodgings for a year if the value of the premises was over £10. The lodger was enfranchised, at least in theory, a good fifty years before his landlady.

More men than women demanded lodgings. Although some might be lodgers or boarders all their lives, for the youthful majority this was a phase before marriage and setting up a home on their own. Lodging for young men, like residential service for young women, was part of the nineteenth-century pattern of delayed marriage. In turn, for couples in late middle age, lodgers could replace grown-up children who had left home. But lodgers might also make up a shortfall when the children were too young to earn. They were the mainstay of widows or other unsupported women. In a provincial market town in 1851, while around a fifth of all household heads were women, they constituted a third of households taking in lodgers.[65]

In the 1900s, the suburban London hatter Fred Willis rented a house with six rooms and scullery. When he first married, the whole top floor was let unfurnished, but as the four children made their appearance, the lodgers decreased. When the eldest child had reached school-leaving age the family hoped the compositor who inhabited the front room upstairs and shared meals with the family would be the last, but he was clean, quiet and orderly and they needed his 10s. a week. He also arranged an apprenticeship in his own trade for the eldest boy, a role often otherwise played by family or friends.[66]

As with servants, a wide spectrum of the population had either grown up in a household with lodgers, become lodgers themselves or taken them in. Families running pubs, inns or lodging houses as their main form of income were especially involved with lodgers. The small private schools for younger boys and girls of all ages run by unsupported middle-class women could be little more than

64. Parliamentary Papers (1859), LXXI, Housing of the Working Classes, Report of HM Commissioners, Q 4147.
65. L. Davidoff, Sample of households from the manuscript census, 1851, Colchester, Essex.
66. Frederick Willis, *101 Jubilee Road: A Book of London Yesteryears* (Phoenix House, 1948).

private homes, surviving by taking in boarders or fostering children with a modicum of education, music and training in gentility added. The household at 30 Goodwin Road, Margate, listed in the 1881 census shows some of these possibilities. It was headed by Clara Searles, a widow aged 45, occupation schoolmistress. With her lived her daughter Helen aged 17 (no occupation given) and two servants: Annie Culver aged 15, servant to the schoolmistress, and Sarah Goodall aged 19, servant to the school. Another widow, Catherine Brown, aged 26, lived there as a boarder, with no occupation given. Finally there were seven unnamed children: one boy aged 2, five boys aged 7 to 8, and one girl aged 10.[67] Thus this household contained boarder, pupils, servants and family members, the categories sometimes overlapping.

Close relationships could evolve between landlady/landlord and lodger or boarder. A landlady or housekeeper might become a de facto wife. Or, again, a young country-bred journeyman lodged in the home of a fellow engineer and 'as is the practice of this class with their landladies he calls her "mother" and he strikes her as being like what her first born boy would have been had *he* lived to be three and twenty'.[68] The familial, even Oedipal, overtones in this pattern are echoed in the stereotypes of lodging. The image of the landlady as an older woman could create unease in extracting payment for services freely expected from mothers, wives and other female relatives. Yet the landlady's age and power over house room and food could be experienced as threatening. Unsurprisingly her image veered between the despised, prying, narrow-minded older woman and a combination of maternal warmth and the 'tart with the heart of gold'. The fusing of the maternal and erotic between an older woman and younger man ran against acknowledged patterns, and there were also sexual possibilities between lodgers and the daughters or servants of the house. Both may account for the stock music hall jokes and songs with a 'Roger the Lodger' motif.[69] The 'legitimate' household head might be provoked into jealousy, and a saying of the period claimed that three evils most commonly broke up marriages: selfishness, greed and lodgers.[70]

67. Manuscript census, 1881.

68. Journeyman Engineer [Thomas Wright], *Some Habits and Customs of the Working Classes* (Tinsley, 1867), p. 210.

69. In rhyming slang, 'Artful Dodger' stood for lodger. J. Franklyn, *A Dictionary of Rhyming Slang* (Routledge, 1960), p. 34.

70. Robert Roberts, *A Ragged Schooling: Growing Up in the Classic Slum* (Penguin, 1978), p. 82.

The service positions of master and servant (*older man/younger woman,* or in a few cases *male servant*), landlady and lodger (*older woman/ younger man*), mistress and companion or maid (*older woman/younger woman*) were all archetypal nineteenth- and early twentieth-century relationships. They embraced those living under the same roof, sharing a degree of closeness, sometimes kinship and usually, though not inevitably, cash payments. These were relationships of connectedness and thus potentially undermined individuality and a sense of differentiated self, especially for the one who served. On the other hand, the superior, who demanded and obtained service, could use the release of time, energy and emotion to build his (and it usually was his) sense of self. Yet that individuality was always under threat from his underlying dependence.

Such connections, acknowledged or not, often marked class boundaries but also crossed them. The relation of master/mistress and servant, landlady and lodger, could determine a sense of group identity as much as the usually more overt relations of the workplace. In both domestic service and lodging these quasi-familial links between server and served, which included power, dependence, deference, care, gift-giving, erotic involvement, love and hate, fill a large and largely unacknowledged gap in the history of the family and in the modern period in general.

PART THREE

Families 1914–1960

CHAPTER SEVEN

Changes in family life:
the twentieth century

> *. . . a fifties childhood may be less deeply influenced by the Festival of Britain,*
> *'Contemporary' furniture, working class affluence and thirteen years of Tory*
> *Misrule than by a Victorian grandparent, an Edwardian father and a cluster*
> *of potent family legends and memories which stretch back to the beginning of*
> *the last century.*
>
> Alison Hennegan[1]

Those whose lives spanned the years between 1914 and 1960, like
their nineteenth-century forebears, lived through a period of very
rapid change and innovation in areas which impinged directly upon
family life. They would have experienced the emotional and physical upheaval and destruction of two world wars; a major depression,
with exceptionally high levels of male unemployment, which had
devastating effects upon many households; a dramatic fall in the
birth-rate and in infant and adult mortality rates which altered
the size and make-up of households and familial groupings; and
the rise of a welfare state which, principally through the provision
of a range of health and welfare services, brought singular benefits
to individuals within families.

Employment patterns for men and for women changed through
this period, as did the nature of work itself with the gradual demise
of heavy industry and the burgeoning growth of new industries and
white-collar work, coupled with the decline of residential domestic
service. Successive rises in the school leaving age and increased
access to further and higher education resulted in children remaining economically dependent on their parents for longer, even though,
after leaving school, most working-class children continued to live

---

1. Liz Heron (ed.), *Truth, Dare or Promise: Girls Growing Up in the Fifties* (Virago,
1985), p. 128.

at home and contribute to the family budget until marriage. On a cultural level, family life both influenced and was influenced by the popularity and growing accessibility of radio, cinema and latterly television, and of all forms of printed materials especially newspapers and women's magazines. And, by the end of our period, many, though by no means all, families were enjoying the benefits of improved housing, better standards of living and the greater availability of a wide range of consumer goods.

Throughout this chapter we will be discussing how these far-reaching shifts were experienced by individuals within families and how families were themselves influential in instigating change. Equally important, how did external changes of this kind affect and how were they affected by contemporary ideas about the family and family life? In our discussion we have tried not only to acknowledge the diversity of family forms, but also to expose power relationships between family members and between families and external authorities. Thus it has been important to distinguish between discourses about families, promoted through official sources, the media and elsewhere, and people's personal experiences of family, while at the same time acknowledging a degree of interdependence between the two.[2] However, as the opening quote illustrates, individuals' experiences within families are shaped not only by external factors but also by the lives of other, older members, whose own highly particular histories may be told and retold through generations and help to create specific forms of family identification.

Given both the diversity of personal and family histories and the pace of external change during the twentieth century, it is all the more extraordinary that the model of the nuclear family, discussed in the Introduction, continues to have such a powerful hold over our imaginations. This model has two main roots. First, it has been perpetuated through the institution of marriage which has held such a central role in the upholding of society in general, and family life in particular, not least as an instrument of regulation by the state and other agencies. Nowhere is this better illustrated in our period than in the abdication crisis of 1936 and the demonization of the twice-divorced Mrs Simpson, whose marriage to Edward VIII threatened not only the position of the Royal Family but also that of the Church and the state. Second, much of the nuclear family's influence has come from the increasing value placed upon

---

2. Michael Peplar, 'Family matters: ideas about the family in British culture, 1945–70', Ph.D. thesis, University of Greenwich (1998).

children born during and in the wake of two world wars to a nation which, until the baby boom of the late 1940s temporarily reversed the trend, had a declining birth-rate. This has resulted in a stronger emphasis on motherhood and mothering within our understanding of the family than in previous centuries.

The weight which conjugal and maternal relationships have thus carried within the family during this century has made it hard, brought up as most of us have been within these idealized blinkers, to understand the significance of our own family histories as well as other economic, reciprocal and affective relationships which continued to exist within households and between friends, kin and communities. In this chapter, and the two illustrative studies that follow, we focus not only on nuclear families but also on other shifting structures and groups linked by blood, contract and intimacy in the first half of this century.

Changing patterns of family life

In light of the dominance of the nuclear family model, recent worries about its demise need to be understood in the context of a particular set of demographic trends which coincided to make families in the early to mid twentieth century markedly different from both earlier and later generations. What has been widely mourned is the disappearance, not of an unchanging family archetype stretching back through many centuries, but of a model specific to this century which has acquired a spurious patina of age and permanence.

The most significant feature of the twentieth century has been the dramatic reduction in family size. By the 1920s the declining birth rate had spread to the working classes, who were beginning to exert greater control over their own fertility. Better nutrition, housing and control of epidemic diseases had led, most significantly in the early 1900s, to reductions in adult mortality rates which diminished the numbers of dependent children losing one or both parents. A dramatic fall in infant mortality also meant that the need for families to replace children who died was no longer so pressing.[3]

3. For a discussion of these issues see Wally Seccombe, *Weathering the Storm: Working Class Families from the Industrial Revolution to the Fertility Decline* (Verso, 1993); Simon Szreter, *Fertility, Class and Gender in Britain, 1860–1940* (Cambridge University Press, 1996); Diana Gittins, *Fair Sex: Family Size and Structure 1900–1939* (Hutchinson, 1982).

The declining birth rate, particularly amongst the middle classes, was an issue of great concern to the state. So much so that two parliamentary commissions on population were set up to advise the government, reporting their findings after each world war, in 1920 and 1949.[4] Among several dire warnings about the terminal decline of the British nation, which attracted publicity in the 1930s, the most sensational prediction suggested that by 2033 the population of England and Wales would be the size of the County of London.[5] Concern for child mortality had increased during the First World War when it was realized that if the annual wastage of male infant life over the preceding fifty years had been prevented, 500,000 more men would have been available to defend the country. To address this problem the Maternity and Child Welfare Act was passed in 1918 which enabled local authorities to provide a range of services aimed at improving infant survival rates and child health.[6] This legislation was also influenced by the eugenics movement, whose chief concern was racial fitness, worries echoed in the late twentieth-century obsession with genetics. Good specimens of British manhood were needed not simply as cannon fodder, but also to revive Britain's declining fortunes as an industrial nation, and to populate the Empire with the British race. Pressure was thus exerted throughout the period upon middle-class women to marry and produce children.[7]

There was more ambivalence about encouraging the working classes to limit their families. Strong opposition, both on religious and demographic grounds, was put up during the inter-war years to the spread of the birth-control movement, pioneered by Marie Stopes, following the publication of her best-selling *Married Love* in 1918. Yet it was also argued that denying working women access to contraception, much more easily available to middle-class women, was creating a racially disastrous population imbalance. Giving evidence to the National Birthrate Commission in 1916, Stopes asserted that women needed to rest between healthy births to prevent

4. These were *Problems of Population and Parenthood, being the Second Report of and the Chief Evidence taken by the National Birthrate Commission 1918–20* (Chapman & Hall, 1920) and *The Report of the Royal Commission on Population* (HMSO 1948–49, Cmd. 7695).

5. Enid Charles in *The Twilight of Parenthood* (1934), quoted in Jane Lewis, *The Politics of Motherhood: Child and Maternal Welfare in England 1900–1939* (Croom Helm, 1980).

6. Ibid., p. 29.

7. See Anna Davin, 'Imperialism and motherhood'. *History Workshop Journal*, No. 5 (1978).

both feeble-mindedness and physical deterioration of the child and 'agonizing torture of the mother'.[8] Projects such as the Peckham Experiment, which offered health care and leisure facilities to South London working-class families in the 1930s and 1940s, but excluded those who were single and lived alone, were also influenced by eugenic ideas in attempting to provide optimum conditions for the reproduction of 'normal' healthy families, in order to encourage parents to want to have babies.[9]

Yet many working-class families continued to rely on *coitus interruptus*, abortion or abstinence to control family size, and the state only reluctantly sanctioned greater access to birth control after the Second World War when it was in the country's economic interests to encourage married women into the workforce. By this time the baby boom of the immediate post-war years no longer made the birth rate seem such a pressing issue. Unwanted pregnancies continued to haunt many women in this period. It was not until 1974 that free access to birth-control advice and contraception was fully incorporated into the National Health Service, while, until the reform of the law in 1967, women's access to safe abortions in private nursing homes continued to be restricted to those with sufficient resources and the right contacts. Back-street abortionists and self-administered, but often ineffective, remedies were the most common resort of poorer unmarried and married women with an unwanted pregnancy.[10] Margaret Forster's family memoir *Hidden Lives* tells of her mother's fear of pregnancy and lack of knowledge about contraceptive methods:

> The whole business of birth control upset Lily, but then so did the whole business of sex. But she tried to be brave and after a visit to the doctor had produced no enlightenment, beyond being told it was her husband's business to take care, she felt there was nothing she could do except try to limit intercourse. She got into the habit, when Arthur was ready to go to bed, of staying up, saying she would just finish the darning. Then she would sit close to the fire and darn and wait and listen and hope to hear him snoring when she would at last join him, slipping between covers with the greatest caution.[11]

8. *Problems of Population and Parenthood*, p. 249, quoted in Lewis, *The Politics of Motherhood*, p. 205.
9. See Innes H. Pearse, 'The Peckham experiment', *Eugenics Review* (July 1945); *Mass Observation Britain and her Birth Rate* (John Murray, 1945), p. 78.
10. Maureen Sutton, '*We didn't know aught*': *A Study of Sexuality, Supervision and Death in Women's Lives in Lincolnshire During the 1930s, 40s and 50s* (Paul Watkins, 1992), pp. 88–98, and Barbara Brookes, *Abortion in England 1900–67* (Croom Helm, 1988).
11. Margaret Forster, *Hidden Lives* (Penguin, 1996), p. 124.

Such anecdotes support the view that women's dependence on their husbands' forbearance and/or their own unavailability for sex hardly made for more equal or harmonious marriages and that the methods involved for family limitation were 'often highly conducive to the creation of difficulties and resentments between spouses'.[12]

Connections between demographic change and gender relations can also be viewed more positively. Diana Gittins argues that women's economic position and marital status were critically important in explaining the decline in the working-class birth-rate, and she stresses the variability amongst different occupational groups. Single women's access to jobs in the clerical, factory and retail sectors and the decline of residential domestic service increased their independence and exposed them to new values and knowledge concerning marriage and reproduction. Although after marriage many women's power shifted, as they became more dependent upon a male bread-winner and undertook a heightened domestic role as wife and mother, still their pre-marital experience affected their subsequent marital behaviour, with a new emphasis on communication and joint decision making on issues such as family size.[13]

The growing belief in equality between partners, with husband and wife playing different but complementary roles, was an important element in the development of the 'companionate marriage', a marital model which sought to harmonize the difficulties and conflicts of interest highlighted above by Forster. Promoted in the 1920s, as an argument for legalized birth control and divorce by mutual consent for childless couples,[14] and reinforced even more strongly in the 1950s, this model was based upon the idea of an exclusive emotionally and sexually intimate relationship between a man and a woman, satisfying to both partners. It was a powerful ideal, which stressed the importance of romantic love, sexual attraction and mutual interests, while disguising realities of gendered inequalities of power and access to resources. Yet it set a standard by which it was believed all marriages would ultimately stand or fall.

The increasing popularity of the companionate marriage model coincided with, and may also have influenced, the unique demographic conditions which prevailed for most of our period. With the strengthening of the conjugal ideal, sex was gradually being separated from reproduction and marriage was no longer seen simply as a vehicle for producing and bringing up children, although

12. Szreter, *Fertility, Class and Gender*, p. 566.   13. Gittins, *Fair Sex*.
14. These ideas were promoted by the influential American judge Ben Lindsay in *The Companionate Marriage* (Brentano's, 1928).

this latter function was still regarded as important. Thus in *The Art of Marriage* (1952) Dr Mary Macauley wrote:

> Some young couples think that even when they are married they should live together without sexual intercourse until the time comes for them to have a child; but this implies a totally wrong idea about sex. As well as its biological and reproductive purpose it was 'ordained for our mutual help and comfort.' Its personal meaning between husband and wife – their mating – is as important in their marriage as their possible parenthood.[15]

The marriage rate increased after both wars, in response partly to the gap left by the 'lost generations' of men and to the wartime necessity to delay marriages. So also did the tendency of the majority of women to marry at an earlier age, although the age at which women might marry continued to cover a wide spectrum until the Second World War. After the brief baby boom in the late 1940s, the average two to three children tended to be born in the earlier years of marriage and women's reproductive cycle completed at an earlier age. Not only did this enable many more married women to return to paid employment, it also gave them entry into a phase of marriage more rarely enjoyed by their ancestors, in which the needs of children were no longer their main focus and adult companionship was of greater significance.

The smaller numbers of children in each family and the prolonged period of their dependency through improving educational prospects also meant, not only that children would be an economic liability for longer, but that mothers felt more pressure to do the best for their children. A survey of marriage in the 1950s indicated that 'There is a more generally felt wish to give the child the other advantages that prudence can obtain; better education, apprenticeship or training.'[16] The social acceptability of large families thus declined, and despite the post-war baby boom, the sociologist Chesser declared in 1947, 'Today, "the neighbours" no longer smile benignly upon the large family. The smiles are usually those of derision . . . .'.[17]

The general pattern of small families of children, born closer together to younger parents, created different, more egalitarian family dynamics and thus changes in the nature of parental authority and caring arrangements. Young mothers, with no older children

15. Dr Mary Macauley, *The Art of Marriage* (Delisle, 1952), p. 40.
16. Eliot Slater and Moya Woodside, *Patterns of Marriage* (Cassell, 1951), p. 185.
17. E. Chesser, *The Unwanted Child* (Rich & Cowan, 1947), p. 21.

to help care for their younger siblings, were more closely involved in their children's upbringing. Although war casualties increased the numbers of widows over the period as a whole, greatly improved life expectation, coupled with a still relatively low divorce rate, ensured that the majority of marriages endured longer than those of earlier or later generations. By the 1950s many more married couples could expect to live into old age together and the number of grandparents alive and able to participate in the care of their grandchildren was thus greater in the first half of this century than ever before or since. The common practice among working-class families of naming grandmothers 'nana' or 'nanny' is suggestive of an expectation of their involvement with childcare. Yet this too was a short-lived phenomenon, curtailed by the widespread re-entry of married women into the labour market in the latter half of the century. 'Nanas' are now much less available for the informal care of their grandchildren.

Material and economic developments

The changing demographic conditions outlined above, which shifted the generational balance and composition of households, and influenced the number, age range and gender of family members classified as dependants, coincided with the increasing involvement of the state with the welfare of families, including the introduction of unemployment, health and other social benefits and the provision of housing.[18] The model of the nuclear family, with a male breadwinner and dependent wife and children, is central to debates, disputes and social policy relating to work, welfare and family life through the first half of the twentieth century, which intensified during times of social and economic stress and hardship.

One such period occurred soon after the end of First World War in the wake of the devastating outbreak of Spanish flu in the winter of 1918/19, which killed 150,000 in England and Wales and took a heavy toll on babies, the elderly and other vulnerable members of society.[19] This was followed, after a brief post-war boom, by a sharp economic slump, which meant that although families who remained in work had an improved standard of living, others were faced for the first time with the spectre of mass unemployment.

18. See Appendix.
19. Charles Loch Mowat, *Britain Between the Wars* (Methuen, 1955), p. 22.

Estimates, which include both insured and uninsured workers, put the total number of unemployed in 1921 at over two million,[20] forcing the government to step in to provide relief for families on an unprecedented scale. The fact that state benefits were targeted principally at men and frequently refused to women was not unconnected with the traumas of the war. Horrifying levels of mainly young male casualties made it all the more necessary for the survivors to be perceived as heroes, deserving homes and jobs, and sufficient income to support wives and children who could give them comfort and succour and bolster a shattered sense of masculinity.

These conditions helped to engender what some historians have identified as a crisis in gender relations, exacerbated by the popular perception that women had pushed men off to fight and be killed at the front and then stepped into their jobs. Whatever the truth of this conjecture, it is clear that the absence of husbands, fathers, brothers and sons from home and a rapidly lengthening casualty list greatly increased the numbers of women who became the main source of financial and domestic support for their families. This was followed by the sudden return of a generation of alienated and, in many cases, shell-shocked and disabled men back to their homes and families and out into the labour market.[21]

The prospect for such men of 'walking the streets' was made worse by the belief that it was only through regaining their status as breadwinner that they would be able to protect their women and keep them 'off the streets'. Wives' security could only be guaranteed if their husbands were given work with a high enough wage or state benefits sufficient to maintain them and their children. Reacting to this situation, in 1919 the *Manchester Evening Chronicle* published a report with the inflammatory headline 'Pin Money Swanks', in which women, of 'the low-necked, short-skirted, high-heeled variety', were denounced for taking employment from men and, because they did not have to support themselves, for keeping 'all their earnings for pin money'. Their work was regarded as the means by which women could display their sexuality. 'Pin money', the paper declared, 'means "seemore blouses" and stockings', whilst to married men 'it means a living'.[22]

20. John Burnett, *Idle Hands: The Experience of Unemployment 1790–1990* (Routledge, 1994), p. 201.

21. Gail Braybon and Penny Summerfield, *Out of the Cage: Women's Experiences in Two World Wars* (Pandora, 1987); Gail Braybon, *Women Workers in the First World War* (Routledge, 1981); Susan Kingsley Kent, *Making Peace: The Reconstruction of Gender in Interwar Britain* (Princeton University Press, 1993).

22. *Manchester Chronicle*, Wednesday, 19 March 1919.

The economic and sexual threat which independent young women in their 'seemore blouses' were considered to pose to the male breadwinner, the family and society is evident through the storm of claim and counter-claim which followed this report. The solutions offered were generally focused upon marriage or domestic service, for such women would then be confined under the authority of a husband or the control of a mistress. That this would also solve the 'servant problem', experienced by upper- and middle-class families, explains the more general popularity of this solution, advocated even in the feminist press[23] and used as a reason to deny unemployment benefits to women.

For some women the enforced choice between marriage and work, made under the shadow of war, left a legacy which their children inherited. The author Doris Lessing was born in 1919 to a marriage which was the product partly of the shortage of eligible men. Her mother, a nurse who had married a wounded soldier after her great love was drowned, chose to give up a career as a London hospital matron because she desperately wanted children. But she was unable to protect her child from her own feelings of frustration or her husband's continuing depression which centred on memories of the war, remembered by Doris as a constant refrain in adult conversation. 'I used to joke that the war had given birth to me, as a defence when weary with the talk that went on and on. But it was no joke. I used to feel there was something like a dark grey cloud of poison gas over my young childhood.'[24]

Debates about women's place in the home, in the labour force and in society more generally erupted during other periods of social crisis throughout this period. They were evident during the Depression of the 1930s, which particularly affected families living in areas of traditional heavy industries in the North of England, Wales and Scotland and increased the general trend of movement to the South where employment appeared to be more widely available. In the face of such high levels of male unemployment, women were increasingly marginalized in the workplace because of a determination to keep men in work which in turn upheld the norm of the male breadwinner.[25]

23. See e.g. *The Woman's Leader,* 5 August 1921.
24. Doris Lessing, *Under My Skin: Volume One of My Autobiography, To 1949* (Flamingo, Harper Collins, 1995).
25. Susan Pederson, *Family Dependencies and the Origins of the Welfare State in Britain and France 1914–45* (Cambridge University Press, 1993).

This norm was maintained throughout our period by working men, who, despite the move towards more egalitarian family dynamics, continued to believe that their status and authority depended on being able to support a family. Trade unions' reluctance to support equal pay measures and their opposition to family allowances, which would give women a measure of financial independence, were motivated by the fear that male wages would be cut if women were acknowledged to be family providers rather than dependants. Equally, some women were also concerned to keep men in this position for fear that they might otherwise evade their family responsibilities. Assumptions that, whatever their marital status, men should be paid as if they had families to support and women treated as if they had none, worked in favour of bachelors, who were more prone to detach themselves from their families, and against single women, many more of whom were supporting elderly parents or other relatives.[26]

Yet despite these pressures, many women resisted the curtailment of their employment, particularly as a result of economic necessity, and sought to establish themselves in new areas of the workforce. Women were increasingly unwilling to become domestic servants and have their personal and social lives regulated and constrained by employment which was noted for its low wage rates, poor working conditions, long hours and lack of insurance benefits. Other forms of work may have had little better reward but they were invariably more attractive than a life in service. Thus through the 1920s and 1930s domestic service amongst women slowly declined as other opportunities opened up with the growth of white-collar clerical work amongst the developing service industries. However, most middle- and some working-class women were forced by marriage bars in professions, such as teaching and the civil service, and in some factories, to choose between paid employment and a husband and children.[27]

Employment amongst married and unmarried women increased gradually during the inter-war years but burgeoned, as it had during the First World War, through the war years 1939 to 1945, as

26. Eleanor Rathbone noted this paradox in relation to single men in *The Disinherited Family* (George Allen & Unwin, 1924).
27. Jane Lewis, *Women in England: Sexual Divisions and Social Change* (Wheatsheaf, 1984); Kay Sanderson, '"A pension to look forward to...": women civil service clerks in London 1925–1985', in Leonore Davidoff and Belinda Westover (eds), *Our Work, Our Lives, Our Words: Women's History and Women's Work* (Macmillan, 1986).

women were recruited into all areas of the labour market to replace men who had entered the armed services. This demand for
female labour continued after 1945, with the developing public
sector, and particularly the National Health Service, seeking to
employ unskilled and semi-skilled workers, and with the continued
growth in white-collar industries such as banks and insurance companies. At the same time there were very serious shortages in the
teaching and nursing professions, which had recruited extensively
from the diminishing inter-war cohort of single women, but which
were now unable to meet the employment needs of the growing
public sectors of health and education. As a result married women,
particularly those over the age of 30, moved increasingly into the
labour market, but they remained for the most part in part-time,
low-paid and low-status, non-unionized work.[28]

All employment for married women had to be balanced with
their continuing domestic role, as 'the prime minister of the home'.[29]
This conflict is evident in the problem page of a woman's magazine
at the end of the Second World War. A correspondent, who wanted
to keep her job because of 'the stimulating atmosphere of business
life, and all the contacts I make with fellow workers', against the
wishes of her soldier husband, was advised that:

> The idea of home to men fighting is the strongest feeling in their
> hearts as all their letters prove. And when they think of home, they
> tend to think of it as the shrine of the wife. The place where she
> reigns and works and where she goes in and out of rooms which
> have a trace of her personality or her handiwork. That to most of
> them epitomises the word home, and your husband is evidently one
> who thinks like this. To such men, home would lose all meaning if
> it were merely the place to which another worker came hurrying
> back after office hours, to give perfunctory attention to his meals.
> And if that young family does come along, they would have to be left
> to hired helpers, while you earned that extra money which you could
> use as you pleased.[30]

Despite the continuing identification of home as the woman's shrine
at which men returning from abroad could worship, and the
workplace as the symbol of women's irresponsibility and frivolity,
this letter indicates the change in focus in debates about women's
employment after the Second World War. Unlike the inter-war years,

28. Jane Lewis, *Women in Britain Since 1945* (Blackwell, 1991) and Elizabeth Wilson,
Only Half Way to Paradise: Women in Postwar England 1945–68 (Tavistock, 1980).
29. BMA, *A Charter for Health* (Allen & Unwin, 1946) p. 59.
30. *Woman's Weekly*, 10 February 1945.

they were less concerned with its effects upon the male workforce, and more focused upon the potential damage such widespread employment of women might do to family life.

Smaller families and the decline in domestic service meant that women had increasingly little help available either in the form of outside paid help or from family members. Worries about the poor domestic environments in which women struggled to rear their families began to receive attention, as did the time and energy demanded of women to meet the growing standards of cleanliness and nutrition which family life necessitated. However, the needs of some women, the single, widowed, divorced and separated, to support families and maintain these appropriate domestic standards remained unconsidered or ignored. Rather the primacy of the male breadwinner became institutionalized by the implementation of post-war social reforms and the construction of the welfare state.[31]

These gendered inequalities were taken for granted in the emphasis upon the country's improved standard of living and high levels of employment, which resulted in households which conformed to this norm having two, three and sometimes four wages with husband, wife and teenage/adult children in employment. Such employment patterns among some families, combined with the opportunities for shift work and overtime, resulted in unprecedented affluence. Opportunities increased equally for the purchase of domestic goods, now freely available following the rationing and cutbacks in production during the war years, and the material standards of family life where there was at least one waged worker rose accordingly. Thus between 1951 and 1959 average consumption increased by 20 per cent per head – the same increase in nine years as in the twenty-six years between 1913 and 1939.[32]

The quality of life for the unemployed was also improved by the post-war reforms. The development of unemployment insurance benefits under the Insurance Act of 1911 had guaranteed many families with an unemployed breadwinner some level of security. They had, however, been inadequate to cope with the high levels of unemployment during the 1930s, forcing the government to introduce the much hated means test. The adverse effects on families in industrial areas, such as adult children being obliged to leave home to avoid having to support unemployed parents, graphically

31. Willliam Beveridge, *Social Insurance and Allied Services Report*, Cmd. 6404; E. Abbott and K. Bompas, *The Woman Citizen and Social Security* (Compass, 1943), and Pat Thane, *The Foundations of the Welfare State* (Longman Group, 1982).
32. Harry Hopkins, *The New Look* (Secker & Warburg, 1963), p. 311.

illustrated in Walter Greenwood's novel *Love on the Dole* (1933), overshadowed much of this period. Yet although the economic position of the jobless was enhanced following the introduction of the post-war national insurance schemes, still the stigma of the Poor Law, only gradually dismantled during the 1930s, left a long-lasting legacy. While statutory benefits were implemented in 1945, they remained centred on the waged worker so that those without sufficient insurance contributions – most women, the disabled and many more – were eligible only for national assistance, which was set at purely subsistence levels and again often means-tested.

The social and welfare reforms introduced by the newly elected Labour government of 1945 in the wake of the war brought unprecedented financial and medical benefits to families, in recognition of the extra demands which children placed upon the household budgets and to strengthen and develop post-war family life. These included a maternity grant for all married women, thirteen weeks' maternity benefit for those who had been insured workers before pregnancy, and a new widow's pension which acknowledged the extent to which the needs of many widows and children had remained unaddressed by inter-war legislation covering only those whose husbands had been in insured work. Most significantly the new family allowance of 5s. a week, awarded for second and subsequent children, gave mothers who had previously depended entirely on their husbands' earnings some level of financial independence.

Still widowed fathers had no pension rights for their wives' unpaid labour, while unmarried mothers were awarded no benefits other than the means-tested national assistance and, with generally only one child, were unable to claim any family allowance. Tax allowances, benefit rates and the organization of the national insurance scheme thus operated to support the nuclear family, financially and ideologically. Married, employed men were aided by the state in the maintenance of their families, but there were no similar provisions made for those outside these boundaries.

Discrimination of this kind was less evident in the much trumpeted new National Health Service. This guaranteed free medical treatment for all, including specialist hospital care, free eye tests, spectacles and dental treatment. In addition mothers were entitled to ante-natal and post-natal care, attendance by a doctor or midwife at delivery and health visiting services during the first five years of the child's life. Such provisions particularly benefited working-class mothers, whose welfare had been an important focus of inter-war feminist campaigns. Despite major improvements in health and mortality rates in the population as a whole, their general health from the beginning of the century had remained relatively poor, as they had struggled to cope with repeated pregnancies, the demands of young children and laborious housework in substandard homes.[33]

One of the major areas in which governments sought to aid the health and welfare of families was in improving the nation's stock of housing, thereby also providing for the needs of an increasingly mobile society. From the nineteenth century to the end of our period, patterns of wider mobility of families were common, responding to changing demands for labour in the local, national and even global employment markets. For the majority of families, however, the most significant shifts in location were first from the countryside to the city in the first quarter of the century and then on again out to the suburbs in the second quarter. To move geographically was often also a way to move *up* the social scale and was, for this reason, a deliberate choice taken by many families. Such a choice was facilitated by better public transport, the greater use of the motor car – there were over a million cars on British roads by 1930 – and the increasing availability of mortgages for the middle classes to purchase new homes.[34] As Carolyn Steedman's *Landscape for a Good Woman* illustrates, this mobility allowed individuals to shed existing relationships and to re-create new families in new locations:

> My parents were immigrants. Strangers to a metropolis during the great depression, they left a northern country, impossible stories left behind them: a wife and children abandoned. In London they created a new set of impossibilities, the matter of terrible secrets.[35]

The mobility of families was forced equally by the attempts of government through the inter-war and post-war years to eradicate the slums and to provide new housing better suited to the needs of accepted family structures or acceptable family organizations. For the first time local councils were charged with the public provision of housing,[36] while the mutual benefits offered by building societies increased the numbers of owner occupiers. By the early 1930s the old system of renting rooms in tenement blocks and lodging was in

33. See Margaret Llewelyn Davies, *Maternity: Letters from Working Women* (Virago, 1978); Margery Spring Rice, *Working Class Wives* (Virago, 1981); Rathbone, *The Disinherited Family*.

34. John Burnett, *A Social History of Housing 1815–1970* (David & Charles, 1978).

35. Carolyn Steedman, *Landscape for a Good Woman* (Virago, 1986), p. 65.

36. M. Daunton (ed.), *Councillors and Tenants: Local Authority Housing in English Cities 1919–1939* (Leicester University Press, 1984).

decline. It was hoped that council housing for the lower classes would lead to a general improvement in their habits, especially in childrearing. With the promotion of the 'ideal home', working-class women in the new housing estates were encouraged to spend more time looking after their own families and less social space was available for lodgers. They were further discouraged by the policy of many councils, who either opposed subletting rooms or levied extra charges. The fall in the age of marriage and increased marriage rates also meant that more independent nuclear households were being set up, while improved short-distance transport – trams, buses and bicycles – enabled young single people to remain living in the parental home and still get to work.[37]

Four million houses were built in the inter-war years, with the most rapid growth in the suburbs around London and Birmingham. But it was still only the more affluent among the population who were able to take advantage of the newly built garden estates, whether owner occupied or rented, privately or from the council. Moreover, family life on such estates was less than ideal in the inter-war period. There were few recreational opportunities provided for adults or children, and a general absence of community services at a wider level. Local authorities struggled to provide the most basic of facilities demanded of them, such as roads and schools, and had few financial resources to develop other amenities, particularly libraries, cinemas, theatres, clinics and community centres.

As a result many families, who had moved to the suburbs to improve the quality of their lives, led a more restricted existence than they had anticipated. The housewife's experience in the suburbs was particularly narrowly defined by and through the home, leaving her isolated during the day when children and husband were at school and in the workplace, and with few recreational or leisure opportunities to be enjoyed during the evening.[38] Nevertheless, the middle classes continued to move away from town and city centres and congregated together in the commutable suburbs of purchased, detached and semi-detached houses.

The phenomenon of suburban living did not affect the upper classes to the same extent, because they generally owned more than one house and had always moved regularly between country estates

---

37. Leonore Davidoff, 'The separation of home and work? Landladies and lodgers in 19th and 20th century England', in *Worlds Between: Historical Perspectives on Gender and Class* (Polity Press, 1995), p. 274.
38. See Alan Jackson, *Semi-Detached London* (Allen & Unwin, 1973).

and town houses. Although a number of large houses were demolished and estates broken up after the Second World War, other landowners managed to hold on to their property despite prohibitive death duties, the difficulties of recruiting domestic staff, and the financial problems of maintenance and repair. As Evelyn Waugh notes in the Preface to his novel *Brideshead Revisited*, which charted the decline of one fictional aristocratic family and household, 'It was impossible to foresee, in the spring of 1944, the present cult of the English country house. It seemed then that the ancestral seats which were our chief national artistic achievement were doomed to decay and spoliation like the monasteries in the sixteenth century.'[39]

The overall shift of families away from city and town centres was not, however, universal. Large areas of inner-city slum dwellings persisted throughout this period despite the forcible movement by government of four million people from slum housing between 1930 and 1939. The Second World War halted this process, and the bombing raids on major British cities, which destroyed large swathes of housing, exacerbated the pre-war housing shortages, as did the general increase in the number of households in the post-war years.[40]

This chronic housing shortage, when combined with fears for the future of family life following the upheavals of the Second World War, spurred on the post-war building programme and contributed, in the 1940s and 1950s at least, to the development of high-quality council housing. However, to meet the immediate demand for accommodation prefabricated houses were erected on derelict ground. And some desperate people took the situation into their own hands and built rough dwellings from old railway carriages or squatted in abandoned and empty buildings in town and countryside alike. With so little accommodation for nuclear families, the plight of those on the boundaries of family life was even more wretched. The peacetime celebrations of 1945 thus brought little comfort to one unmarried mother, who recalled:

> On the day of the great Victory Parade my landlady told me I should have to get out as my condition was now showing. I spent all of my lunch hour searching out a room and some time in the evening if I wasn't too exhausted – all to no avail. By the time I got there they were all taken. No one knew of a single empty room and just as I was

39. Evelyn Waugh, *Brideshead Revisited* (Penguin, 1945; 1981 edn cited), p. 10.
40. Anne Power, *Hovels to High Rise: State Housing in Europe since 1850* (Routledge, 1993).

thinking I should have to sleep in the woods my landlady said I
could stay on longer as she was going away . . .'[11]

For those such as unmarried mothers, the elderly, the single and
the growing numbers of immigrant families in inner-city areas, the
post-war building programme was to provide little help. They were
not considered priorities for housing or rehousing by local authorities and, as a result, were confined in ghettos in the remaining
slum areas, ineligible for council houses to rent and too poor to
purchase new homes elsewhere. Many suffered discrimination from
landlords and landladies. Caribbean women immigrants interviewed
in Lambeth remembered that no light or heat was allowed in their
rooms in order to conceal their presence from the neighbours.[12]

Nevertheless, the post-war building boom did eventually prove
beneficial for many poor but 'respectable' families who had been
living in run-down, overcrowded accommodation with little or no
indoor sanitation. In 1953 6-year-old Ginny's family was desperate
to get away from their two-bedroom flat in a smoke-blackened
block in Hackney. Her older brother was getting into 'bad company'
and the arrival of a new baby, whose pram had to be pushed up
and down ten flights of stairs, made it impossible for her mother
to keep an eye on the older children playing in the street. Ginny's
account reveals her hopes of a new life (she'd never seen fields
before) and also exposes the darker side of the new housing estates.
On arrival they found their garden destroyed by a spiteful neighbour: 'All that remained now were muddy potholes and the dying
tree. What he couldn't dig up he'd destroyed. Next door, a bird
bath had pride of place at the end of the garden path. A broken
plinth was at the end of ours. But at least we had a garden.'[13]

Because of the background of these families, their move into
council housing was, as in the 1920s, regarded as a means by which
the social skills and habits of the population in general might be
improved. In 1946 the BMA commented about the design of new
local authority family houses:

> Some families like to eat their meals in the kitchen. This habit ought
> not to be encouraged in the home of the future. The kitchen is the
> housewife's workplace and preparation room. From the superficial

41. Virginia Wimperis, *The Unmarried Mother and her Child* (Allen & Unwin, 1960),
p. 224.
42. Elyses Dodgson, *Motherland: West Indian Women coming to Britain in the 1950s*
(Heinemann Educational, 1984), p. 29.
43. Virginia Whitehead, unpublished autobiographical essay (1995), quoted by
permission of the author.

point of view it admittedly saves labour to have meals in the kitchen, but there are serious disadvantages. In the first place, the meal served where it is cooked is apt to degenerate into a service from pots and pans, without decency or order. Secondly, it is almost impossible to train children in good habits at table if they have to take their meals in an environment of sink and cooking utensil. And in the third place, the housewife has no opportunity for a change of scene, for quiet and leisure, if she has to feed at her workbench. The kitchen meal tends to be unrestful, disorderly, and devoid of educational value for the children.[44]

Families, however, generally resisted such attempts at social engineering and used their living space and conditions to suit their own requirements. Too little, unfortunately, has been written on the experience of families adapting to the new domestic spaces provided by council houses, and on how family members fared who were left behind in previously shared households.

Although many local communities were broken up in slum clearance programmes, older class divides were perpetuated through the housing developments of the inter-war and post-war years. Respectable working-class families were rehoused on newly constructed council estates but the broadly defined 'problem' families were less easily accommodated. Their supposed inability or unwillingness to manage their time and resources and to improve their social position rendered them subject to much criticism and sometimes served to deny them the opportunity of rehousing. Even the most supportive of their plight among voluntary organizations, the Pacifist Services Unit, commented judgementally, reproducing familiar stereotypes of working-class laziness and disorder:

There is no clock in most of these homes, and one may visit at ten in the morning and find the entire household asleep . . . Most of the mothers and nearly half the fathers in these families must be regarded as inefficient – the mothers disorderly and incompetent in the management of the home and children, the fathers unable to hold down any better work than casual labouring.[15]

The material, social and cultural poverty of the lives of many families, and particularly those who did not fit the nuclear family model, thus continued throughout the inter-war and post-war period despite the huge improvements to the country's housing stock and especially in wage levels more generally.

44. BMA, *Charter for Health*, pp. 44–5.
45. Tom Stephens, *Problem Families* (Pacifist Service Units, 1945), p. 4.

Inheritance strategies

The range of choices available to individuals has always been constrained by their family inheritance, which 'remains the major determinant of wealth inequality as well as the other life chances which depend on this'.[46] In the twentieth century families continued to provide one of the main channels through which money, goods, names, titles and jobs, and opportunities, ideas, beliefs and traditions were passed on from one generation to the next. Despite the widening ideological chasm separating work and public life from home and family, inheritance patterns and practices continued to straddle and undermine that divide.

Although overt nepotism in large businesses and organizations was no longer considered acceptable, the eclipse of family capitalism, the introduction of rational, objective standards and the growth of the large-scale bureaucratic machines within corporate capitalism did not obliterate family influences. As Michael Roper has perceptively shown in his study of managers in British firms after the Second World War, familial metaphors and fantasies dominated relations in the workplace at a psychic level, with important consequences for recruitment and training. For example, the mentor relationship between older and younger men had strong resonances of the father–son bond and often facilitated promotions.[47]

Jobs or positions were still often inherited through the influence or intervention of a family member or family friend, rather than won through open competition. Traditions and practices relating to employment could also be passed down through several generations. Paul Thompson's interviews with 100 British families revealed that over two-thirds had transmitted at least one occupation over three generations or more.[48] Such transmission is well illustrated in an interview by Peter Townsend with an elderly Bethnal Green resident in the 1950s, whose 'husband was a fish porter, and it should be noted that her son John is also a fish porter. One or two of the informant's brothers and her father had also been fish porters.'[49]

46. John Scott, *The Upper Classes: Property and Privilege in Britain* (Macmillan, 1982), p. 119.

47. Michael Roper, *Masculinity and the British Organisation Man since 1945* (Oxford University Press, 1994).

48. Daniel Bertaux and Paul Thompson, *Between Generations: Family Models, Myths and Memories* (Oxford University Press, 1993), p. 24.

49. Peter Townsend's interview with Mrs Elizabeth McCayna for *The Family Life of Old People*, Box No. 35, National Social Policy and Social Change Archive, Albert Sloman Library, University of Essex.

Similarly, older family members were frequently instrumental in providing the means by which the younger generation were able to move on and create their own homes and households. This may have been through financing education and training, financial loans, the passing on of furniture, or practical help in the renovation of property. Willmott and Young's study of East London in the 1950s, for example, revealed how frequently mothers interceded with housing agents and rent collectors on behalf of daughters, to take over tenancies often vacated by relatives.[50]

Inheritance exchanges, although most common between men, could thus also pass between women and between women and men. Mothers often used influence to improve their children's educational prospects and attempted to find work for both sons and daughters. Male relations or family friends also sometimes enabled the entry of women into jobs and occupations only slowly beginning to admit female workers. One of the first members of the women's engineering society in the 1920s, who had herself been supported through college by her father, recalled a comment that 'to be a woman engineer you have to be able to get into a university, you must have a wealthy husband or father to keep you and an uncle who runs a factory'.[51] However, the small number of women in the society revealed just how few had actually been advantaged in this way.

Despite the widespread practices outlined above, many working-class men and women took active steps not to inherit their parents' ways of life, particularly those who were upwardly mobile and wished to leave behind a poverty-stricken childhood. A Mass Observation Survey reported in 1945 that ' "I don't want to be like my mum" is a frequent motive among young wives for wanting few children'. A woman who had twelve siblings but only one child of her own, and a much higher living standard than her parents, was described as having rejected her mother's ways of upbringing in favour of the rigid rules recommended in childcare advice books.[52]

An important inheritance for male members of the upper classes was the public school system, which continued to offer privileged routes into higher education, politics, the militia and the professions. Still operating largely through family networks and nepotism, even the least intelligent were offered some kind of career, providing

---

50. Michael Young and Peter Willmott, *Family and Kinship in East London* (Penguin, 1966).

51. Interview with Mavis by Katherine Holden.

52. Mass Observation, *Britain and her Birth Rate* (John Murray, 1945), pp. 166–73.

their parents knew the right people and could make generous bequests to the institutions concerned. If they had also inherited a family title, they could take their seat in the House of Lords, although since 1911 their political power-base had been considerably reduced. As mounting taxation and death duties led to the enforced sale of big estates, the landed classes' degree of influence over lower-class families in rural areas gradually diminished. With the advent of the motor car and more mechanized agriculture, patterns of rural employment were changing, lessening the likelihood of inheriting loyal family farm or domestic servants or maintaining traditions of deference.

While family titles were reserved for the aristocracy, family names were a more widespread inheritance. As we saw earlier, until fairly recently a child's right to be considered a legitimate member of society who could take on full powers of citizenship and inherit paternal property was contingent upon being allowed to take the father's surname, acquired through the parents' marriage. Successive changes from the 1920s to the 1950s in the laws on adoption and illegitimacy were designed to give some protection to the 'innocent' child from the consequences of the 'sins' of its parents. It was not, for example, until 1959 that the Legitimacy Act allowed an illegitimate child of an adulterous relationship to be legitimated following the marriage of its parents.

At the beginning of the century informal adoption and kinship fostering was common practice in families across all classes but particularly in working-class families, who would often take in their own rather than see them go to the workhouse. However, in 1939, Margery Spring Rice's survey *Working-Class Wives* found that 'Several women appear to have voluntarily adopted children – not grandchildren or the children of relatives but *only* of friends' (our emphasis), which might indicate that orphaned or abandoned children were taken in out of good will as well as from family duty.[53] Nevertheless, the stigma of illegitimacy, which affected both mothers and children, made it harder for a single woman to adopt or foster children, either of friends or family. And those who did might not allow a foster-child to call them 'mother' for fear neighbours would believe it to be their own offspring.[54]

53. Margery Spring Rice, *Working-Class Wives: Their Health and Conditions* (Penguin, 1939).
54. See Katherine Holden, 'The shadow of marriage: single women in England 1919–1939', Ph.D. thesis, University of Essex (1996), ch. 5.

Until 1926 the rights of the natural parents, which in the case of an illegitimate child would be the mother alone, took precedence in English law. They could recover custody of their children, in spite of any agreement to the contrary, although in the case of neglect the Poor Law guardians might 'adopt' the child, which meant that the mother would lose her rights but might still be required to pay for its maintenance.[55] Parliamentary debates leading to the 1926 Act, which enabled adoptions to be legalized and revoked the natural parent's rights to reclaim their child, should be seen in the context of widespread concern about the supposed breakdown of the extended family. The rival claims of kin and natural parents to make decisions about a child's future were hotly debated. Some believed that the sanctity of family life would be upheld by allowing extended kin to take responsibility and that 'flighty' parents should not be allowed to get rid of a child in face of family opposition. Others had less faith in the unity of interests between kin and upheld the rights of the natural parents to decide their child's fate.

The outcome of this debate, in which it was decided that the courts should arbitrate between the claims of family and an outside adopter, is an indication of the increasing involvement of the state in decisions which would previously have been considered essentially private matters. However, it was not until 1950 that Parliament legislated for adopted children to be taken fully and irrevocably into a new family unit thereby losing all contact with the natural parents and any inheritance that might be expected from them. Nevertheless, it remained impossible for adopted children to inherit a title, for these continued to be passed on only through the *bloodline*.

Social regulation of families

A very important concern in twentieth-century England was the direct legacy children received from their mothers. As both world wars and the Depression helped to prick public consciences over the health and welfare of children, successive generations of professionals – health visitors, welfare workers, domestic subjects'

55. Moira Martin, 'Managing the poor: the administration of poor relief in Bristol in the nineteenth and twentieth century', in M. Dresser and P. Ollerenshaw (eds), *The Making of Modern Bristol* (Redcliffe Press, 1996), p. 175.

teachers, psychologists and childcare advice writers – stressed the importance of women's maternal duties. Our prolonged discussion of this issue reflects the weight attached to it by experts in this period.

Both middle- and working-class mothers were targeted, but approaches varied. Since many professionals associated infant mortality during the inter-war years with a failure of motherhood and not with poverty, they believed that a sense of maternal responsibility had to be instilled into working-class mothers and potential mothers. From 1907 onwards 'schools for mothers' were set up by voluntary agencies, often supported by the Ministry of Health, giving advice and training to working-class mothers on childrearing. However, although few middle-class mothers engaged in paid work, hands-on childcare was still not expected of the better off. As in the nineteenth century, the employment of nursemaids or nannies remained quite common between the wars and mothers did not assume that their children might be damaged by their absence.

For working-class girls, however, mothercraft was included as part of the domestic subjects curriculum studied in elementary and some secondary schools to prepare them for marriage. In her autobiography Joyce Storey remembers the flat in her school's grounds which was used for these lessons. This contained 'a doll in a pram and there was a tin bath . . . and we had to dust and sweep and polish. The baby had to be changed and bathed and rocked to sleep.'[56] But such attempts to train girls for motherhood were not always successful or appreciated. This particular flat failed to fulfil its purpose but enabled the writer and her friends 'to bring out our "penny dreadfuls" and read the spicy bits to one another'. The baby evoked no maternal feelings and 'fared dreadfully, often being upended and its head stuck in the potty, whilst Gladys did the "splits", with her dress tucked into her knickers for decency'.[57]

The training manuals used in schools and welfare centres, such as Mabel Liddiard's *The Mothercraft Manual* (running through twelve editions between 1923 and 1956), were often those popular with middle-class mothers. They adopted a scientific approach heavily influenced by the physician Truby King, who stressed the importance of babies feeding, sleeping, toilet training, and even playing strictly by the clock. It is difficult to assess how closely mothers or nurses followed these prescriptions, but they do seem to have been influential, especially for the first child, in middle-class and some

56. Joyce Storey, *Our Joyce* (Bristol Broadsides, 1987), p. 79.   57. Ibid., p. 80.

working-class circles, and may have replaced the advice of neighbours and relatives for new mothers isolated in the suburbs. One mother recalled the 'universal agony' she and other mothers went through, feeling unable to pick up and comfort or feed their crying babies until the correct time.[58] Many midwives, health visitors and welfare workers, trained during the inter-war years, continued to encourage new mothers to use Truby King's methods. Tensions thus arose between older, professional women and young mothers, who were increasingly influenced in the post-war years by the promotion of psychoanalytic ideas in childcare books and more particularly in women's magazines.

The majority of women still had home births between the wars, assisted by either a professional midwife or a doctor according to their means. The untrained handywomen had been outlawed by the Midwives' Act of 1902 but were still often called in to assist the mother and midwife with domestic chores. However, the trend towards hospital births, which accelerated sharply with the advent of the NHS, was already advanced in some areas before the war. In London in 1934, 60 per cent of births were occurring in an institution compared with a national average of 24 per cent in 1933. Some women spoke of the safety of hospital births, with increased levels of medical intervention and hygiene, as a welcome advance from their mothers' experiences in squalid housing with no modern equipment on hand if anything went wrong. Others felt isolated and intimidated in hospitals where their own and their families' experience and expertise were ignored.[59] Typical hospital regimes in the 1950s separated newborn infants from their mothers, excluded fathers from the birth and still adhered to strict timetables.

At the same time working-class women were subjected to close supervision from health visitors and other authorities on childbirth and childrearing, whose advice often conflicted with traditional wisdom. Experts of this kind were often single middle-class women trained in the latest theories. Oral evidence suggests that their advice might be welcomed or resented depending partly on the nature of the community in which they worked.[60]

58. Dianne Richardson, *Women, Motherhood and Childrearing* (Macmillan, 1993), pp. 34–6.

59. Lara Marks, 'They're magicians: midwives, doctors and hospitals: women's experiences of childbirth in East London and Woolwich in the interwar years', *Oral History*, Vol. 23, No. 1 (Spring 1995).

60. For oral evidence see *Oral History*, Vol. 23, No. 1, 'Health and welfare' (Spring 1995).

Muriel, a midwife who had delivered babies in East London between the wars, had few doubts about her ability to take charge of a birth, stressing the authority she had exerted over the mothers:

> I mean sometimes they had them before we got there; not very often, 'cos if they did they got well told off you see, because that wasted a pupil's case . . . if the baby's born before the nurse gets here then the nurse can't count that baby for her examination, 'cos they had to have so many, so they were frightened. They always sent in good time 'cos they knew they'd be told off if they had the baby beforehand.

But when she moved on to do health visiting in a country district she had more problems. The 'good' mothers who came from London, some of whom 'hadn't got a clue which end the baby was hardly', were 'always all right', but rural women were less willing to accept the dictates of an outsider. They didn't like 'new-fangled ideas like immunization and taking the baby to the clinic', and the influence of grandmas 'mucking about in the background saying "you don't want that done dear"' undermined her authority.[61]

By the 1940s and 1950s the influence of psychoanalytic theories, and especially the work of Donald Winnicott and John Bowlby, was changing the nature of advice aimed at mothers. This was now focused more closely upon the nature of the relationship between mother and child and how the child might be emotionally or psychologically damaged by even minimal separation from its mother. As a result, the role of fathers in the home and in childrearing was seldom discussed, although Elizabeth Roberts's study suggests that the post-war fathers were more involved with their children than the previous generation. Nevertheless, this seems seldom to have extended to physical care, and childcare manuals of the fifties either ignored the father's role or treated his participation in caring as a joke.[62] In the case of John Bowlby's work, he places the mother as the sole parent in his discussion of family life.

> Not only do they [husbands] provide for their wives to enable them to devote themselves unrestrictedly to the care of the infant and toddler, but, by providing love and companionship, they support the mother emotionally and help her maintain that harmonious

61. Second interview with Muriel by Katherine Holden. Nicky Leap and Billie Hunter encountered similar stories of resistance to midwives' authority by older married women in *The Midwives' Tale: An Oral History from Handywomen to the Professional Midwife* (Scarlett Press, 1993).

62. See Elizabeth Roberts, *Women and Families: An Oral History, 1940–1970* (Blackwell, 1995), p. 156 and Lynn Segal, *Slow Motion: Changing Masculinities, Changing Men* (Virago, 1990), p. 11.

contented mood in the atmosphere of which *her* infant thrives [our emphasis].[63]

Although there was a recognition of the strains which the post-war woman experienced in balancing her role as 'good' mother with the heavy domestic workload demanded by her role as housewife and, increasingly, part-time work outside the home, the government was reluctant to fill the gap left by the decline in domestic service and supportive female relatives and recommended in 1951 that day-care provision be refused to any woman who was going to work solely to supplement the family income.

Despite the sympathies expressed for the difficult lives of such women, mothers were largely left to struggle alone in meeting the physical, emotional and psychological demands and needs of their children which the theories of maternal deprivation had now made all important. Alison Hennegan recalls how, in the 1950s, her mother's classroom was used as an informal crèche for mothers with nowhere else to turn. 'They'd gallop in, deposit the infant, give my mother a breathless and embarrassedly apologetic explanation of family emergency and gallop out again, their vehement thanks still hanging on the air as the door swung behind them and the trailing toddler clinging to their skirts.'[64]

Caribbean families who came to Britain during the 1950s to fill the post-war labour shortage had particular problems in this respect. While some men and women came alone, others were accompanied or followed by spouses, with many leaving their children behind to be cared for by their mothers or other female relatives. Women with children in Britain, whether married or single, generally needed to work full-time to survive, and found the lack of reliable childcare in England a source of great anxiety. One mother remembered being told: 'Lord have mercy you mustn't take a baby there 'cause she puts them downstairs on the basement floor.' Some women maintained links with their culture: 'I bring up my child just as how I would in the West Indies . . . I have to tell her the ways of people over here are different.' Others were influenced by disapproval of their white neighbours and concerned at the lack of family support: 'I gave out Linda for about three year next door. One day a white lady said to me, "Linda is better off with you". So you could read between the lines. She was the shopkeeper, so I packed it in. It's no good to give your children out.'[65]

63. John Bowlby, *Child Care and the Growth of Love* (Penguin, 1953), p. 15.
64. Heron (ed.), *Truth, Dare or Promise*, p. 130.
65. Dodgson, *Motherland*, pp. 41 and 59.

Theories of maternal deprivation also helped to support the growth of the child welfare movement. This movement had its origins in the war years as a result of the concerns of Medical Officers of Health about the physical and emotional deprivation experienced by children in day nurseries. But equally influential was the impact which evacuated, malnourished working-class children, with their allegedly underdeveloped social skills and poor personal hygiene habits, had upon the predominantly middle-class households in which they were billeted. The Evacuation Survey carried out by the Fabian Society after the first phase of evacuation in 1940 identified some of the resulting tensions between parents and host families which could so easily backfire upon the child.

> If the hostess was a possessive woman she sometimes resented the evacuee's display of affection for his own parents, especially where she doubted her own adequacy to handle this child or where she needed the evacuee's response to herself for her own emotional satisfaction. One hostess repeatedly told a child of eight that her mother had abandoned her and would never see her again. When the mother arrived to visit she was promptly removed. Alternatively the hostess might have to face hostility on the part of a parent who was jealous that her child was being weaned away from her by a higher standard of living.[66]

By the 1950s beliefs in the inadequacy of working-class families were combined with an ideology of 'bad mothering', and together they informed the thinking of many professionals involved with the care of children. Bad mothering included the dangers of mothers going out to work, which, despite advice to the contrary, was an increasing trend, resulting in supposedly deprived or delinquent latch-key children.

Following the Children's Act of 1948 which created Children's Departments with the brief to protect children at risk, local authorities had a statutory duty to take children into care if their parents were deemed unfit or unable to look after them. Because their priorities were to remove children at risk rather than helping to avert the need to take children into care, the numbers of children in residential care rose.[67] Despite widespread agreement that the most appropriate solution was adoption and fostering, resources were put into building new homes at the expense of training staff

66. Richard Padley and Margaret Cole (eds), *Evacuation Survey: A Report to the Fabian Society* (George Routledge & Sons, 1940), pp. 160–2.
67. B. Watkin, *Documents on Health and Social Service, 1834 to the Present Day* (Methuen, 1975), p. 421.

or supporting families.[68] This legislation and the lack of appropriate funding thus created a problem of institutionalized children, which was all too often seen not as the outcome of social policies, but as yet another indicator of the endemic decline of the family.

The growth of welfare services also included voluntary organizations such as the National Society for the Prevention of Cruelty to Children, the Family Welfare Association, Moral Welfare Associations, and the Salvation and Church Armies. These intervened in a variety of ways to monitor families seen to be at risk. Their work included supporting families whose standards of childcare were perceived to be low, and the provision of homes for delinquent adolescents, babies and unmarried mothers, rehabilitation centres for alcoholic and broken families, holidays for families with severe social problems and homes for the elderly without families to care for them. Nevertheless, the care of the sick and the elderly continued to remain predominantly the responsibility of women, both single and married, kin and outsiders, throughout the inter-war and post-war periods. The very real fear which the elderly had of Poor Law institutions, the only other alternative to the charity or voluntary-run Home until 1947, did not diminish and they remained determined to avoid residential care at all costs.

Although the Poor Law was finally abolished in 1948, attitudes reminiscent of the nineteenth-century 'deserving' and 'undeserving' poor were slower to shift. Many elderly people without friends or relatives to care for them continued to be housed in large institutions. The worst of these were poorly staffed, had unplastered interior walls, stone floors and long spartan dormitories with up to fifty beds. They retained rigid regimes, segregating the sexes, including married couples, and provided institutional clothing. In his study of institutional care for the elderly undertaken in the late 1950s, Peter Townsend argued that 'The failure of the Labour and Conservative Governments after 1948 to replace the former workhouses with small homes helped to perpetuate a form of discrimination between human beings which was neither efficient nor moral.'[69]

Yet the idea, promoted by post-war governments, that ideally elderly people should be housed in Homes that imitated family life had taken root in the post-war imagination, even if relatively few (usually affluent) elderly people were benefiting in reality. The

68. A. Land *et al.*, *The Development of the Welfare State* (HMSO, 1992), p. 201.
69. Peter Townsend, *The Last Refuge: A Survey of Residential Institutions and Homes for the Aged in England and Wales* (abridged edn, Routledge & Kegan Paul, 1964), pp. 223–5.

matron of East Leak Hall, a voluntary home run by Nottingham Council, reflects this attitude: 'I have always been sorry for old people. I applied because I knew I could make myself a Home and I try to run it like a home with a big family.'[70]

Voluntary organizations involved with the care of family life, but particularly those with religious inspiration, had a particular emphasis on the regulation of sexual behaviour in order to protect families, and especially children, from deviant sexualities and evils such as prostitution, unmarried motherhood, homosexuality and lesbianism. However, there was little recognition of domestic violence, sexual abuse and incest occurring within families, particularly if they were middle or upper class. Domestic violence was considered by the police and society more generally to be a private dispute between husband and wife and not, therefore, subject to intervention by external agencies. In 1954, Commander Hathergill of Scotland Yard, in discussing the annual crime figures for London, commented, 'There are only about twenty murders a year in London and not all are serious – *some are just husbands killing wives*' (our emphasis).[71] A study of working-class families in Liverpool between the wars shows that threatened or actual violence was employed to maintain men's autonomy as family providers and women's as household and financial managers and that this situation was largely accepted by women: 'A majority of husbands appear to have insisted that a wife take entire responsibility for "her" duties and violent threats were sometimes used to preserve the boundary as rigidly as possible.'[72]

Although incest was criminalized for the first time in 1908, there were only a handful of prosecutions and by 1914 any recognition of child sexual abuse virtually disappeared from NSPCC records. This was despite the 50,000 cases of neglect and cruelty reported to the society annually during the 1920s.[73] Young people were considered to be most at risk from sexual deviancy outside the family. Marriage manuals such as Van de Velde's *Ideal Marriage*, which appeared in England in 1930 and was reprinted 43 times, stressed the joys of conjugal love and the importance of mutual orgasm

70. Peter Townsend Collection, 'The last refuge', Box No. 36, National Social Policy and Social Change Archive, Albert Sloman Library, University of Essex.

71. Cited in Alexandra Artley, *Murder in the Heart* (Hamish Hamilton, 1993), p. 107.

72. Pat Ayers and Jan Lambertz, 'Marriage relations, money and domestic violence in working-class Liverpool 1919–1939', in Jane Lewis (ed.), *Labour and Love: Women's Experience of Home and Family, 1850–1940* (Basil Blackwell, 1986), p. 211.

73. Stephen Humphries and Pamela Gordon, *Forbidden Britain: Our Secret Past, 1900–1960* (BBC Books, 1994).

between husbands and wives, but the 'Hell Gate of sexual perversion was kept firmly closed'.[74]

A new sexual climate after the First World War is evident in the decline of chaperons for upper- and middle-class girls. Working-class communities, however, often continued to regulate, on an informal level, the sexual behaviour of female family members and of neighbours through gossip and rumour. As Roberts noted in *The Classic Slum*: 'The moralists found it hard to forgive and they never forgot. "I wonder", sniffed one old neighbour to another, after hearing of the outbreak of the Second World War, "I wonder if Mrs J., with her husband away, will go on the game again like what she did last time?"'[75]

Family time: rituals and leisure activities

Nevertheless, new leisure habits, which often centred on the cinema and dance hall, promoted more relaxed courtship rituals, whilst formal surveillance of public sexual behaviour decreased. Although the norm was still pre-marital chastity, there is some evidence of an increase in sexual relations outside marriage. Yet at the same time, with the hardening of divisions between work and home, public duties and private pleasures, recreational time spent within the family was regarded as increasingly important. This was a domain where more time could now be spent by men through the reduction of working hours, the increased ownership of radios and television sets, and the advent of paid holidays for growing numbers of more affluent workers, many of whom had become the proud owners or tenants of the new suburban homes.

But how did families spend their increased leisure time? Rowntree and Lavers's survey *English Life and Leisure*, published in 1951, looked primarily at leisure activities outside the home. Yet their inclusion of a chapter on sexual promiscuity, which they attributed partly to the continuing existence of slum housing conditions 'where normal decency is almost unattainable', also suggests a concern that sex as both a leisure and procreational activity could not be contained within its proper domain.[76]

74. Jeffrey Weeks, *Sex, Politics and Society: The Regulation of Sexuality since 1800*, 2nd edn (Longman, 1989), pp. 206–7.

75. Robert Roberts, *The Classic Slum* (Manchester University Press, 1971), p. 9.

76. E. Seebohm Rowntree and G.R. Lavers, *English Life and Leisure: A Social Study* (1951), p. 208.

By the 1940s and 1950s the companionate marriage ideal was premised on the belief that marital stability was dependent upon sexual pleasure for both partners.[77] Advice in women's magazines suggested that having fulfilled her maternal and domestic duties during the working day and put the children safely to bed, a wife should freshen her make-up, change her frock and entertain her husband with an evening of romantic seduction. Formulated in this way, sex became a leisure activity that could be safely contained within the family, and marital relations were seen as a means of keeping both men and women safely in the home, off the streets and, for the former at least, out of the pubs. Yet concerns are also evident in the campaigns to 'clean up the streets', that men might be unwilling to restrict their pursuit of sexual pleasure within the confines of marriage. Rowntree and Lavers forcefully expressed this fear:

> We should not adequately fulfil our task if we failed to point out that the men who comprise the customers of the prostitutes are by no means only the young and foolish. Many apparently staid and respectable citizens are among them and the sight of such men prowling in search of some favoured prostitute seems to us to be an even greater degradation of human dignity than the peregrinations of the prostitutes.[78]

Thus, although prostitutes were excluded from and defined in opposition to the family, their work blurred the boundaries between public and private, by offering the respectable family man sexual services which could not in reality be confined within the family domain.

The threat of extra-marital sex, which lurked behind images of domestic harmony, seldom emerged in women's magazines and periodicals. Rather they tended to project, during the inter-war years, what Alison Light has characterized as quintessentially English images of 'pipe-smoking "little men" with their quietly competent partners, a nation of gardeners and housewives', which, she argues, are reflective of a tension between conservatism and modernity.[79] Retreat into cosy domestic bliss was much advocated after the traumas of each world war. Wounds might be healed through the

77. Janet Finch and Penny Summerfield, 'Social reconstruction and the emergence of companionate marriage, 1949–59', in David Clark (ed.), *Marriage, Domestic Life and Social Change* (Routledge, 1991), pp. 12–14.

78. Rowntree and Lavers, *English Life and Leisure*, p. 211.

79. Alison Light, *Forever England: Femininity, Literature and Conservatism between the Wars* (Routledge, 1991), p. 211.

promotion of leisure activities that could be enjoyed by families together at home, though still largely gender segregated: gardening and do-it-yourself home improvements for men; sewing and other domestic crafts for women. Yet the iconic status of the film *Brief Encounter*, with its hugely popular representation of extramarital romantic love and repressed female sexuality, indicates perhaps that marital life left many as unfulfilled and unhappy as the character played by Celia Johnson.

Modernizing forces, not least the speed of technological change, were also having radical effects on the kinds of leisure activities which families pursued together, and also served to blunt distinctions between public and private life. In contrast to the relatively slow provision of domestic technology (as late as 1949 it was found that one-third of British households heated all their water for washing on the stove), radio and television spread with unprecedented rapidity amongst all social classes: 75 per cent of all households owned a radio by 1943 and a television by 1961.[80]

The act of listening in together to the wireless, and later watching television, brought a heightened shared consciousness of public affairs. This was especially useful to the government during the Second World War when Churchill's rhetoric inspired the nation. The radio brought news from the front into the home while simultaneously idealizing work on the home front. Propaganda films showed families working together to 'dig for victory', which boosted morale but obscured the fact that many households and families were actually being destroyed or fragmented through military recruitment, mobilization of the workforce, evacuation, and war casualties, both abroad and in the Blitz. Later, the screening of the Coronation of Queen Elizabeth in 1953 brought families together in an unprecedented, shared viewing experience, while the long-running popular wireless programme *Family Favourites* linked up families who were dispersed across the world, particularly those serving in the armed forces.

Cinema was another important medium of communication for families. Advances in film technology from silent films to talkies in the 1920s and later from black and white to colour were accompanied by a steady rise in audience figures. By 1952 there were 5,000 cinemas and 150 million estimated attendances. Not only was it the

80. Christine Zmoroczek, 'The weekly wash', in Sybil Oldfield (ed.), *This Working-Day World: Women's Lives and Culture(s) in Britain 1914–1945* (Taylor & Francis, 1994), p. 10; Sue Bowden and Avner Offer, 'Household appliances and the use of time: the United States and Britain since the 1920s', unpublished paper (April 1993).

most popular leisure form in our period, but it was one that could
be cast as family entertainment, transcending age and sex divisions
even though most popular amongst women and the young. While
the very old attended rarely, a survey by Kathleen Box in 1946
showed that although 77 per cent of children under 4 never went
to the cinema, 5 per cent were taken more than twice a week.[81]
These figures suggest its importance for married women, who often
attended in the afternoon before the return of children from school,
and used Saturday cinema clubs for children as a childminding
service.

Cinemas were palaces of escape which promised warm, comfortable, red plush surroundings and an opportunity to enjoy the
depiction of alternative, often American, ways of life. Complaints,
summed up below by Len England in 1944, that film families did
not accurately represent the real families of the 1940s and the
realities of their lives were thus ignored by audiences and film-
makers alike.

> Love at first sight with the handsome hero works excellently on the
> screen; the steady monotony of suburban life, however, is a little
> different to the glamour of the film romance. The couple who marry
> impetuously in the film manage to get on very well; in real life they
> may find an unexpected doctor's bill or hire purchase payment throws
> a spanner in the works ... The realism of such family films only
> increases such danger.[82]

The mundanities and irritations of work and home life could be
forgotten in watching comedy, romance, thrillers or adventure stories unfold, and there was little popular appeal in such films as *Love
on the Dole*, which did represent the plight of the poorest families
in society, but which was 'one of the biggest box office failures in
years'.[83]

Young people, emerging into the new category of 'teenager'
with increased spending power, were regular cinema goers also.
The picture palace offered an opportunity to escape from parental
authority and to meet friends. As the narrative of the central male
character of *A Kind of Loving* reveals, the cinema's back row offered
many opportunities for young couples:

81. Quoted in Rowntree and Lavers, *English Life and Leisure*, p. 228.
82. Len England, 'The film and family life' (1944) cited in Jeffrey Richards and
Dorothy Sheridan, *Mass-Observation at the Movies* (Routledge & Kegan Paul, 1987),
p. 298.
83. Ibid.

As the bint with a torch sees us she flashes us up into the back where the courting couples are snogging away among the empty seats . . . We push past a couple sprawled out holding on to one another and they take no notice of us. We sit down in a double seat with no arm rest between us, which I think is a bit of all right . . . There's a snap like elastic breaking from the couple on the row and the bint giggles and wrestles with the bloke.[84]

As in the novel, many marriage pacts were cemented through such early romantic encounters.

Improved transport and communications also revolutionized the scope of family leisure activities, most importantly through the rapid spread of the motor car, but also with the advent of air travel, which by the 1960s meant that foreign holidays were no longer the preserve only of the wealthy. With the spread of the telephone to increasing numbers of private households, family news and travel arrangements among middle- and upper-class households could also be communicated more quickly and directly. Still its high cost left most working-class families reliant on the postal service, mainly letters, with telegrams used for deaths, emergencies or messages of congratulation for rites of passage such as births and marriages. In 1921 a woman teacher, parted for a few days from an intimate friend with whom she shared her work and life, described a six-minute phone call to her as '5s 6d and *cheap* at the price'[85] – but that was still more than half the weekly living allowance for a pensioner between the wars.

Community networks continued to be of material importance, particularly to women in the older inner-city districts, who relied on neighbours and relatives living close by for support and survival when times were hard. Despite steadily declining church attendance rates, religious organizations still performed important social functions, especially for women and children. Often segregated by age and gender, groups like the Mothers' Union and the Girls' Friendly Society (the latter described by one informant as having been dubbed the godforsaken spinsters)[86] offered women-only spaces and opportunities for companionship, mutual aid and activities, which men more often found in pubs or in working or business men's clubs. Sunday schools were usually mixed-sex and were joined as much for their social as religious functions, such as the prospect of a picnic or outing. Children were frequently encouraged by

84. Stan Barstow, *A Kind of Loving* (Corgi, 1974, first published 1960), p. 52.
85. E. Lawrence, *You Will Remember* (Oxford University Press, 1933), p. 265.
86. Interviews with Miriam Glucksmann, by permission of the interviewer.

parents, who may themselves not have attended church, but who were keen to escape the constant presence of their offspring and to ensure that they be taught moral values that had always been more difficult to assert unequivocally in the context of home and family life.

Most of the activities discussed above fall under the umbrella of 'family time': that is, time spent away from the workplace and negotiated with other members of family and household; although for women situated in the home, distinctions between work and leisure time were often meaningless. As the twentieth-century festivals and rites of passage, such as Christmas and weddings, became increasingly private affairs celebrated by families rather than communities, their symbolic importance increased. These rituals, together with the idea of a regular family dinner hour when all members ate together, and family holidays when they went away from home to play together, whether in seaside boarding houses, the new holiday camps or holiday cottages owned by increasing numbers of middle-class families, all became symbols of family, and by extension national, unity. Even the annual hop-pickers' migration which served as a holiday to many Cockney families was idealized as 'a picturesque and on the whole enjoyable interlude in the ordinary existence of thousands of the poorer families of East London labourers'.[87]

In such 'imagined families' differences in race, gender, age and access to power and resources were invisible. Many of the examples highlighted in this chapter reinforce the idea that the nuclear family, both numerically and as a value system, dominated English society in the earlier part of this century. But what we have also shown is both its transience in demographic terms and some of the ways in which as a model it worked to marginalize individuals and family forms that did not fit. These ideas will be developed further in the two chapters which follow. The first looks at how single women, generally defined as being outside families, gave vital material support to families and also subjectively drew upon the idea of family to make sense of their lives. The second explores the underbelly of the family. Here we bring to light the many areas of secrecy that exist within families, thereby undermining the idea of an entity with a unity of interests.

87. *The New Survey of London Life and Labour*, Vol. 3 (London, 1932), p. 341.

CHAPTER EIGHT

Family shadows: unmarried women

I write of the High Priestess of Society. Not of the mother of sons, but of her barren sister, the withered tree, the acidulous vessel, under whose pale shadow we chill and whiten of the Spinster I write. Because of her power and dominion. She unobtrusive, silent, shamefaced, bloodless and boneless, thinned to spirit, enters the secret recesses of the mind.

The Freewoman, 1911[1]

To throw further light on how the self and identity are forged in the crucible of family, we turn now to a category of identity that in the modern period has often appeared anomalous and even at times infamous. New light can be shed on our understanding of families by unravelling the meanings attached to the term 'spinster' and listening to some of the family stories told by childless unmarried women, who as a group are conspicuous by their absence from most nineteenth- and twentieth-century family histories.[2]

The spinster's relationship to family has many guises. Cast as the old maid, alone, lonely and without family, she was the despised family drudge, or even, as adulterous mistress or frustrated schoolmarm, an enemy of families. Yet she has also been seen as the family standby. In the part of beloved aunt, dutiful daughter or fairy godmother, her gifts of money, goods, care and love have been acknowledged in private within families but seldom deemed of value outside.

How can we understand this paradox? First it is clear that the power of images of the spinster and the old maid to invoke feelings

---

1. 'The spinster by one', *The Freewoman* (23 November 1911).
2. See e.g. Elizabeth Roberts, *A Woman's Place: An Oral History of Working-Class Women 1840–1940* (Blackwell, 1984) and *Women and Families: An Oral History 1940–1970* (Blackwell, 1995).

of pity, fear, ridicule and scorn lies in their categorization as out-siders, evident in the chilling quotation above, taken from the lead article in a pre-First World War feminist journal. In this story, families were threatened by the destructive influence of the 'High Priestess'. As on the eve of war, fears of racial decline were intensi-fying, the British nation was perceived to be withering under the shadow of the empty womb, destroyed by the woman who was no longer willing to mother a son, to cradle that highly prized mascu-line individual. But there are also elements of latent sexuality in the imagery employed. Although she is represented as pale, bloodless and asexual – an enemy of the joys of heterosexual love – her status as a priestess, whose power could either lie in her virginity or in her fertility, points to the temptation a single woman's presence within families offered to married men, and her potential to undermine familial hierarchies.

Such images sent strong messages to women that only marriage and motherhood could give them a completely fulfilled and happy life and fed into a tradition of concern about the problems of the 'redundant' or 'superfluous' woman, which intensified in the years after the First World War. The surplus of women over men in-creased in the generations most affected by war casualties, peaking in 1921 at 1,209 women per thousand males aged 25–30 in England and Wales. Although the surplus declined thereafter, many women in this age group never married. Their numbers widely reported and exaggerated in the press, single women were urged, as they had been since the 1850s, to emigrate to find husbands and multiply the British race in the Empire. For those who 'failed' to marry, work caring for children or domestic service was recommended as a sub-stitute for marriage.

For despite imagery which set the spinster in opposition to families, she was in reality far from being excluded. As she cast her malevolent pale shadow, 'the barren sister' was held within the family shadow. 'Shamefaced, unobtrusive and silent', she could still be perceived as a figure of power and influence. Many single women capitalized on the need families had of their services; the family could become a refuge from the shame of spinsterhood, or a cause which offered them alternative identities and justifications for not marrying.

The parts single women played were not insignificant, especially during the inter-war years. Benefiting from improved health and longevity, they provided a large body of active labour for the ex-panding welfare and educational services and were widely available as family carers. Some middle-class women may have actively avoided marriage and motherhood in order to be able to concentrate on careers and women-oriented lifestyles, although this possibility has consistently been ignored by demographic historians attempting to explain the fertility decline in Western countries.[3] However, by the 1950s the declining birth-rate and increased marriage rate meant that there were fewer unmarried women available to take on these roles.

To understand better why single women's identities were so closely tied into family we need briefly to return to our earlier discussion of the gendered self. While until the late nineteenth century a married woman was legally subsumed into the person of her husband, the possibility for a single adult woman to lay claims to full citizenship on the same basis as the male individual was on the surface greater and she was therefore a potential threat to masculine power. Yet just as the male individual's rights to citizenship concealed his dependence on familial and domestic support, so also the single woman was all too easily locked into a pattern of providing that support by virtue of her gender.

It has been argued that with the impetus of late nineteenth-century feminism, many middle-class women broke free from supporting or being supported by kin, and saw themselves as 'independent women'.[4] It is certainly true that some single women were claiming citizenship and creating alternatives to the family in their lifestyles, although often still making use of familial language and structures, as we saw in our discussion of girls' boarding schools and institutions in Chapter 4. Yet in their work, rather than sharing the fruits of industrial capitalism with 'the self-made man', they were more likely to be rescuing its casualties. Much of their work consisted of monitoring and regulating working-class families through philanthropy and social activism, and their claims to the vote were made partly on the basis of carrying out 'their mission as "social housekeepers", to help to shape the domestic lives of the nation'.[5] The possibility for working-class single women to claim an autonomous

3. Alison MacKinnon 'Were women present at the demographic transition? Questions from a feminist historian to historical demographers', *Gender and History*, Vol. 7, No. 2 (August 1995).

4. See Martha Vicinus, *Independent Women: Work and Community for Single Women 1850–1920* (Virago, 1985); Alison MacKinnon, *Professional Women and the Reshaping of Personal Life* (Cambridge University Press, 1997).

5. Jane Rendall, 'Women's politics, *c.*1780–1870', in 'Major Themes in Women's History: From the Enlightenment to the Second World War' on *Core Resources for Historians* (CD Rom) (Glasgow TLTP History Courseware Consortium, 1998).

self was even more restricted, strung as many were between giving
financial and/or domestic support to their own families and providing domestic service for other families, which, as we have seen,
was the principal employment area for women until the Second
World War. In working-class communities, a woman's decision to
marry, or not, may have depended on her family's financial circumstances, her employment opportunities, and whether her contribution to the family income was regarded as essential or if she might
be needed as a carer. A youngest daughter's sense of value to her
family is caught in the following interview. Born in 1904, Dora
eventually gave up paid employment completely to care for her
mother because:

> Mum had heart trouble and so Dad says well I don't want you to be
> in service, I want you to be here to help Mum. So he got me an
> office job and it was only five minutes walk from home ... I had
> Saturdays off, well Saturday afternoons off, and that's when I used to
> have to go out with mother doing the shopping and that, and that's
> why they wanted me to be there so that any time, like in evenings
> and that, I could help her you see.[6]

The multiple parts played by single women in families cross and
blur the boundaries of blood, contract and intimacy. By virtue of
being kin by blood or marriage, whether as sisters, aunts, daughters, nieces or cousins, they were often expected, as in the extract
above, to provide financial and/or domestic support and physical
care for their young, sick or elderly relatives. But such tasks were as
frequently contracted to women who, though they lived within families, were defined as outsiders employed in some kind of service
position.

Although residential service was declining, domestic service remained the principle occupation for single women in the first half
of this century, and wealthy elderly women, without relatives to
look after them, still often employed live-in nurses or companions,
as they had done in the nineteenth century. Until the Second World
War, working-class single women were also still routinely employed
to undertake much of the physical care of children, as nannies,
nurserymaids, governesses, or general servants in middle- and upper-
class homes, and as matrons and house mothers in institutions.

Whilst bonds of love and intimacy might be created between
children and single carers, these could be compromised by the

6. Dora, interviewed by Katherine Holden (21 February 1994).

carer's status as an employee. This is suggested in an article satirizing middle-class family life which appeared in *Good Housekeeping* in 1933, entitled 'Four in the Family', which number excludes nanny, nursery governess and cook, who are the chief objects of ridicule. The narrator, who is the wife, mother and mistress, acknowledges the comfortless and transitory life endured by the family's nanny:

> when she thinks of all the intimate clutter that constituted Miss Jenkins's private life now neatly arranged in another's chilly bedroom in someone else's house, she must be forgiven if she rails a little over the cruelty of life. Six years of whole-hearted service. Six years of as passionate devotion as Miss Jenkins's mild frame can house: six years of a woman's life, and then one day the children look bigger than usual, school bills are heavier than they used to be and reluctant parents decide they must part with her. So off she goes with her neat trunk to begin all over again.[7]

It was not only working-class single women whose employment contracts brought them into close contact with families. The increasing professionalization and state involvement in welfare services after the First World War also, as we saw in Chapter 7, gave single women opportunities to become experts in family life. As teachers, by far the largest women's profession and subjected to a marriage bar, middle-class single women were responsible for the education and daily supervision of a large proportion of the nation's children. Yet, paradoxically, because they were spinsters, they were frequently derided, regarded as sexually frustrated or sexual inverts, i.e. lesbians, and their influence over children, especially girls – who, it was believed, might be put off marriage by their example – seen as unhealthy.[8]

As nurses, midwives and health visitors, they not only gave advice to mothers, but increasingly presided over rites of passage such as births, deaths and illness. Finally, single women often drew upon family relationships such as mother/daughter or sister within institutional life, especially in schools and hospitals, or the married couple in partnerships with friends and siblings. Imagery redolent of marriage is suggested by a teacher writing to a woman friend with whom she lived and worked about the problems of being in

7. Lorna Rea, 'Four in the family', *Good Housekeeping* (June 1933).

8. See Alison Oram, ' "Embittered, sexless, or homosexual": attacks on spinster teachers 1918–1939', in Lesbian History Group (eds), *Not a Passing Phase: Recovering Lesbians in History 1840–1985* (Women's Press, 1989).

single harness: 'When we are both together and pulling together the cart moves more easily.'[9] From these illustrations it appears that single women were important for the survival of many families and that, although categorized as marginal or dangerous, they could still draw upon the idea of family in a multitude of ways to give their lives purpose and meaning. Their presence in this book reflects our view that, like domestic servants, most of whom were recruited from their ranks, the single should be regarded as an important object of study for family historians.

To illustrate the many and complex ways in which single women in the twentieth century drew upon family in the creation of their identities and were integral to family life, we shall follow the life stories of four women born in the earlier part of this century or at the end of the nineteenth. The stories of the first three, Daisy Brown (born 1908), Ellen Stephens (born 1909) and Bridget Perkins (born 1906), all from southern England, were told in oral history interviews. The fourth, Alice Baker (born 1889), who died in the 1970s, also from the south, is from an earlier generation. Her personal papers were generously made available by a niece, with whose help we have reconstructed her aunt's story.

A principal object in making use of these stories has been to give a voice to members of a marginalized group. But the stories do not simply speak for themselves. Rather they are a dialogue between interviewee and interviewer, shaped both by the nature of the questions asked and the interpretative framework which has subsequently been imposed upon them. Here it has been important to look beneath the surface of individual narratives in order to explore ambivalence and unconscious desires which reveal much about the inherent contradictions of being both single and female.[10] This sense of reading between the lines has been even more necessary in the final case where the subject's own voice barely appears and our interpretation relies heavily on evidence of friends and relatives who were close to her.

9. E. Lawrence, *You Will Remember* (Oxford University Press, 1933), p. 269.
10. Katherine Holden, 'The shadow of marriage: single women in England 1919–1939', Ph.D. thesis, University of Essex (1996). See also Raphael Samuel and Paul Thompson, *The Myths We Live By* (Routledge, 1990). For a discussion of the ethical issues in interpreting interviews see Miriam Glucksmann, 'The work of knowledge and the knowledge of women's work', in Mary Maynard and June Purves (eds), *Researching Women's Lives From a Feminist Perspective* (Taylor & Francis, 1994).

The sister's tale: Daisy Brown[11]

Daisy was interviewed when she was 85, in a suburb of the southern city which had always been her home. Her solid, comfortable, easygoing appearance belied her description of herself as someone with strong opinions and tempers who liked to speak her mind. A voracious reader, Daisy commented that 'one often is read by the books you read'. Yet the books she mentioned, the detective stories of Agatha Christie and Dorothy Sayers, the novels of E.H. Young and Mary Webb which she had devoured in her youth, and now Georgette Heyer's historical romances, whilst they offered her narrative forms which may have helped her tell her life story, hardly reflected the full breadth of her experiences and relationships.

Daisy was the youngest of three children, with a sister May eight years older and a brother Bert ten years older. Her parents had both been in service until they married, her father as a butler and her mother a maid. Her father had been forced to leave service on marriage – his employers refused to keep a married butler – and from then on had done odd jobs mainly in the building trade and was sometimes unemployed. Lying about their ages, her father and brother Bert – who married at the age of 18 – had joined up at the beginning of the war. But her father was later invalided out with TB and remained in poor health thereafter, although he did not die until just before the start of the Second World War.

Her mother, whose health was generally poor and who died of cancer aged 65 in 1933, didn't work outside the home after marriage. However, during the First World War (when Daisy was between 6 and 10 years old) she had fostered war babies, helped by her eldest daughter May. Not long after the war ended, the family adopted George, a war baby whose father was an Australian soldier. Although the arrangement could not at that time have been legalized, the birth mother had apparently signed a paper agreeing to pay £100 if she wanted her child back.

Although she spent the majority of her working life in service living away from her family home, Daisy maintained very strong links with her family, and her positions as youngest daughter and younger sister were significant in shaping her life path. She was a bright child, and at 14 her headmistress had urged her parents to let her try for a scholarship, but the family could not afford it:

11. Daisy Brown, interviewed by Katherine Holden (4 October 1993).

My mother was ill more often than not. My sister was at home most of her life looking after my mother and then my father became an invalid after she died, so she spent most of her life looking after invalid parents. That's why when I was fourteen it was decided, right, she'd looked after . . . she was eight years older than me, that she was to be at home when mother was ill and I was to start out.

As a result of both her parents' ill health, the older sister May's employment history was spasmodic. Daisy's image of her sister was of someone who was always at home. Her father had needed extra care after he had left the army and:

> after mother died, my sister was home with him all the time. He had kidney trouble. He had one kidney removed and that often affects the brain a little bit. She had to sort of keep an eye on him, so she's always had an awful lot to do, my sister.

Yet this was not in fact the whole picture. As Daisy later let slip, the 'awful lot to do' after her mother died had included for May daily paid employment as a char, and she had also worked when her mother was still alive as a waitress at the staff canteen for a tobacco factory, when 'she used to provide a tremendous lot of her money to clothe George'.

Daisy's story placed her sister as carer in the home and herself as the outside wage earner. However, it appears that both sisters made important financial contributions to the family budget, whilst their parents maintained ultimate control of their earnings and their pattern of work and lifestyles. Daisy stressed that she had always given her money to her parents, and it was clear that she felt she had little choice to do anything other than remain in service.

But how constraining was the model of dutiful daughter for the fiery young woman that Daisy recognized in her past self? When asked what had happened if she had ever disagreed with her parents, she told of her long-standing hopes to become a missionary, which had culminated in her taking a correspondence course:

> When it came to the end they thought, well I didn't quite come up to scratch, I'd done very well. They suggested would I care to come to London to work in a mission home, where I could carry on learning and be working in the home? My word! *Go to London!* I shouldn't think so . . . Well I was very fit to be a missionary because I said to my sister what I could do to my mother for not letting me go. That was a lovely missionary spirit wasn't it. But oh no, definitely. Well in those days you did as you were told and your parents were your parents.

It was hard for Daisy to admit any justifiable anger against her parents for exerting so much control over her life, which she also frequently insisted had been very happy. When recounting her small acts of rebellion, she usually followed them with a statement of self-recrimination such as 'it was very wrong of me' or 'I don't know how X put up with me'. Expectations of obedience and sacrifice from daughters set up barriers which Daisy and many others like her felt they could not easily escape. It was a position which Daisy could also have recognized in the fiction of the period. Although there was overt criticism of adult daughters who remained tied to their parents and families, stemming in part from the growing influence of psychoanalysis,[12] inter-war women's magazine fiction still frequently valorized the heroic self-sacrificing daughter, and Flora Mayor's well-reviewed and popular novel *The Rector's Daughter* (1924) had transformed the despised role of the spinster daughter into a vehicle for sainthood.[13]

Daisy saw her relationship with her sister, who died in 1982, as the most important in her life: 'We meant everything to each other. All our lives we have been.' She told how in the past when she was ill:

> I was so afraid I might die. All I was afraid of was because May wouldn't be there, because to me if May's there when I die, to see her first, I know I'll be all right, I always relied on May. She was my one great chum you know.

Although she admitted to some childhood resentments, Daisy felt that her sister had brought her up almost more than her mother. May had been there nursing her when she had toothache and 'leg ache', rubbing her legs and face and singing to her.

Other important relationships in Daisy's life were also mainly with women and drew upon her experience of sisterhood as a model. She declared that she had never been interested in men, except as vehicles for political discussions, but talked openly about feelings she had for older women. These had started early with a crush on the cook in one of her first jobs. Later, in her main employment as cook for two unmarried sisters from a wealthy and distinguished

12. Winifred Holtby, *The Crowded Street* (1924); Radclyffe Hall, *The Unlit Lamp* (1924); May Sinclair, *The Life and Death of Harriet Frean* (1922); E.M. Delafield, *Thank Heaven Fasting*; Sylvia Townsend Warner, *Lolly Willowes* (1926); George Orwell, *The Clergyman's Daughter* (1933).
13. *Woman's Weekly* (27 January 1923); *Modern Home* (June 1930); *Good Housekeeping* (July 1933); Sybil Oldfield, *Spinsters of this Parish: The Life and Times of F.M. Mayor and Mary Sheepshanks* (Virago, 1984), pp. 240 and 315 n. 1.

family, Daisy fell for the younger sister Freda: 'I developed an absolute crush on her. I adored her. If she was cross with me for anything, my day was in ashes, and if she was pleased with me I was in seventh heaven.' It appears that Daisy's devotion to her employer continued throughout their association, which lasted thirty-seven years, and was reciprocated by Freda, who used to write to her when she was on holiday, signing her letters 'with love from Freda'.

Daisy's model of sisterhood, which crossed class divisions, could also encompass the notion of conflict and rivalry. After Freda's elder sister had died, Daisy felt secure enough to express some of her anger at being in a subordinate position. Here she could transcend her sense of powerlessness as a servant by telling stories which placed herself in the light of a recalcitrant younger sister who would always be forgiven. She was also able to demonstrate the power she held over her 'big sister' employer's affections, when, after her father died, she persuaded Freda to let her real big sister May move in with them. May stayed there in a most unusual arrangement as a lodger, sharing Daisy's bedroom whilst she went out to work each day and paying Freda for her keep.

> It was a difficult situation in some ways. The three of us. I loved my sister. I loved Miss Freda. Miss Freda liked me very much, she quite liked May but, she liked me and you see it was three. I had to be canny.

While there are many possible interpretations of this triangular relationship in which class, employment status, kinship, money, affection and passionate feelings were inextricably entwined, it seems likely that Freda knew that she would only be able to hold on to Daisy if she was willing to accept her sister as part of the bargain.

Another story which suggested Daisy's need as a little sister to establish a sense of physical and emotional power over Freda is told by invoking the solidarity of her real siblings. In this scene, Freda and her other maid Rona were with Daisy and May, sheltering in the larder during an air raid.

> Rona was knelt down with her head in May's lap terrified . . . and Miss Freda was there with her head in my lap: 'Our Father which art in heaven, hallowed be thy name. Oh Daisy is that another one?' May and me were in hysterics above them 'cos we weren't afraid for some reason or another, and we were together, that's all that mattered to us. George was in England, he wasn't abroad. I know he could have been killed in England but we knew he was here.

This story inverts class relations between Daisy and her employer. She is without fear and in control, supported in her imagination by her sister and adopted brother.

Daisy's feelings about men and marriage were ambiguous. Whilst it was clear from her story that her primary emotional attachments had always been to women, it seems that her parents' need of their daughters' services and the difficulties her mother had put in the way of them meeting men had been influential in encouraging her daughters to identify so strongly as sisters. When Daisy was asked by one man if she had ever thought of getting married, May interceded: 'Oh no she says, we never have either of us. We've never had any wish to be married.' Thus, despite the restrictions Daisy's parents had placed upon their daughters' early life, by drawing upon a model of sisterhood, Daisy had been able to form satisfying relationships with women, where she could both challenge the class and power relations within domestic service, and maintain a long and happy partnership with her real sister May.

The area in which Daisy showed most ambivalence was in her feelings about children. Her position as the youngest daughter had clearly been threatened by the stream of war babies taken in by her mother and she had reacted by denying she had any maternal instinct, supporting this with a story about pretending to shoot her dolls (who may have represented her foster brothers and sisters) as if they were Germans. In retrospect she found it hard to understand why these children's mothers had given them up: 'Well I know quite well if I'd been in the position, if I'd had a baby, that's mine, you know, what ever condition I'd had him.' Yet she also showed her awareness of the harsh treatment meted out to unmarried mothers.

> Well there was this hospital in St Thomas's Hill. The young girls, who were treated to make them realize they sinned, they worked in the laundry. The babies were in cots in a ward, and the nurses would come around . . . and push a bottle into their mouths, mother's been into the ward and seen it, and of course very often you know with a baby you know, a bottle would slip but when the time was up for feeding, the nurses would come round, remove the bottles. The mothers were down in the laundry.

One of these mothers, Annie, had boarded with Daisy's family, going out to work to support her child whilst Daisy's mother cared for it. Daisy suggested that Annie's baby was fat ''cos when the nurses weren't looking she'd take some milk from the kitchen and she'd up and feed her baby'. But Annie, 'who adored her baby', was also believed to have 'a very jealous disposition', and was eventually asked to leave under suspicion of having poisoned a dog.

These stories, told in a rather disjointed way, recalled by Daisy from memories of herself as a 10-year-old, suggest some of the tensions that existed between single mothers, forced to let other women care for their babies, and the nurses and foster mothers who did the caring. In light of her childhood experiences it is hardly surprising that motherhood held such an uncertain position in the formation of Daisy's sense of self and identity.

The daughter's tale: Bridget Perkins[14]

Bridget Perkins, youngest of ten, with an elder full brother and eight elder half-siblings, grew up in a medium-sized south-eastern town, and was still living in the house where she was born. Her father had been in the building trade and her mother, who was his second wife, had been in poor health and had depended on her only daughter for care. Although Bridget had been close to her much older half-sisters, they were more like aunts, since they had not grown up together.

Bridget's main image of herself, in contrast to the rebellious Daisy, was of a shy dutiful daughter who had been kept back by her parents, not allowed out to mix with men, and who in any crisis was always called upon to give up her work and help at home. She had mixed feelings about this, for she clearly loved her parents and the safety of the home, and took some pride in being the special youngest daughter, recounting stories of her elder half-siblings' jealousy because her mother wasn't their mother, even though 'they all thought the world of her'. Yet she also felt that her parents and upbringing were responsible for her not marrying, for her lack of confidence and reserve and complete ignorance about sex. She quite openly declared herself to be a virgin:

> See, being restricted and only with older people makes a difference didn't it. If I'd been a family with several sisters and that and gone out with them, it would have been a bit different I expect.

She described the metamorphosis she had undergone after her parents died and 'I had my freedom', how much more outgoing

14. Bridget Perkins, interviewed by Katherine Holden (16 December 1993).

and friendly she now was, and how she had been in great demand to go on holidays with other family members.

Bridget's position in the family, as a youngest daughter, always seen as the family carer, had also influenced her feelings about children. She had no experience of childcare when she started as a daily nanny to 2-year-old twin boys, whom she looked after for four years. But she gave up the job when they became unruly because she had been unable to prevent their mother from spoiling them:

> You can't when the mothers go in and make them wild and that, and the trouble is that was just the time when my father was dying and I think I hadn't got the patience with them then because of what was happening here you see.

Although she justified her decision to leave on the grounds of her family's need, Bridget's feelings of guilt that she hadn't been any good as a nanny, which were perhaps also related to her loss of the children, remained with her. Years later these feelings were assuaged when she met one of her charges again and he started to visit her regularly. Hearing of his subsequent tragic life after she had left the family (his twin had died at 15, both his parents were now also dead, and he had later had a breakdown while he was teaching), Bridget started to realize, though still could not explain, her value to him:

> He recognized me and spoke to me and he got in touch and he comes and visits me now, so I couldn't have been such a bad nanny as all that could I? . . . Strange after all these years he wanted to get in touch again. He wanted to know more what I could remember than he could. He seemed to like coming to see me . . . He used to say 'I'm going to marry Nanny': that's the only proposal I've had.

Unmarried nursemaids and servants could often awaken a child's early sexual and emotional feelings through the physical care they gave.[15] This child's Oedipal desires had been directed towards his nanny rather than his mother, suggesting the strength of his attachment. However, Bridget's parents' needs for care made it difficult for her to maintain her primary position in the twins' life, particularly when rivalry with the birth mother, who was also her employer,

15. See Leonore Davidoff, 'Class and gender in Victorian England: the case of Hannah Cullwick and A.J. Munby', in *Worlds Between: Historical Perspectives on Gender and Class* (Polity Press, 1995), p. 109.

became too strong. Unsure of her position and unable to assert her authority to 'mother', she quickly lost touch with her charges without knowing how important she had been to them.

To understand the problems inherent in the mother–carer–child triangle which made it difficult for Bridget to value her role as nanny, we need to examine more closely its economic basis. The significance of lower-middle- and working-class single women's labour in bringing up children within upper- and middle-class households has been insufficiently acknowledged because of the difficulty for all parties concerned in reconciling a relationship based partly upon financial gain and the workings of the labour market with its situation in the private sphere and the emotional economy of the family, where, despite the brisk, detached tone of inter-war childcare manuals, children and their carers might still become closely attached.

Employing a nanny was important in preserving a family's middle-class status, but while, as we saw in the *Good Housekeeping* article, the anxieties and conflicts mothers may have felt about these arrangements could be aired and displaced by referral to the servant problem,[16] the interests and needs of the women employed in these capacities were rarely articulated. We still do not know enough about how either children or their carers coped with relationships in which much affection might be invested on each side, but whose beginnings and endings often depended on the financial position of employers or employees, or circumstances such as the children reaching school age, or, as in Bridget's case, the carer's own parents making demands on her time. Added to this were Bridget's feelings of frustration that her influence over the children would always be secondary and compromised by the more powerful mother. Not only, in the pre-Bowlby era, was the possibility of psychological damage to the child of such arrangements unrecognized, but there was little consideration of the pain and insecurity nannies experienced through such separations. Although some children were able to maintain contact, the comforting story of the nanny who was kept on as a faithful retainer for the rest of her life was a reality in only a small minority of wealthier homes.[17] Bridget's story, echoed by other single women interviewed, was much more typical of childcare arrangements made at that time.

16. Leonore Davidoff, 'Mastered for life: servant and wife in Victorian and Edwardian England', in *Worlds Between*. See also E.M. Delafield, *Diary of a Provincial Lady* (1930), *The Provincial Lady Goes Further* (1932), *The Provincial Lady in America* (1934).
17. Jonathan Gathorne Hardy, *The Rise and Fall of the British Nanny* (Weidenfeld & Nicolson, 1993), p. 216.

For Bridget, as for Daisy and the many other working-class women who went into service, familial identities worked on two levels. Their gender, number and age of siblings, position in the family, and their parents' age, health and need for care, influenced their employment paths, likelihood of marriage and sense of identification as daughters. But being in service had also given them other families with whom they could adopt quasi-familial roles as sisters, mothers or daughters. Bridget had been unable to sustain the position of substitute, rival mother to the twins, but it was easier for her to reproduce the daughter relationship with a rector and his wife for whom she worked for eleven years after her mother died: 'I was quite happy there, it was more like having another mother and father in a way. . . I did everything there for them just as I should have done at home.'

It is striking too that both Daisy's 'big sister' employer and Bridget's parental employers demonstrated their acknowledgement of their servants' quasi-familial status by leaving them money in their wills. This suggests that some material form of acknowledgement beyond the employer/employee contract was owed them for service they had given, and is another example of the ways in which, as we saw in previous chapter, familial inheritance could span the public/private divide.

The midwife's tale: Ellen Stephens[18]

The subject of our next case history, Ellen Stephens, was the daughter of a West Country railway worker, with a sister five years older and a brother five years younger, who went to London in the late 1920s to train as a nurse, specializing in midwifery and health visiting. Yet although she had spent more time living away from home in pursuit of her career than either Daisy or Bridget, family remained as important an element in her story, much of which revolved around the act of not marrying.

Ellen's life was dominated by two expectations: first, that she must 'do good' – 'I liked to feel I was doing something for somebody else you know. I was always . . . taught to do things for other people' – and, second, that among those 'other people', her family would always take precedence. These beliefs enabled her to explain her singleness in several different ways. Her first response, 'I never thought about getting married; it didn't interest me', was modified by an assertion that she had rejected an offer because:

18. Ellen Stephens, interviewed by Katherine Holden (22 September 1993).

I was paying for one of the little boys to go to school, one of my
nephews . . . my brother and his wife couldn't pay for the other
one, they couldn't afford it so that's why I couldn't marry. Well you
can't if you've got that can you, because you've got – and then I
had mother and I couldn't leave mother could I, mother had to be
looked after.

Ellen used a different, yet in some ways similar, reasoning to
explain why she had rejected an earlier suitor, this time by claiming
she had a prior commitment to her work.

You see I wanted to finish my training and if you're being pushed all
the time, well you don't need that do you, if that's what you want to
do. You can't start something and not finish it. So that's why I didn't
marry . . . I think I was right. I mean I've managed.

Beneath these explanations lay some deeper feelings of ambivalence and tension. Ellen was torn by her own and her culture's
conflicting expectations of women in her position. On the one
hand her family's genuine need of her services, both financially
and in terms of physical care, gave her ample justification for a
single life, in which her paid work and voluntary services to family
and community were both expected and valued. Yet she also recognized them as an obstacle: 'I would have married if I hadn't had a
family, but I had a family to consider and I thought that was a
greater tie to me.'

It is also possible to see Ellen's dedication to her work and family
as both a reason for not marrying and a way of compensation, a
word she used on a number of occasions, for her childless state:

I would have loved a family. I would have liked that very much, so
I think I've been sort of compensated 'cos I've had lots of other –
but it's not quite the same is it . . .

The multiple meanings and contradictions embodied in the word
'family' are also brought out here. Ellen could use her family of
birth, and her ties to parents and siblings, as a rationale for not
marrying. Yet this strategy denied her 'a family of her own' and the
possibility of becoming a mother, a relationship which held a much
higher value in her society than the daughter and aunt roles to
which she clung. Ellen's regrets that she had not become a mother
and sense of marginality as a single woman were poignantly revealed in the statement 'sometimes you think it would be nice to
have someone who valued you for yourself alone'. Her reaction to
a married woman who envied her carpets and new car was powerful:

I said my dear don't *ever* envy me. I said I've got nothing. I said you've got two delightful children that I would give the earth for, and I said, think of me in three years time. I've got a lump of tin outside . . . that's the way I answered that.

Ellen's early experiences had shown her the impossibility of having a child of her own outside marriage. In 1927 at the age of 18 she took a job in the workhouse where her father was on the Board of Guardians, where she said they locked up girls who had babies 'who were a charge on the state'. She had felt the injustice of a system in which girls were seen by a psychiatrist once a year, forty in one morning, and their babies sent to sex-segregated children's homes. She had longed to adopt a gypsy baby shortly before the war, but her friend's experience had shown her the pitfalls of such a step. The friend had adopted a child whom she called Penny:

> as she only cost a few pence you see. She was single and she called her Mummy, but then she said, when she got to about ten, it was a bit awkward, there was no man you see, that she must call her auntie, because you see, it looked as though she were illegitimate.

Ellen knew only too well how the stigma of illegitimacy would have been viewed in her family:

> I dread to think what would have happened to any one in my household who had dared to come home with such a baby . . . It couldn't have happened in my house. It couldn't have happened . . . we were too strictly brought up.

Yet Ellen did manage to find ways through her work which would allow her close access to children and to gain status by becoming an 'expert' on the skills needed for marriage and motherhood. Having spent her first few working years as a nanny for two little girls, she subsequently trained first as a nurse and then as a midwife, because she thought it would be 'awful if somebody discovered she was a nurse and didn't know anything about babies'. In her first job as community midwife she started a baby clinic, and after training as a health visitor she taught 'theoretical cookery' to new wives, although she was acknowledged by her family to be a bad cook. She had also taken pride in her ability to give contraceptive advice to women in her village during the Second World War: 'they wanted to know about family planning and they said you see there's nobody else we could ask'. In her off-duty hours she had taught childcare to Girl Guides and looked after the children of a widower whose offer of marriage she had refused.

Ellen's pattern of work had also been shaped by her family's need of her, and especially by her identity as a daughter. After a neighbour had warned her: 'Miss Roberts you must come home. I wouldn't let a dog suffer like your father has', she gave up a job in order that she could live and work from home to help care for him:

> Well who else would? My sister [who had emigrated to Canada] used to write and say I know they'll be all right with you, and my brother wouldn't have done anything . . . he wouldn't think of doing it would he? It wouldn't have occurred to him I don't think . . . he was a very selfish man.

This last comment and many others of a similar tone show that her devotion to family was as much based on duty as love. Although she had idolized her father, Ellen was not close to her mother, who had described her as plain and undervalued her achievements, nor to her sister, 'a beauty' with whom she had little in common. Her selfish brother was 'always spoilt and didn't like her'.

Despite her very open acknowledgement of tensions within her family, they had remained of paramount importance in her life. When she returned to her parents during the war, Ellen brought with her a close friend with whom she had lived and worked continuously since their training days. This friend subsequently married her brother, and all three remained living in the parental home. Perhaps this inclusion in her family of a friend, with whom she had already created a strong bond, helped Ellen adjust to her role, particularly as it enabled her to become an aunt: 'If my brother gave me anything he gave me two delightful boys.'

Ellen was clearly an essential and important provider of services, both in her family and in her local community. Yet although she knew the work she did and the relationships she formed, whether as daughter, sister, aunt, nanny, midwife or health visitor, were of value, Ellen was trapped by her own and others' expectations that she should have married. Her devotion to work and family were primarily a compensation for not marrying and having a family of her own.

The aunt's tale: Alice Baker

Our final subject, Alice Baker, was the fourth of six children and youngest daughter of a businessman, an unsuccessful entrepreneur who had built houses (usually at a loss), and run a pleasure steamer

service to the Isle of Wight and a chain of department stores, finally
going bankrupt. This necessitated a drastic change of income and
lifestyle for his wife and younger children. Initially staying at home
to care for her parents, whose health was poor, Alice had later
worked mainly as housekeeper or domestic bursar in a number of
all-women institutions, including a convent school, a teachers' training college and a girls' high school. After her parents died she
formed a lasting relationship with Betty, a physical education teacher,
who shared a cottage with her in a seaside town and later lived in
an adjoining flat.

Alice's story raises some particularly interesting methodological
issues about the kinds of sources biographers use to re-create a life.
Unlike the other three cases, her own voice is only heard through
an unpublished short story she wrote, but her tale is constructed
through the letters and testimonies from friends and families
and other documents she chose to save and pass on to her family.
It also emerges from a letter written after her death in which Alice's
younger brother revealed previously hidden aspects of the family
past to his daughter Susan, Alice's niece, and from a recorded
conversation with Susan. In recalling her own memories and retell-
ing family stories, Susan offered some important insights into her
aunt's history and what she represented to her family.

The stories which Alice's niece and brother told about her mainly
revolve around her devotion to her family, her sense of duty, her
self-sacrificing nature and her sense of shame at one of her older
sisters' enforced institutionalization, a family secret only recently
discovered by Susan (see Chapter 9). Alice had believed marriage
was a woman's purpose in life, but had apparently missed her chance
in the war:

> We knew that she'd loved someone because she had three watches
> ... that she'd bought and she gave one to my father and she gave
> one to my brother, saying this was [for] someone who never came
> back ... but she told me later on that she had a friend who never
> came back and she also told me that of all their set, all the young
> boys who went off to the 1914–18 war the only three who came back
> were her three brothers.[19]

Interestingly, Alice's papers reveal little of these conflicts in her life.
They consist mainly of letters and testimonials written to her and
suggest a woman who was much loved and valued by her women
colleagues and friends and whose strongest connections were with

19. Interview with Susan by Katherine Holden (27 October 1993).

other women. Amongst them are several emotional letters from a nun who was her former boss at the convent school,[20] although we do not know how Alice felt in return. Susan confirmed this impression of a women-centred life by explaining that Alice had always preferred her nieces, because she 'felt safer with girls: boys were . . . men were mysterious other beings'. Alice had left the bulk of her money to Susan and the daughter of her other niece Jane, whose adoring childhood letters Alice had carefully preserved. Susan said she had done this because she believed 'it was women who needed the money'.[21]

In a birthday letter in the 1950s Betty expresses the depth of her feelings for Alice: 'I am filled with gratefulness for the blessing of your rich friendship, and nothing is so precious to me as that.'[22] Yet Susan saw this relationship with Betty as a definite second best for Alice compared with the position of housekeeper for her brother (Susan's father):

> He looked as though he was going to be a bachelor. She'd envisaged that eventually they would set up house together. My father he knew this, and it took a long time for him to say to her I'm going to marry Elizabeth, and I think it was after that, that she and B.J. [Betty] settled in Rustington. She obviously realized that she was going to be with B.J. and not my dad.[23]

Alice's nieces and nephews were not very comfortable with Alice and Betty's alliance. Susan had never liked Betty, because she could not cope with children and thought of them as rivals for Alice's affection:

> I think there was probably always a bit of jealousy. I know B.J. although she enjoyed our company felt that we were taking Alice away from her, which we were. I didn't like the way she . . . you don't like the smell of people's houses do you. B.J. was a sort of smotherer.[24]

Alice's own voice is largely absent from her papers, with the exception of a short story, 'The Palace of Pearl', written in biblical language in 1915 when she was a bookkeeper for an insurance firm. The story describes a close alliance between women colleagues, Em and Wood, against a male boss, King Abbi. The author, Scribe Em,

20. Letters from Sister Mary to Alice Baker in the private papers of Alice Baker held by Susan (names have been changed to preserve anonymity).
21. Interview with Susan.
22. Letter from Betty Jones to Alice Baker (14 August 1954). Private papers of Alice Baker.
23. Interview with Susan.   24. Ibid.

dedicates the story to her friend, who is a 'kindred soul', and tells how they worked together in strange places doing jobs normally allotted to men. Scribe Wood's departure is poignantly recorded:

> And their labours together in the Palace of Pearl were for the space of one year and in all that time they did serve together, yea not once were they divided. And when the time came for Scribe Wood to depart was close at hand for she was taking unto herself a husband, there was sorrow in the Palace of Pearl, howbeit the sorrow was only in the heart of these two Scribes for none other did know of these tidings for verily these scribes were wise in their day for if these tidings had come to King Abbi then would he have said, 'Let the Scribes Em and Wood be parted it pleaseth me not that they find much pleasure in serving together' yea such a one was the King.[25]

It is noticeable that Alice also draws upon the language of hetero-sexual love. Her story is suggestive of lovers carrying on an illicit relationship which tragically had to give way to the superior claims of a future marriage partner. Yet it is not easy to draw any conclu-sions about the sexual content of Em and Wood's relationship, since there may have been no other language available to Alice to show the importance of women's friendships in the workplace and their fragility in the face of demands made by male bosses and husbands. The story seems curiously at odds with Susan's picture of her aunt's traditional and compliant views of men and women's roles at that time:

> I think really she felt that you know it wasn't a woman's place to go to work, until they were needed . . . it was the war effort. She would have gone for the war effort and as soon as the men came back she willingly relinquished because the men must have the jobs.[26]

While not wishing to challenge Susan's view of her aunt, it is worth considering the problems the institution of marriage posed for Alice in her relationships with other women. These were not insignific-ant. Not only did she have to grapple with her society's confused and contradictory expectations of unmarried women in relation to sex, but, lacking the ties and obligations bestowed through the mar-riage bond, it was not always easy to know how to name or attach meaning to relationships whose claims carried no sanction of law and custom. What space could they occupy if the alternative to be-ing a wife was to be dubbed a sexual invert or a frustrated spinster? What meanings were available for them to attach to friendships in

25. Private papers of Alice Baker.   26. Interview with Susan.

a society where celibate women were in danger of inferiority com-
plexes, where strong expressions of emotion between women could
only be made in private correspondence, and where marriage was
regarded as the only important 'happening' in a woman's life?

If we look at Alice through the eyes of her brother and niece we
see a loving, self-sacrificing aunt, devoted to her relations, who had
missed out on marriage, and who carried the shame of her sister's
mental illness with her to her death. It is a picture which to an
extent reproduces both the positive and negative aspects of the
stereotypical spinster. But there is also another Alice. This is reflected in the correspondence she preserved from the women friends
with whom she lived and worked, and with whom she appears to
have experienced an emotional if not physical intimacy which may
have rivalled or complemented her kin relationships.

The absence of Alice's own voice telling us what those friendships meant for her is typical of the silence surrounding the living
arrangements of many single women in this period. This was true
even of the feminist campaigner Eleanor Rathbone. Tireless in her
campaigns for the autonomy of married women and their families,
she gave little away about her relationship with Elizabeth MacAdam,
with whom she shared her life.[27] That such women were cautious
about saying too much lest their friendships be ridiculed or stigmatized is indicative of the dominant position marriage held in
early and mid twentieth-century England.

Each of these case studies suggests how important identification
with particular kin relationships as daughters, sisters and aunts could
be in the formation of single women's identities, not the least as a
means of escape from the shadow of 'the withered tree' which
denoted spinsterhood. The experiences of nannies and other
primary carers show that relationships of intimacy were also forged
between unrelated children and adults, as they were between women
friends living in female partnerships and communities. Still the
powerful links forged between marriage and biological motherhood,
which left the nuclear family as the sole legitimate forum for intimacy, made it harder for women publicly to acknowledge relationships which lay outside.

Daisy had been able to transcend this in her relations as a servant by drawing upon a model of sisterhood, but the nature of
Bridget's contract with her charges' mother made it difficult for

27. See Mary Stocks, *Eleanor Rathbone* (Victor Gollancz, 1949).

her to value herself as a nanny. Ellen's longing to have children had been frustrated by the stigma attached to unmarried motherhood, and though she had experienced compensations in her work as a midwife and health visitor and in her role as an aunt, she was acutely aware of the disadvantages of her unmarried state. Remaining attached to the identity of daughter was important for all three women interviewed, but it had also limited their autonomy, their geographical horizons and their chances of more challenging work. More mobile than the other women, beloved Aunt Alice, carrying the shameful secret of her sister's illness, left no written record telling us what her friendships outside the family meant to her, although they may have been an important factor in maintaining her health and mental stability.

CHAPTER NINE

Untold stories: family silences

Family secrets are the other side of the family's public face, of the stories families tell themselves, and the world, about themselves. Characters and happenings that do not slot into the flow of the family narrative are ruthlessly edited out.

Annette Kuhn, 1995[1]

As the previous case studies have illustrated, some aspects of family life, certain familial and quasi-familial relationships and particular family members, have been largely ignored by historians of the family and by historians more generally. This has produced silences and absences in the story of the family which we have sought, by shifting the focus of our work, to articulate and to reveal. It must be remembered, however, that families themselves have also been and continue to be active agents in the formation of family stories and, for a multiplicity of reasons, in the creation of silences within those stories. This last chapter, therefore, looks at some of the silences and secrets which have been constructed by families, highlights their impact upon the identity of family members, and considers how an investigation of such silences and absences can enrich our understanding of the history of the family.

Family secrets cluster around what is considered to be the most intimate core of the family – the physical, social and cultural reproduction of its members. They are dominated by the intensely private subjects of sex, money and behaviour, on which, in turn, are focused so many powerful family myths, particularly that of the nuclear family in which couples are devoted and sexually fulfilled, children are loved and wanted, wives are proficient home-makers,

1. Annette Kuhn, *Family Secrets: Acts of Memory and Imagination* (Verso, 1995), p. 2.

and husbands are willing and capable economic providers. Such myths, as Chapter 1 illustrated, hold an encompassing sway over our understanding of *normal* family life and the ways in which familial relationships *ought* to be experienced. Although potentially subversive, secrets have generally operated to allow the individual family and its members to retain their own position within this notion of normality which has, at the same time, continued to uphold and leave unchallenged the myths about family life.

Where there is only minimal disjuncture between the myth and the experience of family life, then privacy, as opposed to secrecy, provides an adequate boundary between the public and private worlds which families straddle, so that, for example, financial difficulties can be hidden behind the closed doors of the home. As one working-class woman remarked, 'I always used to say well I've paid me rent and if I've got nothing, nobody'll know.'[2] But other issues have been more difficult to contain successfully within the private, domestic space of the home because of the public world's power to demand the documentation and registration of the private events of family life, especially of births, marriages and deaths, and because of the ways in which an individual's rights to financial and medical benefits provided by the state were dependent upon these records. At the same time the symptoms and effects of mental illness, the physical visibility of illicit pregnancies, the birth of a child from an 'interracial' relationship, or the evidence of extra-marital sexual activity could not always be successfully concealed inside the home, especially in poor, close-knit neighbourhoods where much of family life was by necessity shared. In cases such as these, privacy was not effective, and secrecy provided the only means to protect the individual and his or her family from rumour or gossip in the local neighbourhood or to deflect direct intervention by voluntary and statutory welfare services.

Family secrets thus work on different levels, for different reasons, and differ through time and across classes and communities. In the first half of the twentieth century silenced areas of family life have included illegitimacy, adultery, divorce, cohabitation, criminality, domestic violence, abortion, adoption, homosexuality and lesbianism, incest, suicide, mental and physical handicap, and mental illness. The list is almost endless and the majority of readers will be able to add to it their family's secrets which have formed, overtly or covertly, part of their own particular family history and myth. Yet

2. Melanie Tebbutt, *Women's Talk* (Scolar Press, 1995), p. 94.

despite their incidence throughout our period, any one of these issues would have been regarded as shameful by *most* families and, as a result, denied if present or discovered within their midst. For example, incest is almost impossible to uncover historically because its existence has been denied within most families and communities. Incest was, and still is, usually located elsewhere, believed to be only an unfortunate problem for isolated rural areas rather than, as recent revelations from incest survivors have shown, common in every class and locality.

It is difficult to speculate about the extent to which families through history have sought to conceal particularly shameful events from the wider community and, indeed, what events were understood to be shameful and in what context. The work of John Gillis has shown, for example, that the problem of unmarried motherhood in the eighteenth and nineteenth centuries was defined differently, not only according to the social class of the woman but also depending upon the region in which she lived. It has also shown that the recipients of direct community intervention changed from the seventeenth century, with its focus on henpecked and cuckolded husbands, to the nineteenth century and its targets of 'moral offenders', who came to include child abusers, homosexuals and wife beaters.[3]

The forms of such intervention, commonly known as rough music, changed very little over these years, and men and women who had transgressed their community's norms were subjected to a rowdy, public denunciation of their actions in which they were verbally abused and held up to ridicule or, for offences considered more serious, physically attacked. However, the incidence of rough music as a regulating force diminished during the early years of the twentieth century, as did the influence of the Church, so that these dual aspects of control over family life declined. At the same time the gaze from the public world, as discussed in Chapter 7, became all the more focused on families with the growth not only of voluntary organizations concerned with the moral and social regulation of family life but also of state involvement.

Yet, as Gillis illustrated, the relationships between social problems and family life have been neither constant nor coherent. The boundaries of acceptable and unacceptable behaviour continuously shift to incorporate and recognize changing cultural and social mores with respect to individual conduct, family life and the public

---

3. John Gillis, *For Better, For Worse* (Oxford University Press, 1985), pp. 126–34.

world's intervention in that life. Thus the questionable ways in which child welfare organizations, of both the state and voluntary sector, reacted to family problems in the first half of the twentieth century are now being regularly uncovered by the press and the media. Most recently we have had reports of illegitimate babies being sold by convents;[4] of Magdalen laundries where women, admitted as unmarried mothers and rebel girls in the 1940s and 1950s, still live after becoming too institutionalized to move out;[5] and of allegedly orphaned children being deported from children's homes to Australia up until 1967. In this latter case, relationships between parents and children were deliberately silenced and denied so that 'Many [of the children] were told their families were dead; the parents too were deceived believing their children had been adopted at home.'[6]

Secrecy, sexuality and society

Throughout our period the ideals of the nuclear family model, of monogamy and of heterosexuality were so dominant and so rigorously upheld that other intimate and sexual relationships were marginalized, even criminalized, and alternative family forms stigmatized. Much of the secrecy relating to family life in the first half of the twentieth century can, therefore, be explained by the powerful, central position which the marital relationship had as the legal site for sexual activity and by the resultant condemnation of sexual relationships outside marriage as illicit or deviant.

Much moral and social regulation sought, therefore, to curb premarital sexual activity and homosexuality, although psychology and psychoanalysis were gradually beginning to challenge the definitions of so-called sexual degeneracy and to seek 'psychological' causes for such behaviour. Nevertheless, and despite greater degrees of tolerance being expressed by particular elements of society, few homosexual men dared to display their sexuality in public since prosecutions for homosexual offences continued to rise steadily through the 1930s. For many homosexuals, therefore, and particularly amongst the working class, secrecy remained a necessity.[7]

---

4. 'Convents "sold Irish babies": 2,000 illegitimate children taken to US in Fifties and Sixties', *The Observer* (10 March 1996).
5. 'Washing away their sins', *The Guardian* (30 October 1996).
6. 'Child slaves of Bindoon', *The Guardian* (30 August 1995).
7. Jeffrey Weeks, *Sex, Politics and Society* (Longman, 1989), pp. 220–1.

Similarly, although lesbianism was never made illegal, the alleged
dangers of lesbianism were brought to the attention of the public
when the novel *The Well of Loneliness*, published in 1928, was declared an obscene libel and its author Radclyffe Hall, and publisher
Jonathan Cape, became the subjects of an obscenity trial. Girls were
considered to be especially at risk in the closed worlds of boarding schools, either from passionate friendships between older and
younger girls or from the unhealthy influence of their spinster
teachers. Moreover, as the previous chapter illustrated, whilst there
were still in existence many female partnerships and communities
which offered women employment and models of lifestyles outside
marriage and the nuclear family, the significance of these relationships was difficult to articulate or celebrate openly during the inter-
war years.

The determination to rebuild the family after the Second World
War brought a renewed stress on monogamous heterosexual love
and further demonized the so-called twin evils of prostitution and
homosexuality. A Mass Observation Survey in 1949 suggested that
homosexuals provoked the strongest expressions of disgust from its
respondents, with homosexual behaviour being reputedly the least
understood and most condemned of sexual practices in post-war
Britain.[8] Within this moral climate homosexuality remained a particularly well-kept secret, for, despite the recommendations of the
Wolfenden Committee in 1957 that private homosexual acts be
decriminalized, the law was not changed until 1967. Moreover, in
the years prior to this legal reform, prosecutions against homosexual men were rigorously pursued and sentences were severe.
Not surprisingly such men kept their public and private lives firmly
compartmentalized. As Allan Horsfall noted:

> If you could have written a survival guide for gay men at that time
> it would have said: never, never give anybody your surname or
> address. Never tell anybody where you work. Never take anybody to
> your home and never write letters, whether affectionate or other-
> wise, to anybody you're sexually involved with or even anybody you
> know to be gay.[9]

This era of sexual conformity also produced a moral panic about
the extent of prostitution within cities and the visibility of vice.

8. See Steve Humphries, *A Secret World of Sex* (Sidgwick & Jackson, 1988), pp. 193–215.
9. Cited in Alkarim Jivani, *It's Not Unusual: A History of Lesbian and Gay Britain in the Twentieth Century* (Michael O'Mara Books, 1997), p. 100.

As a result there was a drive to 'clean up the streets', particularly during the Festival of Britain (1951) and Coronation year (1953), which greatly increased the number of prosecutions and harshened the penalties.[10] Despite complaints from women MPs that 'No one has yet referred to the disgrace caused by men who pay these girls to stand in our streets',[11] prostitutes, and not their clients, remained the target of fears about the effects of prostitution on monogamous sexual relationships and on family life.

The double standard of sexual behaviour thus remained largely unchallenged through the first half of the century. A wall of silence continued to be preserved in most families on the subject of sex and contraception, and unmarried mothers were either hidden – often by passing their child off as the offspring of another family member – or delivered into the hands of voluntary organizations concerned either to punish or reform them, and to rescue their children. In the 1920s and 1930s the most extreme punishment for some unmarried mothers, often those without any family support or financial resources, was their incarceration for life in mental asylums. This physical removal of unmarried mothers from their homes enabled some families to deliberately erase not only such women's disgrace from their family history but also their existence and that of their babies. Where a girl or woman had become pregnant because of sexual abuse by a family friend or because of incest, then her institutionalization ensured the successful silencing of the twofold nature of the family's shame.

Through the 1940s and 1950s, female sexuality continued to be closely regulated. Transgression of this regulation, which positioned sexual activity for women and the birth of children firmly within the confines of marriage, was commonly regarded as deviant behaviour. Thus adultery or the birth of an illegitimate child frequently necessitated secrecy, for this provided the most effective form of protection for women in the face of societal and familial discrimination, prejudice and, at times, punishment. For men, fathering an illegitimate child might be equally denied, but that denial was more often rooted in a reluctance to pay maintenance costs than in a desire to protect the father's or his family's reputation.

One way in which women might conceal the birth of an illegitimate child was through its adoption and so, with the first Adoption Act of 1926, the legal adoption process was constructed to ensure

10. David C. Marsh, *The Changing Social Structure of England and Wales 1871–1961* (Routledge & Kegan Paul), table 57.
11. Street Offences Bill, *Hansard* (Col. 1319, 29 January 1959).

that privacy was guaranteed only to the adoptive parents and not to the natural mother. The married woman with an illegitimate child, for example, would be forced by the courts to obtain her husband's, but not the father's, consent if she wished to have the child adopted. The insistence on this consent was in some cases due to confusion over the legal requirements. But local magistrates were also determined to ensure that the birth of an illegitimate child from an adulterous relationship could not be hidden from a husband, even where husband and wife were separated. Thus magistrates regularly refused adoption orders because a married woman's husband had not signed the adoption form, even though the child had been registered at birth as illegitimate.

There was little recourse for such mothers because the court's powers under the 1950 Adoption Act were discretionary and, as the journal *Child Adoption* noted:

> Some legal authorities on adoption would agree that although with proof of non-access, the husband's consent should not be required, it was nevertheless right that he should be served with a notice of proceedings to avoid any appearance of the court's assisting the wife to deceive him. This moral consideration may influence the judgement of the court in some cases.[12]

The married woman who refused to ask her husband for his consent to the adoption of another man's child was left in an impossible situation, as was her child, for there was a resolve that she should not be allowed to evade the social and moral consequences of breaking the norms of female behaviour and of disrupting the ideals of monogamy. Little wonder, therefore, that such women concealed the birth of an illegitimate child where possible.

The law was equally judgemental towards unmarried mothers who sought to adopt their own illegitimate children because, as with married mothers, it was considered to be a means by which they might avoid the stigmatization of both themselves and their child. Applications for the adoption of illegitimate children by their own mothers were therefore regularly turned down by magistrates who believed that such adoptions were an attempt by mothers to conceal the true status of their children. One County Court judge expressed fears that such an order, if allowed, 'would no doubt soon become common form and illegitimacy would automatically be abolished in this country'.[13]

12. *Child Adoption* (May 1954), p. 5.
13. *Re* D (an infant) Court of Appeal in *All England Law Reports*, Part 3 (1958), pp. 716–19.

Self, family and society

The previous section has illustrated in general ways the reasons why individuals and families might choose silence or denial to protect themselves from social stigma or condemnation by the law. Such silences and denials formed protective boundaries which served either to defend the individual from a combination of familial and social disgrace, or to encompass an entire family and its members and thus deter intervention from the public world. Drawing upon a range of biographical and autobiographical extracts, the remainder of this chapter illustrates how the nature and permeability of such boundaries between and around the self, the family and society shift and overlap depending upon what issues are being concealed, by whom and for what reasons.

The reclamation of silenced aspects of family and personal history is not always an easy or benign process, for, as the following examples illustrate, it demands transgression of long-protected, interwoven familial and quasi-familial boundaries. Individuals who have concealed a particular event to protect their reputation or that of their family can be reluctant to acknowledge the event, and to have their personal and family history 'rewritten' as a result. Personal identity may become threatened by this rewriting process or, where there has been a *family* conspiracy to conceal some perceived disgrace, the status of both the family and the individual may be undermined. The case of Truda and her son, David Leitch, demonstrates the tensions and difficult negotiations which result from the revelation of a secret past.

The journalist and writer David Leitch was adopted at birth in 1937 but it was not a legal adoption. His parents were married and he was a legitimate child, but for unknown reasons they advertised in the *Daily Express* for foster parents and, after handing him over to the Leitches, seemingly disappeared before the legal arrangements could be finalized. However, as David Leitch was to discover after the death of his adoptive mother, normal adoption procedures could not have been pursued as, contrary to the more common scenario, it was his *adoptive* parents who were unmarried and not his natural parents. In order to ensure that they retained the child, the Leitches also disappeared and 'set up afresh in a new neighbourhood called Northwood a few miles further along the Metropolitan line, and resumed life with the baby everyone assumed was the natural child of Ivy's comprehensive loins'.[14] In this instance,

14. David Leitch, *Family Secrets* (Heinemann, 1984) p. 14.

concealing the circumstances of the child's birth suited both sets of parents.

David Leitch traced his mother, Truda, when he was in his thirties and they developed a companionable relationship. But for the following seven years Truda remained adamant that the second child of her marriage, his younger sister Margaret, should not be told of their meetings nor even of his existence. The extent of this determination became all the more evident following her death:

> Why else had Truda tried to wipe out all traces of me and my family before her death? Except for the entries in her address book, and here I was identified only by initials as if she had deliberately used a code (which I was sure she had), it was as if I had never been. We had only been out of touch since before Christmas, a matter of three weeks, and I had sent her a card, just as she had sent me one. Yet there was no trace of it in Truda's apartment, or any other evidence that might have led to me. There was a parallel with the events of my adoption. Three or four weeks after I was born everything had been rearranged in such a way that it was as if I had no existence at all.[15]

As a result Leitch was forced to recognize that the reunion with his mother had not restored him to a place either in her past or into her family, and that she had refused equally to acknowledge his identity as her son.

It was only his sister Margaret's conviction, following a child-hood conversation with her father, that her mother had concealed the birth of a child that led to their eventual meeting. Ironically, however, David Leitch was not that child. Margaret's knowledge was about a younger, illegitimate half-sibling, not an older, legitimate brother, whose birth and adoption had always been kept a closely guarded secret by both her parents. As a result David's existence proved to be as surprising to Margaret as that of the younger half-sister's did to David.

To her family and to the outside world, Truda only ever acknowledged that she had a daughter. To have admitted that she had given away a legitimate son for adoption would have arguably thrown into question her suitability to be mother to Margaret, while to have confessed to an adulterous affair, the birth of an illegitimate child and its adoption would have labelled her as both promiscuous and, again, an uncaring mother. Truda had broken the two most powerful norms of female behaviour and, in her eyes at least, only total silence about her two other children guaranteed her

15. Ibid., pp. 221–2.

reputation. She thus ensured, to her death, that undisclosed events in her past were revealed only when there were no alternatives, and consistently protected herself and her identity with a 'deep-seated caution which she had cultivated like a privet hedge round the borders of her life'.[16]

Elements of Truda's past were discovered in her lifetime, but more commonly such secrets were kept to death as the story of Lily Buck illustrates.[17] While sorting through his mother's personal effects after her death, Colin Buck found a photograph of her as a young woman together with a child, and was curious about the inscription on the back which read 'To my little sweetheart whose picture will always be in my heart forever'.[18] On checking the registrars' records he discovered that, before her marriage to his father, Lily had married a John Burton in 1937 and had had a daughter, Rita, in 1938.

Buck's parents had 'always seemed to stay well away from their brothers and sisters',[19] but he was able to trace his mother's youngest brother, who, since Lily's past had been discovered, was willing to discuss this part of her life but acknowledged that he would not have done so otherwise. The brother revealed that Lily's first marriage had been unhappy, that there were allegations of domestic violence and that ultimately she returned to her parents leaving Rita with her husband and his family. Eventually, and despite the attempts of Lily and her father, custody of Rita was awarded to John Burton and, as far as Lily's brother was aware, mother and daughter were never allowed to meet again.

The need to conceal the existence of this daughter was necessary, however, for reasons other than the disgrace of a failed marriage. Lily and John Burton had never divorced and Lily's second marriage was, therefore, bigamous and her son, Colin, illegitimate. In a period when a woman's identity and reputation were so closely defined by her marital status, neither divorce nor cohabitation offered the security, protection and respectability which remarriage brought to women such as Lily, and their children. By concealing her first marriage, Lily ensured that her second child was not subjected to the stigma of illegitimacy, safeguarded herself from the

16. Ibid., p. 48.
17. See also Paul Thompson, 'Family myth, models and denials', in Daniel Bertaux and Paul Thompson (eds), *Between Generations: Family Models, Myths and Memories* (Oxford University Press, 1993).
18. Colin Buck, 'Many years too late', *Family Tree Magazine*, Vol. 13, No. 11 (September 1997), p. 25.
19. Ibid.

shame of divorce and was able to develop a new set of familial
relationships which, without a divorce, would have been denied to
her. As her son poignantly notes:

> My parents kept these secrets from me for the whole of their lives
> and, I suspect, had my mother known she was going to die so sud-
> denly, the photograph would have disappeared, and with it the only
> link with events of the past. I suppose they felt frightened and ashamed
> of those events and could not bring themselves to tell me . . . I am
> not ashamed of my mother's actions. She acted then as would many
> in a less tolerant society.[20]

All too often, because guilt, shame and fear demanded total silence
during the lifetime of the secret holders, it has been the next generation who have been left to speculate about the social, cultural
and moral norms which demanded such emotional sacrifices from
their forebears, and which forced the construction of insurmount-
able divides between family members. Such was the experience
of Susan, whom we met in the previous chapter. In 1966 she was
informed by her father about an aunt, Elizabeth, who had been
institutionalized for almost fifty years, because of a mental breakdown, but whose existence had never been previously mentioned
by their family. So great was the sense of shame experienced by the
family, but especially Alice, Elizabeth's sister, about this breakdown
that all information relating to Elizabeth was kept secret. Indeed,
even her death was silenced, for, as her brother recalled, 'we did
not put it in the papers for there would have been nobody who
would have seen it who would recall her as a girl, but Alice rang me
up and said "you won't of course put her death in the papers there
is no need to recall our shame." '[21] It was only after Elizabeth died
that Susan was informed of her existence. Yet although Alice lived
another ten years and continued to have a close relationship with
her niece, 'our shame' formed a barrier of silence between them.
Susan never felt able to mention Elizabeth's name nor to admit
that she now knew she had another aunt. Only when that entire
generation had died was Susan able to speak openly about the
enormous pressures which had compelled a family to conceal one
of its members for so many years.

Where family stories were less comprehensively censored but, at
the same time, transmitted only in partial forms, autobiographies

20. Ibid., p. 26.
21. Interview with Susan by Katherine Holden (27 October 1993) and personal
correspondence.

have revealed that the burden of knowing yet not knowing lies heavy upon children. In order to protect the family's status children often unconsciously absorb the necessity of either silence or denial, without knowing about the origins or reasons for that silence. In such ways family secrets shape and mould the identity of individual family members who, although they might be denied knowledge of particular events or discover them at a later date, understand the significance of the secret and the importance of its maintenance to their own or their family's reputation.

The fear of revelation of such secrets can often encompass the child, who becomes an unwitting, powerless player in the family conspiracy but who, in turn, takes on the role as 'keeper of the gate'. Such responsibility, however, both isolates and frightens the child, and that sense of separation from other family members and from the local community has been described by Carolyn Steedman, drawing upon her own experience (but at the time unawareness) of being an illegitimate child:

> Very occasionally, children from the street passed through the narrow corridor to the kitchen and the back yard. This wasn't encouraged, though: we played in general in other children's houses... Enforced isolation was due to the adults keeping their heads down, out of the geographical firing line of censure from the North, preventing possible leakage of information, the door closed against any discovery of their secrets.[22]

Where children do know the significance of their family's silenced past, its effects are equally constraining, as Margot (not her real name) illustrates. Her father, a solicitor, had embezzled money and then fled to South America, leaving his wife and three children to manage as best they could. Margot's mother led a very confined life as a result and Margot herself recalls that 'it was a very tough upbringing... I remember we were so restricted at school, I mean you couldn't talk about things.'[23] So powerful was the determination to maintain this silence that Margot was very reluctant to discuss this episode in her family's history some eighty years later.

But children are not always passive victims. Although they can frequently and deliberately be denied knowledge about particular family events and disgraced family members, they are able to employ strategies of their own to root out and piece together information withheld from them. One young child, for example,

---

22. Carolyn Steedman, *Landscape for a Good Woman* (Virago, 1986), p. 67.
23. Interview with Margot by Katherine Holden (3 November 1993).

was not told what had happened to her mother, who had died suddenly. 'She consequently used to sit under the table at night, hidden by a long chenille cloth, listening to her aunts "because otherwise you got told to get out, you weren't allowed to listen or read the papers." '[24] Equally children have always kept secrets themselves, not least about their life at school and at play, about their friends and about their relationships with siblings and other family members. These secrets cultivate feelings of companionship, of power and of shared experience which, in turn, help develop a sense of personal and familial identity.

But for members of a family which has become a site of enforced secret-keeping because of an internal abuse of trust and power, the disclosure of that abuse can be almost as traumatic and distressing for the victims as the very activities which demanded their silence. The ties of family are such, however, that they rupture only where strained to their very limits and are thus able to contain and withhold the most dreadful of secrets including rape and murder.[25] The boundaries between the family and the public world appear, therefore, to be at their most impermeable when there are secrets to be maintained, with the result that, in the most extreme situations, individual family members find the transition to the outside world almost impossible to realize, and society's ability to cross into the family's inner sphere is equally difficult to achieve.

The case of the Thompson sisters, who murdered their father after more than thirty years of sexual and physical abuse, is particularly illustrative of the ways in which seemingly impenetrable boundaries can be constructed around individual families. From the 1950s Tommy Thompson, the father, terrorized his wife and daughters and subjected them to a reign of extreme mental and physical cruelty. The women's access to life away from the 'family home' was closely regulated, while opportunities for intervention by the outside world, either through neighbours, police or the social services, were regularly disrupted by rapid and frequent changes in address. As their biographer wrote:

> constantly moving house was one of the more laborious ways in which Tommy kept firm control over the family, emotionally and physically undermining his wife and daughters . . . Tommy may not have been doing it consciously, but moving house so often certainly

24. Tebbutt, *Women's Talk*, p. 53.
25. So horrifically illustrated in 1996 by the case of Rosemary and Fred West, who were charged with the sexual abuse and murder of several young girls, including their own daughter.

had the effect of keeping the Thompson family enclosed by disrupting any tentatively developing contact with outsiders.[26]

At the same time Tommy Thompson sought to portray 'normal' family life through family photographs and his daughter's diaries because:

> [He] seems to have believed in the power of the written word and in family photographs almost as if they were forms of magic to ward off the intrusion of the outside world, while 'controlling' external appearances and inner reality... Consequently from Thursday, 30 April 1970, until the last entry on Friday, 11 March 1988 (the day before his murder), Tommy made June Thompson keep a daily diary, sometimes reading what she had written, to ensure that a 'proper' record was being kept in case any outsider should ever begin to seek the truth.[27]

These photographs and diaries, together with the 'love letters' that his wife was ordered to write to him while hospitalized because of his violence towards her, reinforced Tommy Thompson's defences against the outside world. Throughout their school years and their periods in work, his daughters June and Hilda Thompson were compelled to maintain two lives in which they were secretly and seriously abused at home but expected to behave 'normally' outside. In early middle age, these inner and outer lives began to implode with Hilda suffering from escalating bouts of severe depression which neither anti-depressants, alcohol nor ECT halted, and with June desperately seeking to protect her sister and mother from Tommy's ongoing violence. Hilda's mental illness proved impossible to contain, 'leaking and oozing round the house like vapour',[28] and threatening the ability of her father to maintain his hold over the family by threats and violence. A breakdown of his authority was inevitable, but it was by shooting their father that the Thompson sisters literally blew apart the boundaries which their father had constructed around the family and which they themselves had been forced to maintain.

Yet the boundaries created by the silencing of events do not operate only to protect individuals from family and society, or families and their members from the public world. Families set up internal boundaries between generations and (especially during the nineteenth century) between servants and employers which serve to withhold information about aspects of family life from particular

---

26. Alexandra Artley, *Murder in the Heart* (Hamish Hamilton, 1993), p. 82.
27. Ibid., p. 218.   28. Ibid., p. 220.

strands of household members. In such ways an older generation might protect the reputation of one of its members through the suppression of behaviour still conceived of as shameful, or uphold an individual's right to privacy from perceived intrusion by a younger generation. Some family members are thus allowed only a censored version of their family story even though both narrator and audience acknowledge its deliberately partial nature.

Margaret Forster, for example, suspected that her mother had had a mental breakdown in 1943, which at that time had 'the same sort of stigma as attached to the bearing of an illegitimate child, the same sort of pressure to find this shameful'.[29] Nevertheless, she was unable to elicit any information from her family about the reasons why her mother had been hospitalized. Forster writes:

> Nan and Jean [Forster's aunts and her mother's sisters], when in adult life I tried them, when I asked what kind of illness my mother had requiring Pauline and me to be sent to Motherwell for two months, pretended forgetfulness which was obviously at odds with their notoriously sharp memories. Jean would say, 'Oh, you don't want to go bothering yourself about that. Dear me it was centuries ago. What does it matter?' and Nan, who in general loved to tell things that shouldn't be told, said, 'It's Lily's business,' and resisted temptation for once. My father is still alive. He is ninety-four and his mind is as clear and vigorous as ever, but he plays dumb. He doesn't say he *can't* [original emphasis] remember, I notice, but that there is nothing to remember, and that has to be that.[30]

By such silences, the Forster family's older generation protected the reputation and the memory of Lily. Her illness remained a private issue – it was *her* 'business' – and for other family members to intrude into that privacy was clearly considered inappropriate.

A well of silence: Tony's story[31]

This final example comes from a brief autobiography which focuses on the childhood years of Tony and provides much detail about how a family secret is maintained and negotiated within a household. Tony sets the scene in the following way regarding the circumstances of his birth:

29. Margaret Forster, *Hidden Lives: A Family Memoir* (Penguin, 1996), p. 134.
30. Ibid., pp. 133–4.
31. Tony Foley, unpublished autobiography (1997), cited with permission of the author.

In 1920 the eldest daughter now aged twenty seven married a civil servant . . . They set themselves up in a rented house not far from that of her parents. So far the family appeared to be set to progress and extend along conventional lines. When the recently married couple announced the impending arrival of the first grandchild in 1921 the news was received with the usual interest and fuss that most families express when an addition is expected. What was not expected was the revelation that the twenty year old unmarried daughter was also pregnant and into the bargain was two months ahead of her older sister. As happenstance would have it I was to be the first grandchild in the family.

Families at the extremities of the social scale usually cope with situations such as this with a certain amount of equanimity. For those families with social aspirations the effect is likely to be more traumatic. I had no way of knowing how the grandparents, uncles and aunts reacted neither had I any means of finding this out. It was as if the whole incident was wrapped up and dropped into a well of silence.

There was a hasty marriage ceremony most probably performed in the vestry of my mother's Roman Catholic parish church. This was something I found out when I came across their marriage certificate years after my mother's death. The date of the marriage was exactly one week before the day I was born. As far as I am concerned whatever happened after that wedding remains a mystery. I have never been able to find out whether or not my parents actually lived together after I was born. If they did it must have been for a very short time. My earliest childhood memories only recall the home of my grandparents.

I am sure my mother and father would have come under a great deal of pressure from both of their immediate families. They were after all quite young, in their early twenties. In addition the stigma of illegitimacy was more damaging in those times than it is today. So there would have been compulsion to have a quick marriage.

I was never told anything whatsoever about my father's family. It was as if they did not exist. So effectively were the circumstances of my birth suppressed that at no time did it occur to me to ask any questions about my paternity. I was about ten years old when my mother for the first time mentioned my father. She said she left him because he would not get a job to support her and me. That was why she returned to her parents' home. She showed me a photograph of him. He was in the uniform of a ship's officer. Thinking back about it I must have been unimpressed. I did not ask her any questions. She told me where he lived but did not say she ever stayed there. My lack of response to all this could have been childish indifference or more likely it was something I could not handle.

Only when late in life I obtained a copy of the census returns and discovered that my father was the youngest of seven children, that I had three uncles and three aunts as well as paternal grandparents. This side of my life has been completely blanked out. Thinking about it afterwards I could not help feeling some sadness and a certain amount of resentment over the bitterness between two families depriving me from knowing anything about an important part of my genealogy.

The family in which I grew up consisted of my grandparents, an uncle, an aunt and Jane. Jane was the one who only appeared in the house occasionally. She was also the one who would come to my room when I was in bed to talk to me and kiss me goodnight. In the morning she would be gone. I looked forward to her visits. I do not recall anyone ever telling me that Jane was my mother.

Tony's autobiography illustrates the ways in which children know and don't know their history. The circumstances of his birth are likened to 'a mystery' and 'a well of silence' which neither himself nor his family were able or willing to discuss, but at the same time the language he deploys demonstrates the accident and chance by which knowledge can be acquired. He discovered the proximity of his mother's marriage and his birth when he 'came across' the marriage certificate, although other information he has 'never been able to find out'. His childhood was a succession of silences and absences in which he 'was never told anything' and did not even 'recall anybody ever telling me that Jane was my mother'. Small opportunities were presented for him to fill in these silences but he lacked any framework in which to operate. How could a child ask questions about what was clearly a painful and delicate subject – for why else would it not have been discussed earlier? – without causing more pain and distress? Tony's assumption that he 'must have been unimpressed' by the information about his father is corrected by the later statement that 'My lack of response to all this could have been childish indifference or more likely it was something I did not know how to handle.'

Such are the nature of silences, however, that it is unclear what Tony's family were concealing. Was it the precipitate marriage of their younger daughter and Tony's near illegitimate status? Was it the new husband's inability or unwillingness to take up the role of breadwinner? Or was it the shame of having a separated daughter? Most likely it was the combination of these three events which determined the family in its refusal to discuss Tony's father or his family and to behave 'as if they did not exist'. By ostracizing their daughter's husband, the family re-created its boundaries to incorporate their married, but separated, daughter and her child. The marital relationship and the relationship between father and son were thus severed, and the ties of blood between parents, child and grandchild were reinforced.

But consciously or unconsciously, Tony's relatives filled the absences in his life which his missing father had created. His grandfather encouraged him to read, helped him with his school-work and tried to teach him to play the violin. His mother's brother introduced him to the worlds of sport and entertainment, particularly the cinema.

> This uncle brought me to see my first football match. He also took me to my first boxing match, to my first horse race meeting, to TT car races and Grand Prix motor cycle races. He was extremely generous, providing me with pocket money and I also knew he helped with some of the expenses arising from my education.

Other relatives also included Tony in their family's lives.

> My uncle by marriage, the husband of my mother's elder sister, was a slightly more distant character. He only seemed to notice me when I was in the company of his own children, my first cousins. However I was always included when he arranged treats for the 'kids' holidays at the seaside and pantomimes at Christmas . . . He held my mother in high regard. As I grew older he and I developed a more relaxed relationship.

Tony also maintained close relationships with his cousins:

> My first cousins, three girls and a boy, the children of my mother's elder sister, provided as much of a sibling relationship as I would ever experience. Because we lived beside each other and were reared under the authority of the same group of adults the first part of our lives virtually moved along parallel lines. I felt we were as close as brothers and sisters. It never occurred to me to consider whether or not they felt the same about me. Nevertheless that close relationship remained even when as grown-ups we went our separate ways.

As a young child, Tony felt that his unconventional family was not easily incorporated into the local community. He himself had many friends at school and in the neighbourhood but he was not able to 'recall being invited into their homes or meeting their parents'. Later this was rectified by a friendship which lasted into adulthood.

> It was not until I was approaching my teens that I became a close friend of a boy only a little younger than me and whose family welcomed me into their home. My friend was the youngest of three brothers and a sister, all of whom were as gregarious as their mother and father who were, from my perspective, extremely rich. They

literally made me one of the family. They knew my mother and
uncles and aunts very well but neither my friend nor his family ever
asked about my absent father. It was much later in life that it dawned
on me that they may have known the circumstances of my birth. Be
that as it may I was always treated in the same way as the other young
people in the house. I dined at their table, often I stayed the night
and each year when the family took a house for the month of August
at a popular resort I was invited along. And when the mother thought
the youngsters were being too rowdy I, as well as the others, got 'a
clip on the ear.'

On one level Tony's missing father appears, therefore, not to have
disadvantaged either his life or that of his mother. After returning
to her parents, who persuaded her 'to enrol in a training hospital',
Jane qualified as a midwife in 1924 and built up a practice in the
locality. In this she continued to be aided by her parents, who cared
for Tony while she resided in the households of expectant middle-
class mothers who employed her for the last days of their pregnancy
and for up to ten days after their baby was delivered. As a result
Jane became not only a financially independent woman but also a
much respected and valued member of the community. It is doubt-
ful whether she would have been able to achieve this level of personal success as a married woman, or as a separated woman living
alone and with sole responsibility for her child.

Similarly Tony's childhood was enriched by the contribution
of not only his mother and grandparents, but also aunts, uncles,
cousins and friends, and he comments that he benefited, not least
musically, from 'being a child in a household of articulate adults'.
In adult life he became a successful trade union official and, after
retirement, gained a degree in politics as well as acquiring a local
reputation as a talented artist. He has four children, eleven grandchildren and in 1997 celebrated fifty years of marriage.

But yet Tony's identity continues to be tinged by the absences in
his family story. He did meet his father later in life but: 'I was
reluctant to ask too many questions about the past nor did it
appear that he was prepared to say anything about the rift between
himself and my mother'. At a second meeting, after becoming
convinced that Tony was seeking some inheritance from him, his
father decided that they should not see each other again and Tony
reluctantly agreed.

Tony's narrative remains, therefore, incomplete. He questions
whether not having a 'proper live-in father' was an element in the
formation of his character but decides not, for, as he acknowledges,

'In the formative years of my life I had two surrogate fathers in the persons of my grandfather and my uncle.' But the significance is not that he lacked a live-in father but that the existence of his father was all but denied. It was the secrecy surrounding the circumstances of his birth which affected him and, particularly now in later life, the lack of knowledge 'about an important part of my genealogy' which disturbs him. The extent to which the importance of the blood line within our understanding of this sense of self is socially constructed remains unclear, but blood relationships continue to be a powerful determinant in conceptualizing identity, as Tony's story illustrates and as the numbers of adopted adults searching for their natural parents confirm.

The boundaries which silences, absences and secrets create between self, family and society lap and overlap in complex ways but they revealingly illustrate the tangled, interactive relationship between personal identity, family experience and the social world. The investigation of silences and absences within the history of the family can, therefore, be useful for two reasons. First, the nature of issues which were considered shameful by families, and were thus hidden or denied, provides much evidence about the social and moral climate of a particular historical period. Where it is possible, for example, to trace evidence about the ways in which women with illegitimate children were treated in different communities, at different points in time, then a clearer picture may emerge about the reasons behind the definition and construction of illegitimacy as a social problem.

Secondly, greater light can be shone on the ways in which the private lives of the individual and the family were negotiated within the shared space of the home. Secrets protect not only the boundaries between the private and public lives of families but also the privacy of the individual within the family. They thus operate between husbands and wives, parents and children, families of birth and families by marriage, and across and between generations. The ways in which family or personal events are silenced reveal much about the dynamics of family life but also point to the complexities of familial relationships in which horizontal blood ties can be stronger than intergenerational ones. Our understanding of families, as Chapter 3 argued, predominantly foregrounds the intergenerational relationship and especially the mother–child dyad. More work, however, on the silenced aspects of family life may well illustrate the ways in which, for example, siblings or cousins developed and maintained their relationships over time and distinct from other familial ties, and how loyalties and ties between family members came into conflict when the privacy of the individual was at stake.

In the second half of this century, a determination to expose the secret life of the family appears to be in vogue. The sexual double standard and some of the stigma around mental illness have declined, and an awareness of the emotional, financial, physical and sexual power which fathers and men have been afforded in families has increased. There have been, as a result, growing public declarations about private family issues which had been kept secret for decades, and a resolve both to rid families of past shames and taboos and to fill in the silences within family histories. For example, First World War soldiers shot for cowardice are now being reclaimed by their families as society and government acknowledge the physical and mental stress experienced by such men, and reassess the definition of coward. And politician Clare Short was able publicly to proclaim her reunion with her 31-year-old son, whom she had had adopted at birth, declaring, 'I want everyone to know. I want to show him off.'[32]

This opening up of the family story is demonstrated through the extremely popular and rapidly expanding literary genres of biography and autobiography, which have become increasingly focused, often contentiously and sometimes pruriently, on the hidden or silenced aspects of their subjects' lives and families.[33] And a determination to reclaim 'absent' family members is to be found equally in the popular task of producing family trees in which seemingly complete histories of familial relationships are traced through the public records. However, official records, like the census, can do just as much as personal memories and family stories in creating silences and absences about the nature and process of family life in the past.

Nevertheless, it would be wrong to believe that an end to family secrets is imminent, as the ongoing work of counsellors, psychiatrists and psychoanalysts with individuals who have suffered many different forms of familial abuse demonstrates. Moreover, changing codes of behaviour and patterns of family life continue to emerge in the late twentieth century, and new stresses and tensions are uncovered. The incidence of 'granny bashing', the numbers of

32. 'Reunited after 31 years', *The Independent* (17 October 1996).
33. As for example in Garry O'Connor, *The Secret Woman: A Life of Peggy Ashcroft* (Weidenfeld & Nicolson, 1996) and Humphrey Carpenter, *Robert Runcie: The Reluctant Archbishop* (Hodder & Stoughton, 1996).

children caring for invalid parents, and the reported incidence of women abusing their own children are but three examples which have been recently 'discovered'. The rapid changes to reproductive technology have already created scenarios in which the seemingly simple divide between social and physical parenting has been irretrievably dissolved. A recent case in Italy, for example, in which a surrogate mother was pregnant with the foetuses of two different couples illustrates the social and familial complexity of such births.[34] The ties of blood, contract and intimacy are almost seamlessly woven around children born of this technology, and how their families will narrate the family's story has yet to be negotiated.

Today, as in the past, boundaries continue to be constructed to protect families and their members' relationships from social norms and expectations. There will always be silences and absences in the family story, but, since family lives provide the experiential detail of demographic trends, of culture, of medical and scientific progress and of social and political change, investigation into the form and nature of these silences will ensure that a richer, more detailed narrative can be produced.

34. 'Two babies, one womb and five parents', *The Guardian* (8 March 1997).

CHAPTER TEN

Conclusion

. . . until very recently, solid family life could be taken for granted. But today family life is breaking down.

David G. Green, 1993[1]

How is it possible to conclude a story that has no ending? Although our discussion closes in 1960, family stories continue to unfold and to challenge attempts to fix their form and content. Not least in the last twenty years, demographic patterns have changed the experience of family life immeasurably. Childlessness has doubled in a generation, and the incidence of women having their first babies over the age of 30 has soared. Because of increased participation in higher and further education and the financial costs of independent living, more children are remaining in the family home until their early twenties. Out of 3.8 million women in their thirties, almost a million are single or divorced. The last generations of larger families with their substantial numbers of siblings, aunts, uncles, nephews and nieces are slowly disappearing and, with the elderly now forming a significant sector of society, there are fewer potential carers as a result.

These changing demographic patterns affect not only the immediate relationships between parents and their children. Wider networks of family, kin and friends are similarly touched, and their relationships equally shaped. One example is the experience of being a grandchild and of grandparenting, which, if it occurs at all, will undergo an important shift as the average age of grandparents

---

1. David G. Green, 'Foreword', in Norman Denis and George Erdos, *Families Without Fatherhood*, 2nd edn (IEA Health and Welfare Unit, 1993), p. vi. See also Francis Fukuyama, *The End of Order* (Social Market Foundation, 1997).

266

rises to 60, in line with the age of mothers having their first children. And with the present high incidence of the divorced and single, individuals can no longer expect to have lifelong, intimate relationships with marital partners, so that friendships and even relationships with work colleagues may move to the fore and provide an alternative source of long-term emotional support and practical assistance through adulthood.

But it is not only demography which has altered the meaning and expectations of family and familial relationships. Economically, the ideal of the male breadwinner with his 'family wage' is disappearing, and family members of appropriate age and ability are now generally expected to contribute to the household's income. Growing public acknowledgement of the extent of child abuse, and particularly sexual abuse, within society has challenged our perception of fatherhood, manhood and the innocence of childhood.[2] Social and political changes in the conceptualization of individual rights and personal freedom have also been significant. The notion of service, not just in the form of domestic service but also in the ways in which family members understood their position and their relationship to other family members, is a concept which has all but disappeared. Children are now no longer bound in lifelong duty to their parents, and wives do not expect to 'service' the domestic, sexual and financial needs of their husbands.

In conjunction with this belief in individual rights, relationships between family members are increasingly conceptualized as contractual in their nature. Couples living together define themselves as 'partners' and in some cases pre-nuptial agreements are drawn up to formalize personal claims by respective partners-to-be over money and property should the marriage fail. The potential tensions between the rights of children, as individuals in their own right, and those of parents over their children have been recognized by the Children Act of 1989, which recommended that children be involved as fully as possible in actions and decisions about themselves. Adopted children are now entitled to seek out information about their birth families. And the development of reproductive technologies has, at least according to media coverage, brought about a spread of formal and informal contracts in which surrogate mothers, the donors of sperm, and of eggs have to negotiate and agree their particular biological and social relationship to the 'parents' and the child born of such technology.

2. See Diana Gittins, *The Family in Question* (Macmillan, 1993), pp. 169–82.

Despite these very real and substantial changes to family life and to the relationships between family members, our emotional and psychological investment in the family has not diminished. Our understanding of the meaning of motherhood, the responsibilities of parenting and the ties between generations has undoubtedly shifted, but who we are and what we achieve continues to be largely inherited through the financial, educational, material, emotional and social resources of our families and our most deep-rooted relationships are still predominantly familial.

Yet neither the extent of these changes nor the ongoing centrality of family in our lives and in the organization of the public world has been incorporated into debates about late twentieth-century society. Discussions about 'the family' continue to be principally focused through the lens of the nuclear family and its perceived decline. Rates of divorce, of cohabitation and of lone motherhood are thus deemed central to the political, social and moral analyses of contemporary family life. Little attention is paid to the growing numbers of dependent, elderly relatives or to the potential effects of an increased age gap between children and parents, which late motherhood dictates, while the effects of medical advances in genetic screening, and the new, potentially cataclysmic meaning which this scientific research brings to a family's blood relationships, are only just being appreciated. By and large these and other such issues have remained peripheral to contemporary analyses, for none of them are considered essentially threatening to the nuclear family model.

This model and its maintenance continues to be a central feature of late twentieth-century society and, as a result, the vocabulary available to us to describe other formations is inadequate. In the face of the ongoing grouping and regrouping into families of individuals with their past and current marital, familial and quasi-familial relationships, experiences and backgrounds, the definitions of 'reconstituted' and 'blended' families have come into current usage. But such terms provide little insight into the particular experience of life in such households and of the ways in which their relationships are negotiated and sustained. Rather they operate to define these families as *other*, that is, not the norm of 'the family' – a norm which, in its strictest sense, arguably constitutes less than 1 per cent of the family types in England in the 1990s.[3]

3. Jon Bernardes, *Family Studies* (Routledge, 1997), p. 10. See also Linda Nicholson 'The myth of the traditional family', in Hilde Lindemann Nelson (ed.), *Feminism and Families* (Routledge, 1997).

We must continue, therefore, to question the dominance which the nuclear family retains over our imagination and our ideas about family life. The historical story has an important role to play in the task of unravelling the meaning of family and family life at the experiential, metaphorical, political and social level, and of querying the stereotypes which hold us in their sway. Such a questioning will pull in from the margins of history the very different patterns of family life, practices and relationships which have existed in the past but which have been silenced or overshadowed.

The dangers of a narrow approach to the history of the family and to the meaning of the family in the present are evident in the two commonly held assumptions contained in the opening epigram, which disregard and discount the many other significant relationships which have bound people together over time. The family story which we have narrated demonstrates why the family of the past can never be taken for granted. Its conceptual framework offers readers a means by which to question assumptions that 'the family' is in terminal decline, and to listen for other stories which, though too often unheard, tell of its continuing importance to society, our relationships and ourselves.

Appendix: Legislation affecting the family

1834 Poor Law Amendment Act
1842 Mines Act
1844 Factory Act
1845 Bastardy Act
1857 Matrimonial Causes Act
1863 Births and Deaths Registration Act
1870 Education Act
1870 Married Women's Property Act
1873 Custody of Infants Act
1882 Married Women's Property Act
1885 Housing of the Working Classes Act
1886 Guardianship of Infants Act
1889 Prevention of Cruelty and Protection of Children Act
1891 Custody of Children Act
1906 Education (Provision of Meals) Act
1907 Notification of Births Act
1907 Matrimonial Causes Act
1908 Children Act
1908 Old Age Pensions Act
1911 National Insurance Act
1914 Affiliation Orders Act
1918 Maternity and Child Welfare Act
1919 Housing and Town Planning Act
1919 Housing Act
1920 Adoption Act
1923 Bastardy Act
1923 Matrimonial Causes Act
1925 Guardianship of Infants Act
1925 Old Age and Widows' and Orphans' Contributory Pensions Act
1926 Adoption Act
1926 Legitimacy Act
1929 Infant Life Preservation Act

1933 Children and Young Persons' Act
1937 Matrimonial Causes Act
1938 Holidays with Pay Act
1944 Education Act
1945 Family Allowances Act
1946 National Insurance Act
1946 National Health Insurance Act
1948 Children Act
1948 Matrimonial Causes Act
1948 National Assistance Act
1948 Nursery and Child-Minders Regulation Act
1949 Housing Act
1949 Legal Aid and Advice Act
1949 Married Women (Maintenance) Act
1950 Adoption Act
1950 Maintenance Orders Act
1950 Matrimonial Causes Act
1952 Affiliation Act
1953 Births and Deaths Registration Act
1957 Affiliation Proceedings Act
1958 Adoption Act
1958 Children Act
1959 Family Allowances Act
1959 Legitimacy Act
1959 Street Offences Act

Bibliography

General

Abbott, Mary, *Family Ties: English Families 1540–1920* (Routledge, 1993).

Addison, P., *Now the War is Over: A Social History of Britain 1945–51* (Pimlico, 1995).

Anderson, Michael, *Family Structure in 19th Century Lancashire* (Cambridge University Press, 1971).

Baker, N., *Happily Ever After? Women's Fiction in Post War Britain 1945–60* (Macmillan, 1989).

Beddoe, Deirdre, *Back to Home and Duty: Women Between the Wars, 1918–1939* (Pandora Press, 1989).

Bernardes, Jon, *Family Studies* (Routledge, 1997).

Bertaux, Daniel, and Thompson, Paul (eds), *Between Generations: Family Models, Myths and Memories* (Oxford University Press, 1993).

Bourke, J., *Working-Class Cultures in Britain, 1890–1960* (Routledge, 1994).

Braybon, Gail, and Summerfield, Penny, *Out of the Cage: Women's Experiences in Two World Wars* (Pandora, 1987).

Chinn, C., *They Worked All Their Lives: Women of the Urban Poor in England 1880–1939* (Manchester University Press, 1988).

Davidoff, Leonore, *The Best Circles: 'Society', Etiquette and the Season* (Century Hutchinson, 1986).

De Cruse, Shani, 'Women and the family', in June Purvis (ed.), *Women's History: Britain, 1850–1945* (UCL Press, 1995).

Drake, Michael, and Finnegan, Ruth, *Sources and Methods for Family and Community Historians: A Handbook* (Cambridge University Press in association with the Open University, 1994).

Dyhouse, Carol, *Feminism, and the Family in England 1880–1939* (Basil Blackwell, 1989).

Flandrin, Jean-Louis, *Families in Former Times: Kinship, Household and Sexuality* (Cambridge University Press, 1979).

Forster, Margaret, *Hidden Lives: A Family Memoir* (Penguin, 1996).

Forster, R., and Ranum, O. (eds), *Family and Society: Selections from the Annales* (Johns Hopkins University Press, 1976).

Giles, Judy, *Women, Identity and Private Life in Britain 1900–1950* (Macmillan, 1995).

Gillis, John, *A World of Their Own Making: Myth, Ritual and the Quest for Family Values* (Harvard University Press, 1996).

Gittins, Diana, *The Family in Question: Changing Households and Familiar Ideologies* (Macmillan, 1985).

Hareven, Tamara, 'The history of the family and the complexity of social change', *American Historical Review*, 96, 1 (Feb. 1991).

Harris, J., *Private Lives, Public Spirit: A Social History of Britain 1870–1914* (Oxford University Press, 1993).

Ittman, K., *Work, Gender and Family in Victorian England* (Macmillan, 1995).

Jones, S.G., *Workers at Play: A Social and Economic History of Leisure 1918–1939* (Routledge & Kegan Paul, 1986).

Laslett, Peter, *The World We Have Lost* (1965; Methuen, 1979).

Laslett, Peter, and Wall, Richard (eds), *Household and Family in Past Time* (Cambridge University Press, 1974).

Leitch, David, *Family Secrets* (Heinemann, 1984).

Lewis, Jane, *Women in England: Sexual Divisions and Social Change 1870–1950* (Wheatsheaf, 1984).

Lewis, Jane, *Women in Britain Since 1945* (Basil Blackwell, 1991).

Lewis, Jane (ed.), *Labour and Love: Women's Experience of Home and Family 1850–1940* (Basil Blackwell, 1986).

Meachum, Standish, *A Life Apart: The English Working Class: 1840–1914* (Thames & Hudson, 1977).

Mintz, Stephen, *A Prison of Expectations: The Family in Victorian Culture* (New York University Press, 1983).

O'Day, Rosemary, *The Family and Family Relationships, 1500–1900: England, France and the United States of America* (Macmillan, 1994).

Pugh, Martin, *Women and the Women's Movement 1914–1959* (Macmillan, 1992).

Roberts, Elizabeth, *A Woman's Place: An Oral History of Working-Class Women 1840–1940* (Basil Blackwell, 1984).

Roberts, Elizabeth, *Women and Families: An Oral History, 1940–1970* (Basil Blackwell, 1995).

Roberts, Robert, *The Classic Slum: Salford Life in the First Quarter of the Century* (Pelican, 1973).

Roberts, Robert, *A Ragged Schooling: Growing Up in the Classic Slum* (Penguin, 1978).

Seccombe, Wally, *Weathering the Storm: Working-Class Families from the Industrial Revolution to the Fertility Decline* (Verso, 1993).

Smith, H.L. (ed.), *War and Social Change: British Society in the Second World War* (Manchester University Press, 1986).

Stacey, J., *Brave New Families: Stories of Domestic Upheaval in Late 20th Century America* (Basic Books, 1990).

Steedman, Carolyn, *Landscape for a Good Woman: A Story of Two Lives* (Virago, 1986).

Stone, Lawrence, *The Family, Sex and Marriage in England 1500–1800* (1977; Penguin, 1979).

Taylor, Barbara, *Eve and the New Jerusalem: Socialism and Feminism in the 19th Century* (Virago, 1983).

Tebbutt, Melanie, *Women's Talk? A Social History of Gossip in Working Class Neighbourhoods, 1880–1960* (Scolar Press, 1995).

Thompson, F.M.L., *The Rise of Respectable Society* (Fontana, 1988).

Thompson, Paul, *The Edwardians: The Remaking of British Society*, 2nd edn (Routledge, 1992).

Thorne, B., *Rethinking the Family: Some Feminist Questions* (Longman, 1982).

Townsend, Peter, *The Family Life of Old People* (Routledge & Kegan Paul, 1957).

Vincent, David, *Bread, Knowledge and Freedom: A Study of Nineteenth Century Working Class Autobiography* (Methuen, 1981).

Wilson, Elizabeth, *Only Halfway to Paradise: Women in Postwar Britain 1945–1968* (Tavistock, 1980).

Wohl, A.S. (ed.), *The Victorian Family: Structures and Stresses* (Croom Helm, 1978).

Concepts

Davidoff, Leonore, 'Regarding some "old husbands tales": public and private in feminist history', Part I, in *Worlds Between: Historical Perspectives on Gender and Class* (Polity Press, 1995).

Gardiner, J.K., 'Self psychology as feminist theory', *Signs: Journal of Women in Culture and Society*, 12, 1 (1987).

Gilligan, Carol, *In a Different Voice: Psychological Theory and Women's Development* (Harvard University Press, 1982).

Hall, Stuart, 'Introduction: who needs "identity"?', in S. Hall and P. DuGay, *Questions of Cultural Identity* (Sage Publications, 1996).

Jordanova, L., 'Cultures of kinship', in *Nature Displayed: Gender, Science and Medicine 1760–1820* (Longman, forthcoming).

Kitzinger, C., 'The individuated self concept: a critical analysis of social constructionist writing on individualism', in G. Breakwell (ed.), *Social Psychology of Identity and the Self Concept* (University of Surrey Press, 1992).

Klein, David, and White, James, *Family Theories: An Introduction* (Sage, 1996).

Levy, Anita, *Other Women: The Writing of Class, Race and Gender 1832–1898* (Princeton University Press, 1991).

Morgan, David, *Social Theory and the Family* (Routledge & Kegan Paul, 1975).

Morgan, David, *The Family, Politics and Social Theory* (Routledge & Kegan Paul, 1985).

Morgan, David, *Family Connections: An Introduction to Family Studies* (Polity Press, 1996).

Morris, B., *Anthropology of the Self: The Individual in Cultural Perspective* (Pluto Press, 1994).

Nelson, Hilde Lindemann (ed.), *Feminism and Families* (Routledge, 1997).

Pateman, Carole, *The Sexual Contract* (Polity Press, 1988).

Porter, Roy (ed.), *Rewriting the Self: Histories from the Renaissance to the Present* (Routledge, 1997).

Ragin, Charles, and Becker, Howard, *What is a Case? Exploring the Foundations of Social Inquiry* (Cambridge University Press, 1992).

Riley, Denise, *'Am I that Name?': Feminism and the Category of 'Women' in History* (Macmillan, 1988).

Schiebinger, L., *The Mind Has No Sex? Women in the Origins of Modern Science* (Harvard University Press, 1989).

Taylor, Charles, *Sources of the Self: The Making of Modern Identity* (Harvard University Press, 1989).

Taylor, J.B., and Shuttleworth, S., *Embodied Selves: An Anthology of Psychological Texts, 1830–1890* (Oxford University Press, 1998).

Teichman, J., *Illegitimacy: A Philosophical Examination* (Blackwell, 1982).

Weeks, Jeffrey, 'The value of difference', in Jonathan Rutherford (ed.), *Identity, Community, Culture and Difference* (Lawrence & Wishart, 1990).

Yeo, Eileen, *The Contest for Social Science: Relations and Representations of Gender and Class* (Rivers Oram Press, 1996).

Young-Eisendrath P., and Hall, J. (eds), *The Book of the Self: Person, Pretext and Process* (New York University Press, 1987).

Childhood

Ariès, Philippe, *Centuries of Childhood: A Social History of Family Life* (1960; Jonathan Cape, 1962).

Behlmer, George K., *Child Abuse and Moral Reform in England 1870–1908* (Stanford University Press, 1982).

Burnett, John, *Destiny Obscure: Autobiographies of Childhood, Education and Family from the 1820s to the 1920s* (Allen Lane, 1982).

Cunningham, Hugh, *The Children of the Poor: Representations of Childhood Since the Seventeenth Century* (Basil Blackwell, 1991).

Cunningham, Hugh, *Children and Childhood in Western Society Since 1500* (Longman, 1995).

Davin, Anna, *Growing up Poor: Home, School and Street in London 1870–1914* (Rivers Oram Press, 1996).

Gittins, Diana, *The Child in Question* (Macmillan, 1997).

Greven, Philip, *Spare the Child: The Religious Roots of Punishment and the Psychological Impact of Physical Abuse* (Alfred Knopf, 1990).

Hardyment, Christina, *Dream Babies: Child Care from Locke to Spock* (Jonathan Cape, 1983).

Hendrick, Harry, *Child Welfare: England 1872–1989* (Routledge, 1994).

Heron, Liz (ed.), *Truth, Dare or Promise: Girls Growing Up in the Fifties* (Virago, 1985).

Hopkins, Eric, *Childhood Transformed: Working Class Children in Nineteenth Century England* (Manchester University Press, 1994).

Jordanova, Ludmilla, 'Children in history: concepts of nature and society', in Geoffrey Scarre (ed.), *Children, Parents and Politics* (Cambridge University Press, 1989).

Pinchbeck, Ivy, and Hewitt, Margaret, *Children in English Society. Vol. 2: From the Eighteenth Century to the Children's Act 1948* (Routledge & Kegan Paul, 1973).

Richardson, Dianne, *Women, Motherhood and Childrearing* (Macmillan, 1993).

Thompson, Thea, *Edwardian Childhoods* (Routledge & Kegan Paul, 1982).

Demography

Anderson, Michael, 'The emergence of the modern lifecycle', *Social History*, January 1985.

Anderson, Michael, 'The social implications of demographic change', in F.M.L. Thompson (ed.), *The Cambridge Social History of Britain. Vol. 2: People and their Environment* (Cambridge University Press, 1990).

Anderson, Michael, 'What is new about the modern family?', in Michael Drake (ed.), *Time, Family and Community: Perspectives on Family and Community History* (Basil Blackwell, 1994).

Gillis, John, Tilly, Louise, and Levine, David, *The European Experience of Declining Fertility 1850–1970* (Blackwell, 1992).

Gittins, Diana, *Fair Sex: Family Size and Structure 1900–1939* (Hutchinson, 1982).

Halsey, A.H., *British Social Trends Since 1900* (Macmillan, 1988).

Higgs, Edward, *Making Sense of the Census* (HMSO, 1989).

MacKinnon, Alison, 'Were women present at the demographic transition? Questions from a feminist historian to historical demographers', *Gender and History*, 7, 2 (August 1995).

Soloway, Richard Allen, *Birth Control and the Population Question in England 1877–1930* (University of North Carolina Press, 1982).

Szreter, Simon, *Fertility, Class and Gender in Britain, 1860–1940* (Cambridge University Press, 1996).

Wrigley, E.A., and Schofield, R., *The Population History of England 1541–1871* (Edward Arnold, 1981).

Gender

Clark, Anna, *The Struggle for the Breeches: Gender and the Making of the British Working Class* (Rivers Oram Press, 1995).

Connell, R.W., *Gender and Power* (Polity Press, 1986).

Davidoff, Leonore, 'Class and gender in Victorian England: the case of Hannah Cullwick and A.J. Munby', in *Worlds Between: Historical Perspectives on Gender and Class* (Polity Press, 1995).

Davidoff, Leonore, and Hall, Catherine, *Family Fortunes: Men and Women of the English Middle Class 1780–1850* (Hutchinson, 1987).

Edwards, Elizabeth, 'Education institutions or extended families? The reconstruction of gender in women's colleges in the late nineteenth and early twentieth centuries', *Gender and Education*, 2, 1 (1990).

Hall, Catherine, 'The early formation of Victorian domestic ideology', in *White, Male and Middle Class: Explorations in Feminism and History* (Polity Press, 1992).

Leydesdorf, S., Passerini, L., and Thompson, P., *Gender and Memory* (Oxford University Press, 1996).

Light, Alison, *Forever England: Femininity, Literature and Conservatism between the Wars* (Routledge, 1991).

Muscucci, Ornella, *The Science of Woman: Gynaecology and Gender in England 1800–1929* (Cambridge University Press, 1990).

Poovey, Mary, *The Ideological Work of Gender in Mid-Victorian England* (Virago, 1989).

Rendall, Jane, *The Origins of Modern Feminism: Women in Britain, France and the United States, 1780–1860* (Lyceum Books, 1985).

Roper, Michael, *Masculinity and the British Organisation Man* (Oxford University Press, 1994).

Roper, Michael, and Tosh, John (eds), *Manful Assertions: Masculinities in Britain since 1800* (Routledge, 1991).

Smith, S., *Subjectivity, Identity and the Body: Women's Autobiographical Practitioners in the 20th Century* (Indiana University Press, 1993).

Kinship

Brain, Robert, *Friends and Lovers* (Paladin, 1977).

Cooper, Di, and Donald, Moira, 'Households and "hidden" kin in early nineteenth century England: four case studies in suburban Exeter, 1821–1861' *Continuity and Change*, 10, 2 (1995).

Davidoff, Leonore, ' "Where the stranger begins": the question of siblings in historical analysis', in *Worlds Between: Historical Perspectives on Gender and Class* (Polity Press, 1995).

Firth, R., Hubert, J., and Forge, A., *Families and their Relatives: Kinship in a Middle Class Sector of London* (Routledge & Kegan Paul, 1970).

Gellner, E., *The Concept of Kinship: And Other Essays on Anthropological Method and Explanation* (Blackwell, 1987).

Lewis, Jane, and Meredith, Barbara, *Daughters Who Care* (Routledge, 1988).

Reay, Barry, 'Kinship and neighbourhood in 19th century rural England: the myth of the autonomous nuclear family', *Journal of Family History*, 21, 1 (1996).

Schneider, David, *A Critique of the Study of Kinship* (University of Michigan Press, 1984).

Smith-Rosenberg, Carol, 'The female world of love and ritual: relations between women in nineteenth-century America', in *Disorderly Conduct: Visions of Gender in Victorian America* (Oxford University Press, 1985).

Strathern, Marilyn, *After Nature: English Kinship in the Late 20th Century* (Cambridge University Press, 1992).

Yanagisako, Sylvia Junko, 'Family and household: the analysis of domestic groups', *Annual Review of Anthropology*, 8 (1979).

Marriage and singleness

Adams, Margaret, *Single Blessedness: Observations on the Single State in a Married Society* (Heinemann, 1977).

Anderson, Michael, 'The social position of spinsters in mid-Victorian Britain', *Journal of Family History*, 9 (Winter 1984).

Ayers, Pat, and Lambertz, Jan, 'Marriage relations, money and domestic violence in working-class Liverpool 1919–1939', in Jane Lewis (ed.), *Labour and Love: Women's Experience of Home and Family, 1850–1940* (Basil Blackwell, 1986).

Chandler, Joan, *Women Without Husbands: An Exploration of the Margins of Marriage* (Macmillan Education, 1991).

Clark, David (ed.), *Marriage, Domestic Life and Social Change: Writings for Jacqueline Burgoyne* (Routledge, 1991).

Davidoff, Leonore, 'Mastered for life: servant and wife in Victorian and Edwardian England', in *Worlds Between: Historical Perspectives on Gender and Class* (Polity Press, 1995).

Delphy, C., and Leonard, D., *Familiar Exploitation: A New Analysis of Marriage in Contemporary Western Society* (Polity Press, 1992).

Doggett, Maeve, E., *Marriage, Wife-Beating and the Law in Victorian England* (Weidenfeld & Nicolson, 1992).

Ducquenin, Anthea, 'The importance of marital status for women's lives', Ph.D. thesis, Plymouth Polytechnic (1984).

Gillis, John, *For Better, For Worse: British Marriages, 1600 to the Present* (Oxford University Press, 1985).

Gittins, Diana, 'Marital status, work and kinship 1850–1930', in Jane Lewis (ed.), *Labour and Love: Women's Experience of Home and Family, 1850–1940* (Basil Blackwell, 1986).

Hammerton, A. James, *Cruelty and Companionship: Conflict in Nineteenth-Century Married Life* (Routledge, 1992).

Holcombe, Lee, *Wives and Property: Reform of the Married Women's Property Law in Nineteenth Century England* (University of Toronto Press, 1983).

Holden, Katherine, 'The shadow of marriage: single women in England 1919–1939', Ph.D. thesis, University of Essex (1996).

Jalland, Pat, *Women, Marriage and Politics 1860–1914* (Clarendon Press, 1986).

MacKinnon, Alison, *Love and Freedom: Professional Women and the Reshaping of Personal Life* (Cambridge University Press, 1997).

Oram, Alison, 'Repressed and thwarted, or bearer of the new world? The spinster in interwar feminist discourses', *Women's History Review*, 1, 3 (1992).

Parker, Stephen, *Informal Marriage, Cohabitation and the Law, 1750–1989* (Macmillan, 1990).

Perkin, Joan, *Women and Marriage in 19th Century England* (Routledge, 1989).

Phillips, Roderick, *Putting Asunder: A History of Divorce in Western Society* (Cambridge University Press, 1988).

Shanley, Mary, *Feminism, Marriage and the Law in Victorian England, 1850–1895* (Princeton University Press, 1989).

Spring Rice, Margery, *Working Class Wives: Their Health and Conditions* (Virago, 1981).

Stone, Lawrence, *Road to Divorce: England 1530–1987* (Oxford University Press, 1990).

Trustram, Myna, *Women of the Regiment: Marriage and the Victorian Army* (Cambridge University Press, 1984).

Vicinus, Martha, *Independent Women: Work and Community for Single Women 1850–1920* (Virago, 1985).

Weeks, Jeffrey, 'Pretended family relationships', in David Clark (ed.), *Marriage, Domestic Life and Social Change: Writings for Jacqueline Burgoyne* (Routledge, 1991).

Parenting

Banks, J.A., *Prosperity and Parenthood: A Study of Family Planning Among the Victorian Middle Classes* (Routledge & Kegan Paul, 1954).

Bowlby, John, *Maternal Care and Mental Health* (World Health Organization, 1952).

Bowlby, John, *Child Care and the Growth of Love* (Penguin, 1953).

Chodorow, Nancy, *The Reproduction of Motherhood: Psychoanalysis and the Sociology of Gender* (University of California Press, 1978).

Collier, Richard, *Masculinity, Law and the Family* (Routledge, 1995).

Collins, Stephen, 'British stepfamily relationships, 1500–1800', *Journal of Family History*, 16, 4 (1991).

Doolittle, Megan, 'Missing fathers: assembling a history of fatherhood in mid-nineteenth-century England', Ph.D. thesis, University of Essex (1996).

Humphries, Stephen, and Gordon, Pamela, *A Labour of Love: The Experience of Parenthood in Britain 1900–1950* (Sidgwick & Jackson, 1993).

Llewelyn Davies, Margaret (ed.), *Maternity: Letters from Working Women* (1915; Virago, 1978).

McKee, Lorna, and O'Brien, Margaret (eds), *The Father Figure: Some Current Orientations and Historical Perspectives* (Tavistock, 1982).

Riley, Denise, *War in the Nursery: Theories of the Child and the Mother* (Virago, 1983).

Ross, Ellen, *Love and Toil: Motherhood in Outcast London, 1870–1918* (Oxford University Press, 1993).

Strathern, Marilyn, 'Technologies', in S. Hall and P. DuGay (eds), *Questions of Cultural Identity* (Sage Publications, 1996).

Sexuality and reproduction

Bland, Lucy, *Banishing the Beast: English Feminism and Sexual Morality 1885–1914* (Penguin, 1995).

Brookes, B., *Abortion in England 1900–67* (Croom Helm, 1988).

Brophy, J., and Smart, C. (eds), *Women in Law: Explorations in Law, Family and Sexuality* (Routledge & Kegan Paul, 1985).

Ducrocq, Francoise Barret, *Love in the Time of Victoria: Sexuality, Class and Gender in Nineteenth Century London*, trans. John Howe (Verso, 1991).

Fink, Janet, 'Condemned or condoned? Investigating the problem of unmarried motherhood in England 1945–1960', Ph.D. thesis, University of Essex (1997).

Gillis, John, 'Servants, sexual relations and the risks of illegitimacy in London 1801–1900', in J. Newton, R. Rapp and E. Ross (eds), *Sex and Class in Women's History* (Routledge, 1983).

Hall, Lesley, *Hidden Anxieties: Male Sexuality, 1900–1950* (Polity Press, 1991).

Haste, C., *Rules of Desire: Sex in Britain, World War One to the Present* (Chatto & Windus, 1992).

Holzman, Ellen, 'The pursuit of married love: women's attitudes towards sexuality and marriage in Great Britain 1918–1939', *Journal of Social History*, 16 (1982).

Humphries, Stephen, *A Secret World of Sex: Forbidden Fruit: The British Experience 1900–1950* (Sidgwick & Jackson, 1988).

Jeffreys, Sheila, *The Spinster and her Enemies: Feminism and Sexuality 1880–1930* (Pandora, 1985).

Laqueur, Thomas, *Making Sex: Body and Gender from the Greeks to Freud* (Harvard University Press, 1990).

Mason, M., *The Making of Victorian Sexuality* (Oxford University Press, 1994).

Mort, Frank, *Dangerous Sexualities: Medico-Moral Politics in England since 1830* (Routledge & Kegan Paul, 1987).

Oram, Alison, ' "Embittered, sexless, or homosexual": attacks on spinster teachers 1918–1939', in Lesbian History Group (eds), *Not a Passing Phase: Recovering Lesbians in History 1840–1985* (Women's Press, 1989).

Perrot, Michelle (ed.), *A History of Private Life. Vol. IV: From the Fires of Revolution to the Great War*, Eng. trans. Arthur Goldhammer (Belknap Press, 1990).

Porter, Roy, and Hall, Lesley, *The Facts of Life: The Creation of Sexual Knowledge in Britain, 1650–1950* (Yale University Press, 1995).

Silva, E.B. (ed.), *Good Enough Mothering: Feminist Perspectives on Lone Motherhood* (Routledge, 1996).

Smart, Carol, 'Disruptive bodies and unruly sex: the regulation of reproduction and sexuality in the nineteenth century', in Carol Smart (ed.), *Regulating Womanhood: Historical Essays on Marriage, Motherhood and Sexuality* (Routledge, 1992).

Szreter, Simon, 'Victorian Britain 1837–1963: towards a social history of sexuality', *Journal of Victorian Culture*, 1, 1 (1996).

Walkowitz, Judith, *Prostitution and Victorian Society: Women, Class and the State* (Cambridge University Press, 1980).

Walkowitz, Judith, *City of Dreadful Delight: Narratives of Sexual Danger in Late-Victorian London* (University of Chicago Press, 1992).

Weeks, Jeffrey, *Sex, Politics and Society: The Regulation of Sexuality since 1800* (Longman, 1981, 2nd edn 1989).

The state and welfare

Arnot, Margaret, 'Infant death, child care and the state: the baby farming scandal and the first infant life protection legislation of 1872', *Continuity and Change*, 9, 2 (1994).

Beveridge, William, *Social Insurance and Allied Services* (HMSO, 1942).

Crowther, M.A., 'Family responsibility and state responsibility in Britain before the welfare state', *Historical Journal*, 25 (1982).

Davies, Celia, 'The health visitor as mother's friend: a woman's place in public health, 1900–1914', *Social History of Medicine* (1988).

Davin, Anna, 'Imperialism and motherhood', *History Workshop*, 5 (1978).

Finch, Janet, *Family Obligations and Social Change* (Polity Press, 1989).

Finlayson, Geoffrey, *Citizen, State and Social Welfare in Britain, 1830–1990* (Clarendon Press, 1994).

Gardner, Phil, *The Lost Elementary Schools of Victorian England: The People's Education* (Croom Helm, 1984).

Glennerster, H., *British Social Policy Since 1945* (Blackwell, 1995).

Gordon, Linda, *Heroes of Their Own Lives: The Politics and History of Family Violence, Boston 1880–1960* (Viking Press, 1988).

Graveson, R.H., and Crane, F.R. (eds), *A Century of Family Law, 1857–1957* (Sweet & Maxwell, 1957).

Henriques, Ursula, 'Bastardy and the New Poor Law', *Past and Present*, 37 (July 1967).

Jones, Helen, *Health and Society in Twentieth Century Britain* (Longman, 1994).

Land, Hilary, 'Eleanor Rathbone and the family wage', in Harold Smith (ed.), *British Feminism in the Twentieth Century* (Edward Elgar, 1990).

Leap, Nicky, and Hunter, Billie, *The Midwives' Tale: An Oral History from Handywomen to the Professional Midwife* (Scarlett Press, 1993).

Lewis, Jane, *The Politics of Motherhood: Child and Maternal Welfare in England 1919–1939* (Croom Helm, 1980).

Lewis, Jane, 'Welfare states: gender, the family and women', *Social History*, 19, 1 (1994).

Lewis, Jane, 'Dealing with dependency: state practices and social realities, 1870–1945', in Jane Lewis (ed.), *Women's Welfare, Women's Rights* (Croom Helm, 1983).

Lowe, Rodney, *The Welfare State in Britain Since 1945* (Macmillan, 1993).

Rathbone, Eleanor, *The Disinherited Family* (1924; Falling Wall Press Ltd., 1986).

Stetson, D.M., *A Woman's Issue: The Politics of Family Law Reform in England* (Greenwood Press, 1982).

Thane, Pat, *The Foundations of the Welfare State* (Longman Group, 1982).

Wilson, Elizabeth, *Women and the Welfare State* (Tavistock, 1977).

Wimperis, Virginia, *The Unmarried Mother and Her Child* (Allen & Unwin, 1960).

Work

Burnett, John, *Useful Toil: Autobiographies of Working People from the 1820s to the 1920s* (1974; Penguin, 1984).

Burnett, John, *Idle Hands: The Experience of Unemployment 1790–1990* (Routledge, 1994).

Cockburn, Cynthia, *Brothers: Male Dominance and Technological Change* (Pluto, 1983).

Cunningham, Hugh, 'The employment and unemployment of children in England *c*.1680–1851', *Past and Present*, 126 (1990).

Gathorne Hardy, Jonathan, *The Rise and Fall of the British Nanny* (Weidenfeld & Nicolson, 1993).

Hall, Catherine, 'The butcher, the baker, the candlestickmaker: the shop and the family in the Industrial Revolution', in *White, Male and Middle Class: Explorations in Feminism and History* (Polity Press, 1992).

Hareven, Tamara, 'Family time and industrial time: family and work in a planned corporation town 1900–1924', in *Family and Kin in Urban Communities 1700–1930* (New Viewpoints, 1977).

Higgs, Edward, 'Women, occupations and work in the nineteenth-century censuses', *History Workshop*, Vol. 23 (Spring 1987).

Horn, Pamela, *The Rise and Fall of the Victorian Servant* (Sutton Publishing Ltd., 1997).

Horrell, Sara, and Humphries, Jane, 'Women's labour force participation and the transition to the male-breadwinner family, 1790–1865', *Economic History Review*, 48, 1 (1995).

John, Angela, *Unequal Opportunities: Women's Employment in England 1800–1918* (Basil Blackwell, 1986).

Joyce, Patrick, 'Work', in F.M.L. Thompson (ed.), *The Cambridge Social History of Britain 1750–1950. Vol. 2: People and their Environment* (Cambridge University Press, 1990).

Lown, Judy, *Women and Industrialization: Gender at Work in Nineteenth Century England* (Polity Press, 1990).

Petersen, Jeanne, 'The Victorian governess: status incongruence in family and society', in Martha Vicinus (ed.), *Suffer and Be Still: Women in the Victorian Age* (Bloomington, 1974).

Rose, Sonya, O., *Limited Livelihoods: Gender and Class in Nineteenth Century England* (Routledge, 1992).

Summers, Anne, *Angels and Citizens: British Women as Military Nurses 1854–1914* (Routledge & Kegan Paul, 1988).

Taylor, Pam, 'Daughters and mistresses – mothers and maids: domestic service between the wars', in J. Clarke, C. Critcher and

R. Johnson (eds), *Working Class Culture: Studies in History and Theory* (Hutchinson, 1979).

Zmoroczek, Christine, 'The weekly wash', in Sybil Oldfield (ed.), *This Working-Day World: Women's Lives and Culture(s) in Britain 1914–1945* (Taylor & Francis, 1994).

Home, household and housing

Burnett, John, *A Social History of Housing, 1815–1970* (David & Charles, 1978).

Davidoff, Leonore, 'The rationalisation of housework', in *Worlds Between: Historical Perspectives on Gender and Class* (Polity Press, 1995).

Davidoff, Leonore, 'The separation of home and work? Landladies and lodgers in 19th and 20th century England', in *Worlds Between: Historical Perspectives on Gender and Class* (Polity Press, 1995).

Davidoff, Leonore, L'Esperance, Jeanne, and Newby, Howard, 'Landscape with figures: home and community in English society', in Leonore Davidoff, *Worlds Between: Historical Perspectives on Gender and Class* (Polity Press, 1995).

Hall, Catherine, 'History of the housewife', in *White, Male and Middle Class: Explorations in Feminism and History* (Polity Press, 1992).

Higgs, Edward, 'Domestic service and household production', in Angela John (ed.), *Unequal Opportunities: Woman's Employment in England, 1800–1918* (Basil Blackwell, 1986).

Jackson, Alan, *Semi-Detached London* (Allen & Unwin, 1973).

McBride, T.M., *The Domestic Revolution: The Modernisation of Household Service in England and France, 1820–1920* (Croom Helm, 1976).

Index